AUTENTICO

AUTENTICO

Cooking Italian, the Authentic Way

Rolando Beramendi

WITH

Rebekah Peppler

PHOTOGRAPHS BY

Laurie Frankel

St. Martin's Griffin
New York

AUTENTICO. Copyright © 2017 by Rolando Beramendi.
Photographs © Laurie Frankel.
All rights reserved. Printed in the United States of America.
For information, address St. Martin's Press, 175 Fifth Avenue,
New York, N.Y. 10010.

www.stmartins.com

Editor: BJ Berti
Production Editor: Eric C. Meyer
Editorial Assistant: Gwen Hawkes
Design: Level, Calistoga, CA

The Library of Congress Cataloging-in-Publication Data
is available upon request.

ISBN 978-1-250-12497-5 (hardcover)
ISBN 978-1-250-12498-2 (ebook)

Our books may be purchased in bulk for promotional,
educational, or business use. Please contact your local
bookseller or the Macmillan Corporate and Premium Sales
Department at 1-800-221-7945, extension 5442, or by
email at MacmillanSpecialMarkets@macmillan.com.

First Edition: October 2017

10 9 8 7 6 5 4 3 2 1

THIS BOOK IS DEDICATED TO:

{ **ROLANDA TERUZZI**
Fabrizio, Sandra, Saverio, and Aurora
and
Maria and Michelangelo Pistoletto,
for making me understand, believe, learn how to **COOK** and **SHARE**
Italian food, and bestow upon me a life one should be so lucky
to have ever had. . . .

{ **NICOLINA PEDUZZI**
(my Italian mother)
with
Gianluigi, Maria, Stefania, and Giancarlo
(my brothers and sisters)
and
Stefano, Carolina, Piero, Maddalena, and Giuditta,
for making me feel like I have a **FAMILY**. . . . }

{ **ALESSANDRO VALLECCHI,**
who introduced me to
CHIARA MASSIERO,
and to both of them,
for making me feel at **HOME**
in Firenze. . . .

{ **BEATRICE CONTINI BONACOSSI**
(a true sister)
and the entire Contini Bonacossi family,
for teaching me
about **TRADITIONS** and **INTEGRITY** . }

{ **CARLO CIONI**
(the father I never had)
for sharing with me what **AUTENTICO** means
as well as to Franca, Delfina, and Riccardo,
for making me feel **GROUNDED** at **HOME,**
in **PEACE,** and **ALIVE**. . . .

ROSETTA CLARA CAVALLI D'OLLIVOLA
and
Paolo Salvadori di Weissenhoff, for always being TRUE and GENUINE....

LISA MIDDIONE
and
Carlo Middione,
for being the first to BELIEVE in me....

SARA WILSON,
Gustavo Houghton,
Tony Wilson and the entire Wilson Tribe,
for making and allowing me to
CARRY ON, EXIST, PERSIST, and INSIST,
while nurturing
MANICARETTI for over thirty years until this day
and forever after....

LAURIE FRANKEL,
for her amazing support, friendship, photographs,
and eye,
and for letting us BE in ITALY and SEE IT
on the following pages of
AUTENTICO....

And...
CONNIE, PAULINA AND FABIENNE TERRANT,
for
putting my HEART back together and making me
want to go FORWARD.

Contents
SOMMARIO

TORTA DI FARRO (PAGE 195)

Rolando Beramendi simply exudes enthusiasm.

He doesn't just walk into a room, he bounds into it. When he talks to you, he envelops you with his conversation. Enthusiasm just leaks from every pore and it's impossible not to be affected by it. I met Rolando thirty years ago when he came to Barefoot Contessa, my specialty food store in East Hampton, New York, to show me the products he was importing from Italy. I think I bought everything he was selling—how could I not? He taught customers the value of using the best products available—extraordinary olive oils for cooking and for dipping bread, rich syrupy vinegars, the most flavorful canned tomatoes from San Marzano, and so much more.

Many years later, I was lucky to be invited on a food trip to Sicily with friends who knew Rolando. Rolando took us to so many of his suppliers and it was a week that I'll always remember. We visited women who made marzipan the way their ancestors had for centuries, we visited factories that harvested sea salt by hand, we joined cooking school teacher and cookbook author Anna Tasca Lanza at her fattoria and watched her make ricotta with milk from her family's sheep and wine from their vineyard. Each product was special and pure and beyond delicious. Rolando took us for lunch at one of his favorite olive oil producers and who served his own homemade limoncello after lunch. I'll never forget that fresh, sharp lemon flavor that warmed you down to your toes. Rolando's incredible enthusiasm was infectious and touched every place we visited on that trip.

Recently, Rolando invited us to his friends' house and cooked an amazing dinner for everyone. The food was incredibly delicious and, together with his enthusiasm for the ingredients, for laughter, and for his friends, he nourished everyone at the table. What I really love most about Rolando is that he does what he loves—imports and showcases extraordinary ingredients from Italy. But the by-product of that passion is that he has sustained dozens of small producers in Italy who make the finest handmade products by giving their products a market in the United States. It's that giving part that makes Rolando happy—that he's doing what he loves and that love sustains everyone he touches, from the producers of the ingredients, to the customers who cook with them, to the families sitting down to eat together.

This book is imbued with Rolando's enthusiasm. It's about honoring the people who have taught him about food and community and he is doing just what he loves—sharing that joy with all of us.

How lucky are we?

Ina Garten

Barefoot Contessa cookbooks & television

I'm a real nomad and a mutt.

carry an Italian passport (which is my dearest and most prized possession), an expired Argentine passport, and have a United States Green Card. I always seem to be on an airplane, constantly commuting from New York to San Francisco to Florence.

Shortly after I graduated from the University of California at Davis with a degree in economics, I visited some friends in the Italian Alps for the Christmas holidays. One night I cooked a big dinner for everyone. Some of the guests, who owned a gift-basket company in Turin, asked if I could help them find an importer and export their food products into the United States. When I returned, I made some appointments with local importers and distributors, but everyone told me that the products were too expensive (artisanal pasta), too unusual (traditional balsamic vinegar), and too esoteric (arugula pesto). So I decided to open my own company to import Italian foods. While cooking dinner one evening, the company's name popped into my head: Manicaretti! It's an old-fashioned Italian word that means "little treats," "delicacies," or "delicious morsels." Manicaretti was born on April 14, 1989, when I was twenty-five years old.

I was lucky to be in the right place at the right time. The food revolution was just beginning in the early 1990s, and San Francisco, where I was living, was at the center of it all. The first shipment of Italian products was stored in the garage of my house in Sausalito. Now, thanks to the curiosity of American chefs and retailers and the amazing support and camaraderie of my Italian producers, Manicaretti is wildly successful and continues to grow. I travel all over Italy, eating, tasting, asking questions about food, and looking for new products to bring to American tables.

These remarkable producers have taken me in as a family member. They continue to share their traditions and dishes with me so I can share them with my Manicaretti customers. And now I get to share the recipes and knowledge through Autentico.

I cook food in its most authentic form. I cook to break preconceived notions of what food should be—no overcrowded plates, no recipes with too many disparate ingredients, no out-of-season ingredients, no need for a lot of equipment. I make no-fuss food for my guests and myself that nourishes both our hearts and our stomachs.

As I always tell people whom I've met at the lunch or dinner table—the best way to make friends is to share a meal.

An *authentic* meal.

DISCLAIMER
AVVERTENZA

Si, sono cittadino Italiano. Ho casa a Firenze, dove abito, e lavoro negli Stati Uniti sempre a giro con la mia valigia.

Si, questo libro e' parziale nei confronti della mia "vera famiglia."
Si, questo libro e' un libro scritto e fotografato in Italia, e certe immagini potranno offendere qualcuno.
Sono foto di cibo.

Si, questo libro contiene una piccola scelta tra tantissime ricette Italiane che conosco bene, che ho imparato dalla mia famiglia Italiana, e tante di queste ricette si sono evolute e hanno subito delle modifiche e/o sono state aggiornate e adattate al mio stile di vita, gusto e valori.

Si, la mia vera famiglia e' composta di tutti i produttori e fornitori che per la maggior parte sono anche parte della famiglia Manicaretti. Tanti altri produttori del passato sono anche parte della storia di questo libro. Tutti loro mi hanno insegnato le loro tradizioni, segreti, storie e mi hanno aperto tutte le porte sia di casa, ma anche della cucina. Tutti loro, ne settore enograstronomico Italiano, mi hanno aiutato a diventare la persona che sono.

Yes, I am an Italian citizen, live in Florence, and work in the United States of America (where I live out of a suitcase).

Yes, this book is biased toward what I consider my "true Italian family."

Yes, this book is about Italian food in Italy and the photographs were taken there. Some of the images may offend someone. Remember, they are simply pictures of food.

Yes, this book contains a small selection of the many Italian recipes that I know well, which I have learned directly from members of my true Italian family. Many have been modified and/or altered in order to keep up with the times, taste, and values.

Yes, my true Italian family is composed of all the producers—past and present—who have contributed to the birth and existence of the importing business, Manicaretti. All of them have offered me teachings, traditions, secrets, and stories, throwing open their doors at home and in the kitchen to teach me everything I know. All of them, for the almost thirty years of working in the Italian food and wine sector, have made me who I am.

>>>

Si, sono autentico perche le persone che mi hanno fatto conoscere, vedere ed imparare tanto dalla bellissima Italia, le sue tradizioni e usanze, il magnifico cibo e vino, sono tutte autentiche, e grazie a loro, ognuno ha contribuito a farmi sentire piu' Italiano di quanto anche tante volte si sentono loro stessi. La mia autenticita' e stata costruita come un puzzle, e non e' ancora finito il lavoro! C'e' tanto da fare!

Si, questo libro e' stato scritto con la filosofia di riportare il cibo com'e'. Non come modificare, sostituire o variare. Nel caso il lettore gradisca fare delle modifiche, addizioni o altre manovre in cucina, fin che queste scelte siano fatte col rispetto agl'ingredienti, al piatto stesso, ed ai commensali, allora ben vengano!

L'appetito vien mangiando!
RICORDATEVI:
E' il "giusto" cibo e soltanto cibo!

Yes, I am authentic, because the people who have made me are authentic. They shared the beauty and bounty of Italy with me and they all helped me feel more Italian many more times than they feel themselves. They have built me like a puzzle and the job is not yet complete!

Yes, this book has been written with the very Italian philosophy of "it is what it is . . . and that's how it will be." Options, substitutions, and other variations within each recipe have been (mostly) kept aside. In the event that the reader should wish to modify, add, or make any other kind of maneuvers in the kitchen, so long as these choices are made with respect to each and every one of the ingredients in the recipe and those which are being added or deleted, and with respect to the original dish and the actual diners, then let them take place.

MAY YOU BE HUNGRIER THE MORE YOU EAT!
Buon appetito a tutti

Rolands

Remember:
It's "just" food,
and only food!

1

The Pantry

LA DISPENSA

Be and become a supply-side cook.

Wherever you are in the world make sure your pantry is well stocked, organized, and ready to be your support system. By making sure there is plenty of olive oil, vinegars, jarred tomatoes, anchovies, and spices on hand, you can shop daily for perishables and celebrate the arrival of seasonal ingredients knowing your pantry is ready to support turning fresh ingredients into full meals.

Please, pay attention to what you buy to stock your pantry. Make sure you shop at a reliable specialty food shop and that you become best friends with your grocers. And when it comes to Italian pantry items, there are a few things you'll notice. Under current (you never know how long they will last!) European Union regulations, food products carry certain designations to protect their authenticity. These two designations should make you feel very comfortable that you are buying authentic Italian made products:

- **DOP** or *Denominazione di Origine Protetta* **(Protected Designation of Origin)**
The DOP label guarantees that the product is authentic and of the highest quality and integrity. Products grown, produced, and packaged in specific geographical places and using traditional methods can be labeled as DOP, and every step of the process from production to packaging adheres to the strictest rules and regulations.

  For example, *Aceto Balsamico Tradizionale* (traditional Modena balsamic vingegar), *Parmigiano-Reggiano*, and *Prosciutto di Parma* all carry the DOP designation because they are one of a kind. We should only buy these products that are authentically made and developed. The more we support our local farmers, even if they are on the other side of the world, the better off we will be and the more authentic will be!

- **IGP** or *Indicazione Geografica Protetta* **(Protected Geographical Identification)**
IGP is another strict designation like DOP but with a more generous embrace. Products in this category come from a specific geographical area, while respecting one aspect of traditional production or processing. Balsamic vinegar of Modena carries the IGP label, but it's good to be aware that it hasn't been produced according to the stringent requirements of *Aceto Balsamico Tradizionale DOP*.

Think of your refrigerator as part of your pantry. Keep a running supply of stocks, pesto, and sauces on hand and make sure to utilize whatever scraps you have. For now, let's start with the most essential ingredient in any Italian kitchen: extra-virgin olive oil. Learning to cook and eat with only good quality extra-virgin olive oil changes the quality of your food in a way no other ingredient can. And it's so simple!

Olives and Olive Oil

It is impossible to imagine Italy without olive trees.

As passionate as I am about Italian food and wine, I am most obsessed with encouraging the use of high-quality olive oil. You will notice an immediate change in the flavor of anything you eat the moment you switch to a good quality extra-virgin olive oil. Almost every savory recipe in this book starts and, often, ends with extra-virgin olive oil. The quality of the oil used is as important to a recipe's success as any of the other ingredients—even more so when drizzled into a bowl of soup, or on grilled fish or lamb chops just before taking the first bite. The best way to enjoy summer tomatoes, fresh basil, and tender, sweet *mozzarella di bufala*, is only by drowning them with fabulous extra-virgin olive oil full of green nectar and delicious greenness. Why use anything but?

To be labeled extra-virgin olive oil, the oil must contain less than 0.1 percent acidity. Some industrial producers press poorer-quality, late-harvest olives and put the oil through a chemical process that washes away and reduces the extra acid so it can still be labeled "extra-virgin." In other words, that bottle of $7.99 extra-virgin olive oil is heavily processed and nowhere in the same league as a $30 bottle. Olive oil is such an essential product, so make sure you use the good stuff.

In 1990, a group of Tuscan olive oil producers, led by my dear friend Bona de' Frescobaldi, created a consortium called Laudemio, establishing a new set of regulations to ensure that consumers are protected, which has now become the benchmark for quality standards all over the world. The label on a bottle of quality olive oil provides the olive oil's biography, much like a wine label tells about the wine in the bottle, and you'll be able to know if you're buying the real thing.

What's the best way to make sure the olive oil you're stocking in your pantry is the right kind? Check the back of the label and ask your specialty food store staff to advise you.

Whether you're on your own or at a shop with knowledgeable staff, check the label or talk to the salesperson about where the oil is from, the harvest date, and where it was pressed. Here's the information that should appear on the back label:

- The name of the specific estate where the olives were grown.
- The date and year the olives were hand-harvested and bottled.
- That the olives were crushed by mechanical means at the *frantoio* (olive mill) on the estate twenty-four hours from the time they were hand-harvested.
- A "best before" date shown prominently on the label or the bottle cap.

Many different factors can affect the growing of olives. Changes in climate can interfere with the growing season, the harvest, and production. Bad weather or an infestation of the olive fruit fly can result in no harvest at all. Sometimes the size of a farm can prove overwhelming for the family running it.

For example, the Contini Bonacossi family, producer of Capezzana olive oil, owns 1,600 acres of olive trees in Tuscany. Tending to so many trees and so much land is a very labor intensive endeavor and just as anywhere in the world today, when it became too much for the family to care for their thousands of trees and harvest the olives for oil or find enough workers to do so, brother Filippo came up with a solution. Eighty families are allotted large parcels of the olive groves with trees to weed, protect, prune, and manage. When the olives are harvested in the fall, each family brings the fruit to the *frantoio* for pressing and the oil is split 50/50 between the farmers and the Contini Bonacossi family in a fair and rational way. The farmers use theirs throughout the year and gift it to relatives and friends, while the family ships many cases of Capezzana extra-virgin olive oil.

It is very important to buy products that are made by authentic people in an authentic way. Here is an example of what I mean by authentic producers:

In 2015, a fruit fly infestation and hailstorms devastated the entire crop. When the first farmers brought a small batch of the remaining olives to the mill at Capezzana, the oil was of such poor quality that the family had to make the the decision not to press any of the fruit that year. It was unimaginable for these Tuscans to be without their own olive oil for a year, and the Contini Bonacossi family feared that many of the farmers would quit the program the following year, but everyone returned in 2016 to tend their trees and harvest their olives and the oil is, as always, of superior quality.

In addition to the criteria previously mentioned, look for the area the olive oil comes from. *Terroir*—the term used in winemaking to describe the specific soil and climate of a vineyard—is also applicable to olive groves.

It helps to think about olive oil as a seasonal product, much like tomatoes and other fruits and vegetables. You should keep as many types of the four types of olive oil on hand (with a bonus fifth type in the fall) as you can.

Throughout *Autentico*, I suggest the appropriate olive oil for each recipe, but if you only have one good one in your pantry, put it to use!

Cooking with Extra-Virgin Olive Oil

As November approaches and the olive oils on your shelf reach their "best before" dates, begin using them for cooking rather than finishing. The more you use good quality olive oil in your cooking, the better your food will taste. Trust me. There are plenty of great opportunities in the specialty food shops and markets around the world, where good olive oil is sold in specials or "buy 2 get 3." When shopping for cooking extra-virgin olive oil, look for olive oils that are from the previous year, usually sold in February and March by specialty food shops as shopkeepers make room for just-pressed oils. These are ideal for cooking, as long as they were stored at proper temperature—the same as storing red wine.

Mild Extra-Virgin Olive Oil

Soft, lightly flavored olive oil, typically from central Italy, such as Lazio, Abruzzo, Umbria, Molise, and Liguria Tuscany, is used for frying, marinating, or braising meats and vegetables, making *Soffritto* (page 40) or Tomato Sauce (page 42). In spring, drizzle the oil over peas or asparagus so the taste of the spring vegetables is predominant. During the summer, make Pesto (pages 43–46) with delicate Ligurian oils. Pour some on poached or steamed fish to add a perky brightness to it. A bottle retails between $18 and $25.

Medium Extra-Virgin Olive Oil

Medium extra-virgin olive oil enhances seared swordfish, tuna, branzino, grilled vegetables, Mashed Potatoes (page 57), and Caponata (page 313). Whisk with a few drops of fresh lemon juice and sea salt and use on salads of

any variety to brighten them and take them to the next level. Drizzle over fresh summer tomatoes with mozzarella and basil and over rustic soups. A bottle will range in price from $20 to $30.

Robust Extra-Virgin Olive Oil

This is what I call Tuscan ketchup. It is the best type of steak sauce. Powerful and spicy, robust extra-virgin olive oil adds an intense and flavorful green note to your dishes. The more intense and flavorful the oil, the less you cook with it. Instead, drizzle it over sliced steak to take stock of its grassy flavor. Pour it generously over beans, artichokes, steamed greens, and kale salads. Use less robust olive oil when cooking so you can pour more raw oil on top of a finished dish.

Olio Nuovo

Olio nuovo is the first extra-virgin olive oil pressed each autumn. Gutsy, almost angry, and bright green, this oil should be celebrated as a ritual, a rite of passage of the seasons, a gift of nature. Splurge on a bottle every fall if you can find one, or else come to Tuscany as soon as you can to bathe in it. Drizzle it over *Fettunta* (page 73), or copiously pour it over slow-cooked beans (page 29), Simply Sautéed or Roasted Greens (page 60), and Mixed Broccoli and Cauliflower (page 306). Grill a grass-fed steak or fish seasoned simply with salt and pepper, then pour on the *olio nuovo*. Make sure that after two weeks, the bottle is empty. *Olio nuovo* is often the most expensive olive oil you'll have in your pantry, ranging from $35 to $40 per bottle, because it is airfreighted all over the world as soon as it bottled. Splurge on a bottle once a year. Use immediately; pour abundantly.

Storing Olive Oil

• Keep bottles in a cool, dark place where the temperature is a consistent 64°F to 68°F (18°C to 20°C). Temperature fluctuations—hot or cold—affect the aromas and cause eventual deterioration, which is why olive oil shouldn't be refrigerated or kept next to an oven or stove. And, store olive oil away from windows.

• Extra-virgin olive oil will last for one to two years, or forever if kept properly, but its flavor and aroma will start to fade as time goes by. If stored properly, use it as a cooking oil after about a year.

• Quality olive oil is meant to be used and enjoyed, and improves the flavors of everything. Cook with the best olive oil you can afford and you will notice an immediate difference in how good your food tastes.

Olive da Tavola | Table Olives

Sixty percent of Italian table olives come from Puglia and Calabria and the remaining 40 percent from Liguria and Campagna. Olive-eating traditions vary throughout Italy. My Pugliese friend Rossella Florio says bowls of her mother's fennel-cured olives are left out to snack on, while Tuscan Beatrice Contini Bonacossi says olives are used to make oil, not to eat. In the northern Marche region, large Ascolane olives are pitted, filled with meat, breaded, and fried.

When purchasing olives, any variety should come in a range of colors found in nature. For instance, good Taggiasca olives have hues of dark green to deep reddish mahogany to almost gray. Beware of olives that are all the same shade of a particular color; it means they have been cured in water and lye or copper sulfate to make them look homogenous and "more presentable." There is nothing more appetizing to me than a blemished or sunspotted fruit! My favorite cured olives are soaked in salt and water that is frequently changed, then aged in brine for three months to remove some of their bitterness and make them edible. Buy olives in jars or hermetically sealed packages, as olives sold at open olive bars can quickly oxidize and turn rancid.

My favorites for eating and cooking with are:

- **Taggiasca:** A Ligurian cousin of French picholines, these can be mixed with olive oil, lemon zest, herbs, and a bit of pepperoncino for an antipasto. Put two or three dozen olives in a jar of olive oil and use the infused oil as a finishing oil on grilled fish and vegetables. The oil-soaked olives are delicious. Pit Taggiasca green olives, chop into a coarse paste with capers and olive oil, and spread on swordfish or tuna before grilling.
- **Bella Cerignola and Ascolane:** Ascolane olives have a stone fruit and tropical flavor that is very distinguishing. In the Marche, they make one of my favorite aperitivo nibbles in the world: *olive Ascolane*. They pit the olives, stuff them with a little meat—similar to that used to stuff meat ravioli—bread them, and deep-fry them in a mild extra-virgin olive oil.
- **Gaeta black:** Combined with capers and anchovies, these olives from Naples turn Tomato Sauce (page 42), along with an anchovy or two into Puttanesca sauce if you wish. When you eat them in Napoli, Capri, or Palermo, you feel you are truly in the heart of the Mediterranean.
- **Castelvetrano:** Meaty, dark green to navy blue Castelvetrano olives hold their shape in sauces and other dishes and seem to be the ones that have suffered the most of the contamination of industrialization. The unnatural green that these olives have been celebrated for is the best reason why we should ask for better quality olives. They are so full of chemicals and bad stuff, and part of a big scam. I wish I could say something nice about them, but the problem is similar to that of bad, cheap olive oil.
- **Tremiti:** These addictive olives from Puglia taste like salty cherries and easily pull away from their pits in one bite.

POMODORI
Tomatoes

If there is one New World ingredient that dramatically changed how Italians cook and eat, it's the tomato. The arrival of pomi d'ori ("golden apples"), now called pomodori, was wholeheartedly embraced and found an ideal environmental partner in the soil of Italy. Tomatoes in Italy taste like nowhere else, as does the olive oil or wine. It's all about *terroir*!

Pelati | Jarred or Canned Tomatoes
San Marzano tomatoes are essential for making Tuscan *Ragù*, My Way (page 63), soups, and sauces—especially during the winter months.

While San Marzano plum tomatoes can be grown anywhere, those cultivated in volcanic soil near Mount Vesuvius, just south of Naples, are the real deal. While there are fraudulently labeled cans on the market, made in many places around the world, true canned San Marzano tomatoes are protected by European regional food product laws. Each can is assigned an individual number and the label will read "Pomodoro San Marzano dell'Agro Sarnese Nocerino D.O.P." It will also include the symbols of the Consorzio, the group that guarantees authenticity, and the D.O.P. Look for those, use them, and help us protect them.

Passata di Pomodoro

Passata is a crushed, strained, and uncooked tomato sauce that has been strained of seeds and skins. You can do it yourself during the peak of the tomato season, but it is so much work and Italian Passata taste so good and it's so affordable nowadays, why bother? Look for tall 24-ounce glass jars in the same section as canned tomatoes.

Pomodori Secchi |
Sun-Dried Tomatoes in Olive Oil

Some of us of a certain age above fifty years old, were traumatized by terribly tough, chewy so-called sun-dried tomatoes. Then finally they went away. Now they seem to be coming back, and made in a wholesome and real way as once upon a time. The high-quality varieties found today are a delight of sweet tomato flavor that elevate crostini, panini, pizza, farro, and rice salads. Masseria Mirogallo, a farm owned by the Belfiore family in Matera produces perfectly made *pomodori secchi*: bright red in color, marinated in olive oil, with a supple meaty texture that is a throwback to some, and a new flavor to many of the new generations. It feels as if solar energy is trapped into them, and to many in America, they will be the best type of jerky they wish they could have!

Estratto di Pomodoro |
Jarred Tomato Paste

Tomato paste should have an intense tomato-vegetal flavor and be dark maroon in color. A spoonful of estratto imparts sweetness and deep layers of flavor, and is a "flavor burst" to any dish that includes tomato as an ingredient, including tomato-based sauces. Add a tablespoon to minestrone or Tuscan *Ragù*, My Way (page 63). Spread a thin layer on toasted bread and drizzle on some *olio nuovo* to accompany a green salad or add a spoonful when making marinades for grilled meats.

My dear friend Maria Grammatico, from Erice in Sicily, makes *estratto di pomodoro*; ripe tomatoes are crushed by hand and the pulp is spread on tilted wooden planks or tables (*taulieri*) under screens to dry in the blazing heat of the relentless Mediterranean sun. As the pulp dries, the juices evaporate and run off the tilted tables, which are turned twice daily for even drying. Each evening at dusk, the boards are brought indoors to prevent any overnight moisture from damaging the drying paste. Once the boards are brought back outside each morning, the thick paste is folded with a large flat wooden spatula. When the *estratto* is the right consistency and takes on a deep red, almost the color of blood, it is thinned with just a bit of olive oil and then hand packed into jars and kept as a secret weapon to highlight many dishes. But please, don't tell anyone if you are using it!

POMORODI DA DISPENSA
Tomatoes in Your Pantry

• **PASSATA DI POMODORO**

Strained tomato sauce, used for making Tuscan *Ragù, My Way* (page 63), *Calamari in'Zimino* (page 265), or a basic Tomato Sauce (page 42).

• **PELATI**

These tomatoes have been blanched very quickly and had their skins removed. That way the tomato will break up easily and you won't have the skins in the final dish. I particularly love the jarred tomatoes from Masseria Mirogallo, which are so delicious, and packed in their own juice with the addition of a big basil leaf. Use them when making *Tonno alla Pantesca* (page 269).

• POMODORINI IN SALAMOIA

Pacchino tomatoes are somewhat salty on their own, but when preserved in water and salt, it makes you feel that they are always fresh in your pantry. I love to make my Chickpea, Tomato, and Broken Pasta Soup (page 144) with them, as well as to make a different version of Tomato Sauce (page 42).

• SPACCATELLE DI POMODORO

Sliced and seeded tomatoes jarred in their own juice (without salt or water). I use these for making *Spaccatelle di Pomodori* (page 121) and in stews where I want pieces of tomato to stick out and be a part of the dish.

SALE E PEPE
Salt and Pepper

Pellegrino Artusi, whose classic Italian cookbook *The Art of Eating Well* (which has been in print in Italy continuously since 1894) often included the letters "q.b." in his recipes. An abbreviation for *quanto basta*, which means "as much as is needed" or "as much as is enough," q.b. is a philosophy that can still be put to use over 125 years since his book was first published. *Quanto basta* rings true when seasoning with any herb or spice, but is especially apt when seasoning with salt and pepper, which is why specific amounts are rarely given in the recipes in *Autentico*.

Be faithful to your own taste buds, tasting as you cook. Add as much salt and pepper as needed, as much as is enough, or as much as you like. It's that simple.

Sale | Salt
Pure sea salt is as essential to each and every one of us as good olive oil in your kitchen. It is made by evaporating seawater and, depending on where the seawater comes from, contains varying amounts of trace minerals that add distinct flavors and colors. As a result, Cervia sea salt from Emilia-Romagna on the Adriatic Sea has no bitter minerals, giving it a naturally "sweeter" taste than other sea salts like Trapani sea salt from the waters of Eastern Sicily, which have been harvested since Phoenician times.

Keep coarse and fine sea salt in your pantry. Use coarse sea salt in pasta water or long-cooking dishes like Tuscan *Ragù*, My Way (page 63) and stews, so it has plenty of time to dissolve. Fine sea salt is best for sprinkling on finished dishes.

Pepe | Black Pepper
If I had to choose just one spice to keep in my pantry, it would be whole Tellicherry black peppercorns. All black peppercorns come from the same plant, but Tellicherry peppercorns are the largest ones. As they grow larger, their heat dissipates and they develop a nutty, citrus flavor. Always purchase whole peppercorns and try crushing them in a mortar and pestle rather than a pepper grinder for different sized pieces.

ACETO BALSAMICO TRADIZIONALE
True Balsamic Vinegar

In 1992, when I sold a rare, traditional true Balsamic vinegar aged in a batteria from 1892, to Nancy Silverton, co-owner and chef of Campanile restaurant in Los Angeles, the dazzling, complex condiment was virtually unknown in the United States. As chefs like Nancy, Thomas Keller, and Paul Bertolli introduced it to customers, the demand for this precious product rapidly grew, and unfortunately, went astray.

To make *Aceto Balsamico Tradizionale*, cooked Lambrusco and Trebbiano grape must, called *saba*, is aged in attics for twelve, eighteen, twenty-five, or more years in wooden barrels of successive sizes. Varying seasonal and daily temperatures then perform *la maggia*, the magic, that no one can explain. At the end of the aging period, the *acetaio* (vinegar maker) withdraws a small amount from the smallest barrel and tops off each barrel with the contents of the next largest cask. Fresh must is then added to the largest cask, and each year the withdrawing and topping off is repeated. Only when the balsamic vinegar has reached its appropriate age and density is it bottled in a similar way that Spanish Sherry producers and Sicilian Marsala producers make their precious wines (a.k.a. Solera procedure).

Precious, authentic traditional balsamic vinegar is produced in the cities of Modena and nearby Reggio Emilia under stringent European Union regulations. In 1979, the Consortium of Producers of authentic Balsamic Vinegar of Modena established a series of controls, rules, and regulations that delineate the processes for making true balsamic vinegar. In April 2000, the European Union granted this product the highest recognition by awarding it a DOP (*Denominazione di Origine Protetta*), demarcating and ensuring that the very precious and singular balsamic vinegar is a consistent continuation of its centuries-long tradition. A board of *assaggiatori* (expert tasters) guarantees that each bottle of vinegar with a numbered seal is in compliance with all the rules, regulations, and procedures set forth by the consortium.

Authentic and traditional balsamic vinegar has a glossy, mahogany color and a complex flavor that balances the natural *agrodolce* (sweet-sour) elements of the cooked grape juice with hints of woodiness from the aging barrels. Drizzle the precious condiment sparingly over cooked meats, fish, or dark greens as soon as they are done to make sure it loses none of its singular aroma and unparalleled flavor. For dessert, spoon a few drops over mixed berries or shaved ice. I enjoy it the most over chunks of good Parmigiano-Reggiano, strawberries, or just simply by the spoon instead of dessert. It's truly balsamic as a digestive!

An 8-ounce (250ml) bottle—depending on the age—ranges in price from $60 to $500 (only Thomas Keller buys this one . . . it's over 100 years old!) Most stores will sell them for around $125 and you must keep them like a good wine or olive oil: away from the light and in a cool dark place. *Aceto Balsamico Tradizionale* promises a lifetime of enjoyment.

Condimento Balsamico, also called *Condimento* or *Balsamico*, is made with the same grape must and in a similar set of barrels as *Aceto Balsamico Tradizionale* DOP. The finished product, however, may be younger or older depending on the producer. This, yet again, is where your importer, specialty food keeper and chefs are to be your allies. *Authentic Condimento Balsamico* can be just as good, or better at times, than *Aceto Balsamico Tradizionale* DOP. But, as I always say: It's not a Ferrari! It may be bottled from barrels that have undergone as few as three *travassi* to as many as one hundred.

ACETO DI FRUTTA
Fruit Vinegars

Whereas red and wine vinegars are made from wine, fruit vinegar is made from fruit that is selected, crushed, and made into a paste, which then gets inoculated with a special mother in order to start the fermentation. The resulting product adds a much brighter and "alive" ingredient to your food. You will notice immediately the difference because it makes the food spark in your mouth. Brightness, fruitiness, and acidity . . . What could be better?

Red and White Wine Vinegars

To make good wine vinegar, one must first make good wine.

Then the wine needs to be acetified slowly and, finally, aged in a similar way to a fine wine. Finding the right balance between aroma, flavor, and acidity is a delicate task that requires patience and care by the producer. The difference between a high-quality vinegar and one that is more akin to "sour wine" (containing a lot of alcohol and high acetic acid) is drastic and the inflicting results upon your lovely greens, food, or drinks might become quite a piece of conversation among your friends. Please, use good vinegar! Better wine vinegars are matured in wood for up to two years and have lower acidity levels than younger vinegars and there are many out and about in the market. Make sure you try them before you buy them, and make sure you keep them in the same pantry with your olive oil.

Capers

Capers are the unopened flower buds of the caper bush. The shrubby, wall-clinging plant boasts sprigs of shiny, oval, dark green leaves and white fragrant blossoms with violet stamens and flourishes in the wild among the cracks and crevices of rocks and stone walls. The caper plant can tolerate harsh sea storms and thrives in dry heat, allowing it to flourish in the salty breezes that blow in from the seas throughout the Mediterranean basin. You'll find caper plants from the Atlantic coasts of the Canary Islands and Morocco to the coastlines of the Black Sea, the Crimean Peninsula, Armenia, and eastward around the Caspian Sea well into Iran.

Small, tight, firm caper buds are the most prized, and from early April until September, the newly formed firm buds of the caper bush are harvested by hand every eight to twelve days, resulting in nine to twelve harvests during the hot, sunny period. Hard harvesting is painful since most capers are grown in small farms over volcanic lava soil, and because the soil is so dark, the heat so sweltering, and the labor so backbreaking, the buds are plucked at sunrise or sunset before they have a chance to bloom. The buds are quickly packed under salt so they can undergo the lactic-fermentation, and after a few days, the salt is changed and then set to cure for a few weeks more. Capers were once upon a time a form of currency, much like salt. A mechanized cylindrical screen sorts the capers by size on a scale from 6 to 16, which indicate their size in millimeters.

To bring out their complex flavors, capers must be cured in salt (also called a dry cure) or brine (wet cure). Capers packed in salt have a brighter, more intense flavor and a noticeably firmer texture when cooked compared to those bottled in brine, which turn mushy when cooked. Please don't ever use the ones packed in vinegar, which are usually made with very low quality capers and pickled in industrial vinegar!

The large semi-mature seed pods of the plant are known as *cucunci*, or caper berries. Smaller, teardrop-shaped, stemless Sicilian caper berries are distinct, and since they are smaller, they have thicker skins, hundreds of tiny seeds, and a soft, delicate flavor. To prepare them, quickly rinse caper berries in a colander to remove the salt. Add chopped or whole caper berries to caponata. Make a quick sauce of chopped caper berries, cherry tomatoes, torn basil leaves, and robust extra-virgin olive oil to spoon over grilled swordfish. Serve with salumi, in a bowl of olives, with some good robust olive oil and freshly chopped oregano or skewered as a garnish for Bloody Marys or Martinis.

Anchovies

To those who say, "I don't like anchovies," my response is, "Just try a good one," from my dear friend Lucia!

Cetara, an ancient fishing village located south of Naples on the Amalfi coast, is involved in the harvesting and processing of anchovies from the Tyrrhenian Sea, famously known for being a dark, clean, and cold rock-bottom sea. In 1983, Francesco di Mauro's company, Ittica Alimentare Salerno (IASA), was the first to preserve local anchovies and tuna in glass jars. Who would have ever thought? Now it feels so common, but tuna in a can was something we all grew up with. Francesco was truly AUTENTICO, as preserving anchovies and tuna in a jar allows you to see the quality of the meat, which should be plum-colored almost pink.

His three children—Lucia, Francesco, and Salvatore—now run the business, and visit their boats and the factory, and being with them is truly a life-changing experience. I have made so many people fall in love with anchovies and we have so much more to do. A while back, Lucia invited me to join them on the traditional midnight anchovy harvest during the new moon called *La Notte delle Lampare*, the Night of the Lamps. Once our fishing boat was well out of the harbor, the fishermen lowered lamps into the water to attract the silver-blue anchovies. Nets were thrown out by hand to catch tens of thousands of the tiny fish flocking to the light.

Back on shore, the fish were quickly packed in ice and taken to the processing plant, where workers gutted and cleaned the fish by hand at astonishing speeds. Once rinsed, the fish are carefully placed on linen cloths and layered with sea salt in small wooden barrels called "Terzigno," all by hand. After a year of curing in a dark cellar, the anchovies are gently rinsed and removed from the barrels. The visual impact of plump pink anchovies being carefully cleaned and packed by hand is remarkable in this day and age. Notice how many times I wrote "by hand"? No machinery is used, just the fingers of as many as seventy-five women. Amazingly enough, Lucia's family says that women are not allowed on the fishing boats, only men. However, once the anchovies are brought to shore, women only can do the work of cleaning them, curing them, and preserving them. There is no other product I have witnessed being made in Italy such as this. And there are not many producers left who do it this way!

Every tray of anchovies that arrives for processing at IASA bears the name of the vessel, the fishing method, the EU and FAO zoning, and the date the anchovies were caught. This label ensures the sustainability of IASA's fishing practices and the future of these tiny silvery-blue fish in the Mediterranean. And yes, there is a big difference in cost and flavor between the Adriatic and Tyrrhenian seas. Adriatic anchovies can cost as much as 8 Euros per kg and the harvest is about 2 months

earlier than the Tyrrhenian Sea anchovies, which cost as much as 20 Euros due to the fact that they are meatier and less "muddy" in flavor than their cousins from the other side of the boot, which grow in warmer waters. If you are going to cure them and also make *colatura* from them, then you better have fleshy and meaty blue fish with bright neon lights when they get to your plant.

Colatura di Alici | Anchovy Essence

Because the anchovies are pressed and cured in salt, a significant amount of the rich, amber-red fish oil drips down to the bottom of the barrels. Called *colatura di alici*, this essence is one of the most treasured and special ingredients to come out of Campania. Rich with the saline flavor of anchovies and the sea, *colatura*'s roots date back to ancient Rome (when it was known as *garum*). Once the anchovies are packed, the essence goes on to be aged for three to four years in oak barrels before being filtered and bottled.

A little bit of *colatura* goes a long way. Add it drop by drop to a dish until the desired flavor is obtained, and avoid seasoning with salt until you've tasted the final dish. *Colatura* can be spooned over pasta, fish, and vegetables; stirred into braising lamb or beef; splashed on top of braised sea bass with cherry tomatoes, olives, garlic, and parsley; or drizzled over Farro Soup (page 99). Substitute a few drops of *colatura* for anchovy fillets or stir a few drops into a martini.

AROMI E ODORI
Aromas and Scents

At vegetable stands throughout Italy, when you ask a vendor for *aromi e odori* for your broth, she will tie up the *aromi*—one celery stalk, one carrot, and one red onion—and the *odori*—parsley, sage, bay, and rosemary stems—and wrap up your purchase in newsprint. It is always good to have a lot of *aromi e odori* available so you can use them to flavor all your roasted meats, use generously whenever you want, to scent and give more aroma to your kitchen while cooking, and to make your food taste different than the last time you made it!

CIPOLLE
Onions

Ask an Italian cook if she uses onions and garlic in the same dish and she'll give you a suspicious look and answer, *"Mai!"* (Never!) Ask another and she'll say, *"Certo! Chi non?"* (Of course! Who doesn't?) Some use white onions, others red or yellow. "Non c'e' mai una regola" (there are no rules!) and once again, q.b. is yet again a guiding force.

When a recipe calls for raw onions, like Blood Orange, Lemon, and Red Onion Salad (page 88), I prefer *cipolle di Tropea*, a sweet purple-red, oval onion similar to Walla Walla or Vidalia in taste. They are so sweet that you can eat them without blanching. Look for them at farmers' markets. For cooking, I use red onions; they impart onion flavor with fewer tears, and they are more authentic with the Tuscan food I know so well.

When cooking, soft onions should take 4 to 5 minutes; translucent onions, 5 to 6 minutes;

aramelized onions, between 30 and 45 minutes. When making caramelized onions, be sure to stir the onions once they begin to stick to the pan, but not too frequently or they won't brown. If the onions start to burn, lower the heat and stir a bit more frequently, watching that the caramelization is even throughout the pan and using the lowest flame possible to turn them into almost a marmalade.

AGLIO
Garlic

When it comes to garlic, you just want a scent, *una sfumatura*. A small amount goes a long way, even when making Pesto (page 43) or Salsa Verde (page 50). When making sauces, keep the cloves whole, but crush them with the side of a chef's knife and remove the bitter green sprout if one is present. Rub halved cloves on toasted bread for bruschetta. Purchase heads of garlic that are firm and plump.

LE ERBE FRESCHE
Fresh Herbs

Whether used during cooking or torn and sprinkled on top of a finished dish, fresh herbs bring vitality to Italian cooking. The trick is to learn to use them in the right amounts. Too little adds nothing; too much can overpower a dish.

Whenever possible, buy herbs like basil and mint with the roots still attached. To make them last longer, wrap the stems in damp paper towels and store in the fridge or put herbs in tall jars with plenty of water. Tear, rather than cut, leafy herbs into pieces to keep their color and flavor. Herbs like thyme and rosemary last longer, especially if refrigerated in a brown paper bag.

Basilico | Basil
Since basil doesn't stay fresh for very long, make *Brodetto* (page 56), a quick vegetable broth, using the stems and leaves once they start to turn. Basil leaves become soft and less flavorful when watered too frequently. Choose stems with roots attached whenever you can and look for bright green, plump, firm leaves. Remove smaller basil leaves from their stems and use them whole. Larger ones should be torn, never cut with a knife, into irregular pieces.

Foglie di Alloro | Bay Leaves
One of my favorite walks in Firenze is to head up to the Via San Leonardo villas behind the Boboli Gardens, then turn right at Viale Machiavelli, which becomes Viale Galileo. At the Piazzale Michelangelo, the view of the city is spectacular. Along this route—as throughout much of Italy—wild hedges of bay laurel grow prolifically, and I often pick a few leaves on my way and tuck them into my pocket. Fresh or dried, bay leaves release their aromas when added to moist heat like soups, stews, or beans, or fish before grilling.

Erba Cipollina | Chives
Use a pair of scissors to snip chives into small pieces and add them to Salsa Verde (page 50) or Mashed Potatoes (page 57). Toss them with springtime peas, asparagus and salads. Scatter on grilled fish.

Cime di Finocchio | Fennel Tops

Fennel grows prolifically throughout much of Italy, and every part is used. The Wild Fennel Pollen (page 28) and seeds are popular as seasonings. The bulbs can be roasted, panfried, or sliced raw for salads and to accompany *Bagna Caôda* (page 105). The fronds can be added to soups and stews or sprinkled over fresh salads like other fresh herbs. Wrap the fronds in a damp paper towel and refrigerate. Sicilians even craft footstools from the large stalks of wild fennel plants; you can find them for sale all over the island.

Menta | Mint

Store mint in a plastic bag in the refrigerator, and leave the bag slightly open (trapped moisture causes the herbs to mold) or trim the ends and place in a jar with 1 inch of water. I often use mint in place of "nipitella," (catnip), which grows wild in Toscana, when making a simple dish of fettuccine with fresh porcini mushrooms. When sprinkling parsley on grilled fish and lamb chops it's wonderful to add a few torn leaves of mint as a surprise bite.

Prezzemolo | Parsley

Flat Italian parsley is so fresh, bright, and full of green energy that it often ends up being sprinkled on most of my dishes along with robust extra-virgin olive oil. Torn or coarsely chopped, the texture and bitter flavor of the leaves add a surprise burst of flavor to whatever you add it to. Even though the poor little green herb has been relegated to be a simple garnish or sprinkled decoration in many of the Italian trattorie (alongside stale black pepper when serving steaks!) I firmly believe that parsley is one of our most underutilized and underestimated herbs, and we should all be eating a lot more of it. I use more flat-leaf (Italian) parsley—whole bunches and individual leaves—than any other herb. It's fresh, bright, and adds a pop to any dish.

Rosmarino | Rosemary

While many cooks chop up rosemary's thin, spiky leaves and add them to their cooking, I often add whole sprigs of rosemary when cooking potatoes, beans, and mushrooms and remove the wilted sprigs before serving. Layer whole sprigs in a roasting pan as a bed for roast pork, lamb, or chicken.

Salvia | Sage

If you find yourself with too much fresh sage, tie the ends with a bit of kitchen twine and hang the bunch in a cool, dry place. In a few weeks, you'll have plenty of dried sage to get you through the winter. Use fresh sage leaves to make *burro e salvia*, a simple sage and butter sauce that is often served with gnocchi, ravioli, and fresh pasta.

Timo | Thyme

Fresh or dried thyme is used with other herbs in soups, grilled fish dishes, and in Ligurian and some Sicilian eggplant dishes. To easily remove the leaves from the stems, push one stem through a mesh sieve. The leaves will remain in the sieve.

Just as hard as it is to imagine Italy without the tomato, corn, and potato, the same applies to the pepper. In Piedmonte, bell peppers are use profusely in making *Peperonata* (page 49). In Tuscany during the month of May, we have a type of green pepper very similar to a Spanish Pimiento del Padron or Japanese Shishito peppers called "Frigitelle" because they are fried and served with a sprinkle of sea salt. They are quite delicious as part of an antipasti party.

Many parts of Italy, especially in the south, use peperoncini. In Italian, *peperoncini* refers to hot peppers, while sweet ones, like bell peppers or Italian frying peppers, are called *peperoni.*

Peperoncini are small, wrinkled red peppers that measure ½ to 2 inches in length. They are preserved by sun drying, immersing them in olive oil, or packing them in salt to use year-round. Their heat levels range from mild to fierce. Like all hot peppers, the smaller the size, the greater the heat. And the farther south you go in Italy, the hotter the peppers, with sun-dried ones from Calabria and Basilicata topping the heat scale. Add them whole to a stew, or crush them and add while a dish is cooking.

Peperoncini Cruschi | Sun-Dried Cruschi Peppers

When these glossy, deep red Basilicata and Calabrian peppers ripen at the end of July through September, they are hand harvested and strung into large wreaths (called *serte*) to be dried in the shade in open and ventilated greenhouse-style sheds for twenty to twenty-five days until they are dry and wrinkled all over. Once dried, these aromatic and spicy peppers, known as *cruschi*, are fried in local olive oil just until the skins turn a brick red color and take on a soft leathery texture reminiscent of a potato chip. Frying the peppers takes just seven seconds—one second too many, and they will become *carbonizzati*, or charcoal. Once fried, *cruschi* are lightly salted and used throughout the year. In Lucania, the arch of the Italian boot, near one of the most incredible cities of the world, Matera (see pages 112–113), *cruschi* are eaten like chips or toasted nuts with a glass of wine. Serve them alone or stir into braised and roasted meats. Add an additional layer of flavor by crushing with a mortar and pestle and sprinkle over eggs fried in olive oil, *Misticanza, Two Ways* (page 76), or spaghetti with garlic, olive oil, and chiles.

Spices

Since the Renaissance, dried spices like *canella* (cinnamon), *chiodi di garofano* (cloves), *anice stellato* (star anise), and *ginepri* (juniper berries) have been used in much of Italian cooking, especially in savory stews and meat dishes. Although dried, these spices lose their aromas and flavors over time. Store them in dark containers away from sunlight and replace them yearly. Two dried spices in particular deserve a special mention: saffron and wild fennel pollen.

Zafferano | Saffron

Legend has it that the *Crocus sativus* plant was brought to Abruzzo by a thirteenth-century Dominican friar. Today, *zafferano dell'Aquila* is considered Italy's finest and has a DOP (*Denominazione di Origine Protetta*) certification that guarantees the product is locally grown, harvested, and dried by traditional methods. The saffron growers watch the late October/early November weather closely, because the flowers can pop up overnight. The three bright orange-red stigmas must be removed before the flower's sixth petal opens. During harvest time, and due to the fact this is such an old tradition, elderly women sit at tables covered with white tablecloths and gently remove the stigmas by hand. The stigmas are carefully toasted so they remain whole. It takes 200,000 flowers to make 1 kilogram of saffron. Today, saffron is also grown in Chianti and Umbria. Just a little pinch of saffron threads imparts its rich color and flavor to dishes like *Fregola Sarda con Scampi, Piselli e Asparagi* (page 200), and seafood stews. I can't think of a more beautiful and special spice to have (along with the next one, of course!).

Fiore di Finocchio | Wild Fennel Pollen

Fennel flowers are hand harvested all throughout Italy and placed in cloth bags to prevent moisture from collecting and creating mold. The flowers are then spread on paper-lined wooden boards kept under protective netting in a well-aerated, dry room. About ten days later, the fennel is checked for moisture and, although it is not completely dry at this point, is sifted to remove leaves and twigs, and packed in large cotton bags to finish the drying process. When thoroughly dry, the precious pollen is golden-green in color and has a heady aroma of anise. It is used throughout the year in many Tuscan dishes, especially to make salumi and porchetta. Purchase fennel pollen packed in airtight bags and store in an airtight container in a cool, dark place to maintain its aroma and flavor. Like saffron and *colatura* the flavor is so intense it is wise to add a little bit at a time and check for the intensity. It is truly a privilege to add this spice to your pantry. Look for it in specialty food shops, or check in the resource chapter at the end of the book to find out how to order online.

Before grilling, dust thick-cut pork chops or swordfish and tuna steaks with a blend of fennel pollen, sea salt, and black pepper. Scatter a bit over fresh goat cheese to accompany salads. Add a pinch when making salad dressing, salt rub, and sausages.

Beans

Italy has some of the most delicious and wonderful beans in the world. Since ancient times, beans such as cicerchie (a small almost flat and square bean related to lupins) as well as chick peas, lentils, fava beans, and peas were eaten throughout the peninsula. With the arrival of the American varieties, due to the Columbian exchange, the assortment of beans expanded and the love for beans grew to new levels. In Toscana, we eat so much beans! In fact, areas such as the Pratomagno south of Florence and Soranna near Lucca grow some of the best beans in the world, which are sold for 60 Euros per kg. That's more than a T-bone steak! Add beans to soups, salads, and stews, or soak bread slices briefly in the rich bean broth, then top each piece with some beans and drizzle with robust extra-virgin olive oil.

Fagioli Freschi | Fresh Beans

Unlike pole or snap beans, borlotti (cranberry), lupini, cannellini, and other varieties of fresh shelling beans must be removed from their pods before they are cooked. It takes a little time to prepare a pound or two of fresh beans, but once shelled, fresh beans take just 5 to 8 minutes to cook in a pot of abundantly salted water. If you're going to add beans to soups and stews, simmer them for less time so they retain a nice and toothsome al dente bite.

A word about fava beans or *fave* in Italian: Since American-grown fava beans are larger than those in Italy, they must be blanched once they are removed from their pods and then peeled. Italian *fave* have a thinner membrane, so peeling is unnecessary. Large Italian *fave* are dried to use throughout the winter. And if you come to Florence, please ask for "Baccelli," not for fava or fave, which refers to the male organ!

Fagioli Secchi | Dried Beans

Tuscans, who are often called *mangiafagioli* ("bean eaters"), because they often eat beans in place of pasta, on bread, or as a *contorno*, have mastered the art of cooking them. To serve broken beans to Tuscans is like offering a plate of broken spaghetti to a Roman.

To prepare slow-cooked beans: soak them first in water overnight. Once soaked, discard the water and rinse the beans in a colander. To cook, put the beans in a large pot and add enough water to measure "quattro ditta d'acqua" (four fingers of water) on top of the beans (or 3 inches). Add 1 tablespoon cooking extra-virgin olive oil, ¼ teaspoon Tellicherry black peppercorns, 1 garlic clove, a sprig each of sage and rosemary, and a bay leaf. Bring to a boil, then reduce the heat to maintain a very gentle, slow simmer. It is essential that the cooking water barely move. Carlo Cioni, chef and owner of Ristorante Da Delfina in Artimino, Tuscany, insists, "Don't ever stir the beans or they will break. Every once in a while, gently swirl or shake the pot. They should look like they are being cradled in the water as if you are trying to put a baby to sleep in a cradle!"

Just like pasta, the only way to know when beans are done is to taste them (start testing around 30 minutes). If they are evenly cooked throughout with a firm but creamy texture, turn off the heat and let the beans cool in the cooking liquid. Once cool, refrigerate the beans in their broth. Beans should never be salted during cooking; add salt when finished, but not too much and *quanto basta*!

One pound dried beans will yield about 5 cups cooked beans. Look for freshly dried local beans at farmers' markets or purchase them from quality companies like camelliabrand.com or ranchogordo.com.

MIELE
Honey

As with olive oil and wine, fine honey is the product of *terroir*, the environmental factors that impart one-of-a-kind flavors. Some Italian honeys are exceptionally rare and are made from single blossoms, like *rhododreno* (rhododendron) in the National Park of Piemonte, *cardi* (cardoon) from the Tuscan island of Elba, and bitter strawberry bush from Sardinia and loquat flowers. *Miele de melata* is honeydew honey produced from insect honeydew or plant secretions other than nectar. From Piemonte in the northwest to the volcanic slopes of Sicily's Mount Etna, Italian honeys come in endless varieties depending on which blossoms the bees feed on. Also like olive oils and wines, certain honeys are best when paired with certain foods, so keep several different types in your pantry. Throughout Italy, mothers soothe their children's sore throats with a glass of warm milk with a spoonful of acacia honey stirred in.

Robinia del Canavese | Acacia

Native to eastern North America, the seeds of the acacia tree were brought to Europe in the beginning of the 17th century. Now an arboreal fixture in regions throughout Italy along roads and railway tracks, the trees grow from 30 to 70 feet high and burst into white blossoms in May and June, perfuming the air with their sweet scent. Hot, dry weather in Italy means that there will be a shortage of acacia honey in a given year.

Pure acacia honey is transparent and ranges in color from pale yellow and green to light gold. The nose is floral and fruity; the flavor is slightly acidic with hints of vanilla.

Stir acacia honey into yogurt or cream, or drizzle over sliced peaches or fresh cheeses, such as ricotta and stracchino.

Castagne | Chestnut

Since bitter flavors are so pronounced in Italian food, chestnut honey, with its dark, dense, molasses-like color and its bitter chocolate flavor, is popular. There is no better flavor in the world for me than this honey. It is quite shocking for many people the first time they taste it, but after using it on cheese or gelato, the flavors grow on you and you will be addicted to it as I am.

Serve as an accompaniment with fresh ricotta, stracchino, or ripe blue cheeses like gorgonzola dolcelatte. Drizzle a spoonful over pecorino Toscano and sliced fresh pears. Add chestnut honey when making gelato or ice cream. Combine with other ingredients and use as a glaze when roasting or grilling pork chops or guinea fowl.

Fior d'Arancio | Orange Blossom

Orange blossom honey is white, thick, and very sweet with a light citrus finish. With delicate aromas of orange blossoms, it also has hints of marmalade with a slight citric acid tone. Light white color, with amber hues are indications of purity and will darken as well as crystallize into granules of various sizes with time. Orange blossom honey has a surprising characteristic: It contains small amounts of caffeine. In Italy, orange blossom honey is made from blossoms that bees feast on in October and November.

Stir some into a cup of tea or a glass of warm milk. Spread on morning toast. Pair with sharp pecorino cheese or use to glaze fruit tarts.

Millefiori | Wildflower

Millefiori means "a thousand flowers." It is both the most common type of honey and also the rarest, because bees drink the nectars from flowers in a particular place at a particular time, which means it is impossible to re-produce the unique color, aroma, and flavors of wildflower honey from year to year.

Use wildflower honey for everything from spooning on toast to stirring into yogurt to adding to any recipe that calls for honey.

FARINA
Flour

There are significant differences between American all-purpose flour and Italian *doppio zero* ("00") flour. In North America, flours are labeled by how much protein they contain, which affects gluten formation when bak-ing and making pasta. In Italy (and Europe), flours are classified by how they are ground. Coarsely ground flour is labeled "*Tipo 2*," while finely ground flour is labeled "*Tipo 00*."

The gluten in European durum wheat flour is quite strong, but not very elastic. The result: a toothy bite to bread and pasta, but not as much chewiness. North American wheat flour, however, offers both strength and great elasticity. The result: a good bite and more chewiness.

All-purpose flour was used to test the des-sert recipes in *Autentico*. If you want to use *Tipo 00* (which I prefer), slightly more liquid may be required since it has more surface area due to its fine milling.

PINOLI
Pine Nuts

Italian pine nuts are twice the price of less-expensive, so-called pine nuts from China or Russia, which are a completely different spe-cies of a pine tree and often have an odd fuel-like aftertaste. Italian pine nuts are elongated and somewhat crescent shaped, while those from China and Russian are more heart-shaped. The best Italian *pinoli* are grown in the Mac-chia di Migliarino, a magnificent pine forest along the coastline between Livorno and Pisa near the Tyrrhenian Sea, where the old trees look like enormous umbrellas.

PISTACCHI
Pistachios

Hot, sunny, and dry summers make Sicily, especially the areas around Mount Etna and the town of Bronte, an ideal location for growing these nuts, which are recognized by their vibrant green color and violet hues. Pro-duction is alternate bearing or biennial bear-ing, meaning the trees bear the nuts only every other year, which makes these precious nuts more precious and extremely expensive. Check on the Resources pages for sources of authen-tic Sicilian pistachio, which have a noticeable different flavor than any other pistachio.

Equipment

Be and become a kitchen equipment minimalist.

I have very little equipment in mine and therefore you will notice in the recipes of *Autentico* that you don't need to have lots of different tools. Basics such as durable pots, saucepans, and roasting pans in varying sizes; sharp knives (a chef's knife, a paring knife, and a serrated knife); a Dutch oven; and heavy-duty baking sheets are essential. Buy the best quality items you can afford and they will last a lifetime. Here are some other essentials I have in my kitchen in Firenze:

Pentola Per Cuocere la Pasta | Pasta Pot

An 8- to 10-quart pot with a draining insert is an indispensable kitchen tool. With the insert, you can make and easily strain brodetto, broth, pasta, and vegetables; without the insert, the pot can be used for preparing soups and stews. The pot should be wide, rather than tall and narrow, for easier cooking, cleaning, and storage, and the insert should be deep, rather than shallow.

Pinze | Tongs

Nine- and 12-inch tongs are essential for tossing pasta with sauce and salads; turning meat, seafood, and vegetables when grilling; and hundreds of other uses.

Mortaio e pestello | Mortar and Pestle

A mortar is a bowl, made of wood or stone, and a pestle is a long club-shaped tool used to crush or grind herbs and spices or make sauces like Pesto (page 43–46) and Salsa Verde (page 122). They come in many sizes and a range of prices. I have three or four sizes in my kitchen, from a small one to crush spices to a large one to make pesto and pastes.

Stampo | Springform Pan

A sturdy 10-inch round springform pan with a bottom and a locking, removable band is helpful when making savory tortes and many desserts. The band should fit the bottom tightly so there is no leaking.

Pentola con Coperchio | 12-inch Straight-Sided Skillet with a Lid

Italians tend to cook pasta sauces in a large skillet, then add the cooked pasta to the skillet and toss, rather than mixing everything together in a bowl (which keeps the dish warm as long as possible). The skillet is placed on a trivet on the table and the pasta with sauce is dished out into warm bowls. A large skillet is handy for sautéing and braising vegetables.

Forbici | Scissors

While I use my fingers to tear up herb leaves, many cooks snip them with scissors which can also be used to cut up leftover spaghetti for soups. Throughout Abruzzo, scissors and a few spicy peperoncini are placed on the table so each person can add the desired amount of heat to pasta or other dishes.

Grattugia | Grater or Zester

A sharp, stainless-steel rasp zester or Microplane is all you need. It is ideal for grating Parmigiano-Reggiano, Pecorino Romano, as well as lemon and orange zest. And it's essential for grating nutmeg into mashed potatoes as well as cinnamon sticks into panettone bread pudding.

2
Ready to Use
PRONTO PER ALL'USO

Once your shopping is done,

take a little time to make a few simple basics to keep in your refrigerator. Having *Soffritto, Battuto Verde, Salsa Di Pomodoro, Brodo,* and other ready-to-use essentials guarantees a homemade meal in just minutes—no matter how busy the day.

Italian *soffritto*—similar to French *mirepoix* or Spanish *sofrito*—is a classic, simple mix of sautéed aromatic vegetables that jump-starts a slew of recipes from soups and stews to pasta sauces and Tuscan *Ragù, My Way* (page 63). Derived from the verb *soffriggere*, which means "to fry" in Italian, *soffritto* starts as a raw mixture of onions, carrots, and celery called *battuto* (from the verb *battere*), which means "to chop"). Low heat, unhurried cooking, and regular stirring turns a *battuto* into a *soffritto* in 35 to 40 minutes. The longer and slower the vegetables are cooked, the darker, nuttier, and softer they become, and thus the more complex the flavors in the final dish.

The key to *soffritto* is cutting the vegetables into the same size (use a knife rather than a food processor) to ensure even cooking. This recipe yields about three cups, but is easy to scale up (just use equal parts onion, celery, and carrots). I often double or triple the amount and store the cooked *soffritto* in the freezer.

And one last thing: Tuscan cooks prefer to use the inner, lighter-in-color stalks from a bunch of celery for their subtler flavor. The outer green ones have a stronger celery flavor and can overpower the other vegetables. Use whichever is most to your liking!

Soffritto

SOFFRITTO

MAKES 3 CUPS

2 cups (500 ml | 440 g) mild extra-virgin olive oil

2 cups (275 g) very finely diced white onions (about 1 large onion)

2 cups (275 g) very finely diced carrots (about 4 medium carrots)

2 cups (275 g) very finely diced celery (about 8 medium stalks—preferably the lighter, inner stalks)

1 garlic clove, finely chopped

q.b. coarse sea salt and crushed Tellicherry black peppercorns

• Put the olive oil, onions, carrots, celery, and garlic in a large skillet and stir to coat evenly with the oil. Place over high heat until the oil is hot and the vegetables start to fry, about 5 minutes. Reduce the heat to medium and cook, stirring occasionally, until the onions are a deep golden brown, the celery has turned from white to a pale gold, and the vegetables are very tender, 45 minutes to 1 hour. Season with salt and pepper. Use immediately or set aside to cool, then store in an airtight container in the refrigerator for up to 1 week.

While plucking all the leaves from bunches of parsley and other herbs for *battuto verde* isn't the most exciting of tasks, the end result is an all-purpose flavor enhancer that lasts a week or two in the fridge. To make the prep more enjoyable, I pour myself a big glass of wine and pluck a large batch all at once. Then the work is done and it's in the fridge ready to go. The only herb that should stay consistent for *Battuto Verde* is a very large bunch of bright green parsley—the rest is up to you. In the summer, use a bunch of basil in addition to the parsley. In the winter, add a mixture of sage, bay, and rosemary. If you have them on hand, I love the bright-bitter combination of scallions and celery leaves.

Serve in a bowl in the middle of a table, mix a teaspoon into vinaigrette for green salads, smear over Crostini (page 73), stir into slow-cooked beans (page 11), or drizzle over grilled meat and fish.

Shattered Green Herb Sauce

BATTUTO VERDE

MAKES 1 CUP

Leaves from 1 large bunch parsley, stems reserved for another use

Leaves from 1 bunch basil (or a mixture of sage, bay, and rosemary), stems reserved for another use

½ teaspoon fine sea salt

q.b. freshly ground Tellicherry black pepper

Mild extra-virgin olive oil, to finish

• On a cutting board, sprinkle the herbs with the salt and use a very sharp knife or mezzaluna to coarsely chop them. Transfer to a jar and season with pepper. Cover with a thin layer of olive oil. *Battuto verde* will keep in the refrigerator for 1 to 2 weeks (the herbs will start to discolor after a few days, but the flavor remains the same!).

A simple homemade tomato sauce forms the heart of many Italian pasta, braises, soups, and other dishes. Instead of using canned tomatoes, I use *passata di pomodoro*, a puréed raw tomato sauce that has been strained of seeds and skins, for a sauce that is smooth, rich, and flavorful. Popular throughout Europe, *passata* is quickly gaining a following in North America—find it in specialty food shops in tall glass jars next to the tomatoes. If you cannot find it in your store, run pure canned tomatoes through a sieve or a food mill and discard the solids.

Contrary to popular belief, if you use quality ingredients, tomato sauce doesn't need to take all day to cook. My family recipe takes under 30 minutes from start to finish. Cut the recipe in half or refrigerate or freeze leftovers.

Tomato Sauce

SALSA DI POMODORO

MAKES 3 CUPS

¼ cup (60 ml | 57 g) medium extra-virgin olive oil

2 large white onions, finely chopped (about 2½ cups)

2 cups (475 ml | 454 g) *passata di pomodoro*

6 sprigs basil

q.b. coarse sea salt and crushed Tellicherry black peppercorns

• In a large saucepan, combine the olive oil and onions and sauté over medium heat until the onions are transparent, 12 to 15 minutes. Add the *passata* and basil and bring to a simmer. Cook until the sauce has reduced by one-third, 15 to 20 minutes. Remove and discard the basil sprigs and season with salt and pepper. Use immediately or reheat before serving. *Salsa di Pomodoro* will keep in an airtight container in the refrigerator for up to 5 days.

The three recipes that follow range from mild and slightly sweet *(Pesto di Erbe)* to intense and bitter *(Pesto Amaro)* to sweet and salty *(Pesto alla Trapanese)*. Working by hand—I use a large mortar and pestle—allows you to control the texture of the final pesto, but feel free to experiment with a food processor, pulsing slowly so as to not overwork the herbs.

If you're not using the pesto immediately, transfer it to a jar and top with ½ inch of mild extra-virgin olive oil. Refrigerate for up to 2 weeks. Before using, bring to room temperature and stir well.

Pesto

PESTO

When I started my business in 1988, arugula was just becoming popular in America. The vegetable's green leaves were huge, the size some Tuscan farmers call *per i cavalli* ("suitable for horse feed")! and had an overly bitter and metallic flavor. Fortunately, better-tasting and small-leafed varieties of arugula are now available everywhere, ideal for making *Pesto di Erbe* at home wherever you are. Here I use a combination of baby arugula, basil, and parsley (along with green garlic or ramp tops in the spring). The basil—key to the pesto made in Liguria—imparts briny, sweet, seaweed undertones; the parsley, a bright green flavor; the arugula, that distinctive peppery note.

This recipe relies on proportions (3 parts arugula to 2 parts other herbs), making it easy to customize the yield. Spread over crostini, use in a grilled cheese, or add more olive oil to the pesto and use as a dipping sauce when having a *pinzimonio* (fresh vegetables cut into sticks). I also love *Pesto di Erbe* on top of grilled branzino or grilled meats such as *bistecca alla Fiorentina*.

Arugula and Herb Pesto

PESTO DI ERBE

MAKES 2½ CUPS

3 cups (100 g) arugula

1 cup (30 g) fresh basil and/or parsley leaves

1 cup (30 g) green garlic or ramps tops

q.b. fine sea salt

1¼ cups (300 ml | 275 g) mild extra-virgin olive oil, plus more to finish

• In a large mortar, start smashing the arugula, basil, and green garlic with the pestle one handful at a time (if it becomes too dry, add a little extra-virgin olive oil) until a very thick paste forms. Season with salt. Add the olive oil slowly, drop by drop, crushing constantly until combined and the pesto is creamy and thick.

• Transfer the pesto to a jar and cover with the remaining olive oil. If it's not sufficient, top off with more olive oil until the pesto is covered under the oil. Store in the refrigerator for up to 2 weeks.

The ancient seaside city of Trapani in western Sicily and its surrounding hills are home to the Titone family, producers of award-winning extra-virgin olive oil. Nicola and his daughter Antonella are third- and fourth-generation pharmacists, and they use their scientific background to discover innovative ways to farm organically. Rather than use pesticides to deal with pesky olive fruit flies, they poke holes in empty water bottles, add a sardine to each, and hang them on the trees. The fruit flies are drawn to the odiferous fish and drown in the bottles. Antonella's mother's recipe for *Pesto alla Trapanese* includes almonds and tomatoes, but no cheese. She gives a range for garlic cloves; just keep in mind that the more garlic used, the more pungent the pesto.

Toss this pesto with your favorite pasta—such as *Busiate col Pesto alla Trapanese* (page 160)— serve over crostini, or stir into couscous and top with mixed seafood.

Almond and Tomato Pesto

PESTO ALLA TRAPANESE

SERVES 4

4 garlic cloves

q.b. fine sea salt

½ cup (12 g) fresh basil

1 cup (150 g) raw blanched almonds

¼ cup (60 ml | 55 g) robust extra-virgin olive oil

¼ cup (100 g) ripe cherry tomatoes, skinned and seeded, cut into small dice

• In a large mortar, use the pestle to mash the garlic with a few pinches of salt. Once the garlic is finely crushed, gradually add the basil and almonds, a few at a time, and use a gentle circular motion to crush the leaves with the garlic. Add the olive oil as needed to make the mixture easier to crush. Finally, add the chopped tomatoes and continue crushing until it all amalgamates into a beautifully thick paste. The color should be orange-brownish-nutty with specks of green and red.

The word *bitter* has been dealt some ill-deserved connotations. The facial expressions some of my friends make when I serve a bitter dish is so amusing, yet after I encourage them to have three or four more bites, they get it and start eating more and more with enthusiasm! It's one of my favorite flavors. Bitter makes me hungrier. It feels good in my stomach, too, digestive and cleansing.

No matter where I am (my morning walk up to my favorite church in the world, San Miniato al Monte along the beautiful Via San Leonardo; visiting friends in the *campagna*; meeting olive oil or wine producers around Florence), I gather as many wild herbs as I stumble across. Particularly after the first September rains, the earth is brimming with wild herbs. If I don't have enough herbs after carefully cleaning and peeling the tougher roots with a paring knife (the flavor of the roots can be very intense, almost like horseradish or wasabi!) to make a *Misticanza* salad (page 76), I make this pesto.

Pesto Amaro has exactly the bitter, sparkling pungency I love so much: clean, earthy, and spicy in the back of the palate. It never tastes exactly the same, varying with the herbs I find. Therefore, this recipe is just a road map for your own adventures in bitter. It's really all about proportions: Use a handful (about 1 cup cleaned, full-leaf herbs) of each herb you find on the milder side of bitter, and about half that measure (½ cup) for the very bitter varieties.

In my home, spoonfuls of *Pesto Amaro* find their way over beans and steamed broccoli, thickly spread atop steaks (almost as if it's a green mean version of salsa verde or an angry Argentine chimichurri), and as a "secret" final ingredient when I make *Arista di Maiale* (page 245).

Bitter Wild Herb Pesto

PESTO AMARO

MAKES 2½ CUPS

1 cup (50 g) wild arugula or watercress

1 cup (60 g) baby kale

1 cup (25 g) celery leaves

1 cup (25 g) fresh flat-leaf parsley

½ cup (30 g) stemmed dandelion greens

½ cup (30 g) chicory

½ cup (15 g) fennel fronds

½ cup (30 g) chopped scallion tops

2 fresh sage leaves

2 small marinated artichoke hearts, finely chopped

1 garlic clove, finely chopped

1 cup (250 ml | 230 g) robust extra-virgin olive oil, plus more as needed

q.b. fine sea salt and crushed Tellicherry black peppercorns

• In a large mortar, start smashing the greens with the pestle a handful at a time, and mixing in the garlic and artichoke hearts to give some moisture. If the mixture becomes too dry, start adding a little extra-virgin olive oil until the pesto is a coarse paste. This should be a little coarser, more rustic and intense than the smooth pesto used for pasta. Season with salt and pepper.

• Transfer the pesto to a glass jar and cover with olive oil. Store in the refrigerator for a week or two. Use it as a condiment in a small bowl to accompany meats or in the simplest way possible as soon as you make it. If it's been in your fridge for over a week, use it to marinate meat or pork, or flavor a stew.

Once you make these *agrodolce* (sweet-and-sour) peppers and see how quickly they disappear, you'll want to double or triple the recipe. Drape over bruschetta; add to farro or fregola sarda salads; pair with roast pork, rabbit, or fish . . . or eat out of hand. Cut the red and yellow (or all of one color) peppers into different shapes and sizes. This is a dish where cooking each ingredient separately is essential to a successful result.

Stewed Sweet Red Peppers

PEPERONATA

MAKES 3 CUPS

3 tablespoons (45 ml | 40 g) mild extra-virgin olive oil

1 medium white onion, cut into ½-inch slices

4 red and yellow bell peppers, each cut into 4 or 6 sections

¾ cup (175 ml | 170 g) white wine vinegar

2 tablespoons (25 g) sugar

q.b. fine sea salt and crushed Tellicherry black peppercorns

- In a large skillet, heat 1 tablespoon of the olive oil over medium heat. Add the onion and stir to coat with the oil. Cover and cook, stirring occasionally, until the onion is soft, about 5 minutes. Transfer the onion to a bowl and wipe out the skillet with a paper towel.

- Add the remaining 2 tablespoons of oil to the skillet and set it over medium heat. Add the bell peppers and cook, covered, stirring frequently, until the peppers start to soften. Remove the lid and cook until some of the liquid has evaporated and the peppers are soft.

- Whisk the vinegar and sugar together in a medium bowl until the sugar has dissolved, then add the mixture to the skillet and cook over high heat, stirring, until the vinegar has evaporated. Transfer the pepper mixture back to the bowl with the onions and season with salt and black pepper. Set aside to cool to room temperature, taste for seasoning, then use or store the peppers in an airtight container in the refrigerator for up to 2 weeks.

The key to this classic Italian green sauce is parsley. Heaps on heaps on heaps of fresh (the fresher the better), perky, aromatic parsley leaves. Fresh flat-leaf parsley leaves are preferable, but curly works, too. Whichever you use, use the sharpest knife you have to do the chopping, as it slices cleanly through the leaves—all the better to preserve the bright flavor and color.

Tossed with a bit of onion, olive oil, and vinegar, the resulting *salsa verde* adds liveliness to any simple dish. Try with fried eggs, a simple steak, or *Bollito Misto* (page 218).

Green Sauce

SALSA VERDE

MAKES 1 CUP

Leaves from 3 large bunches flat-leaf parsley, very finely chopped

1 small yellow onion, very finely chopped

2 tablespoons (30 ml | 25 g) medium extra-virgin olive oil

1 tablespoon (15 ml | 15 g) Italian white wine vinegar

q.b. coarse sea salt and crushed Tellicherry black peppercorns

• In a large bowl, toss together the parsley, onions, olive oil, and vinegar. Season with salt and pepper. Let the salsa verde sit for at least 1 hour before using. (The flavors will meld and the onion will soften slightly, losing its "edge.") Cover and refrigerate for up to 1 day—just be sure to bring it to room temperature before serving.

Broths

BRODI

Keeping a jar or three of rich, homemade broth in your refrigerator or freezer is the fastest way to ensure that you have the start to soups, pastas, and stews at your fingertips. Following are three simple, classic *brodi* to get you started: hen, beef, and vegetable.

The Italian saying *"Gallina vecchia fa' buon brodo"* ("An old lady makes good broth") has a double meaning in Italian. Literally, it refers to the fact that an aged hen makes a richer, more flavorful broth. Figuratively, it's used to denote that elderly women are wise beyond their years. Regardless, it's true in both cases: the older, the better.

A large, old stewing hen that no longer lays eggs is essential to this recipe. While the meat of an old bird is tough and requires gentle cooking, the resulting broth will be deeply nourishing and satisfying. Once cooked, use the chicken meat in salads or on sandwiches with pungent *Salsa Verde* (page 50).

Some cooks say that celery leaves give the broth a slight bitterness, but my palate craves that flavor profile. If yours craves otherwise, simply omit the leaves. Also, I don't skim the scum from the top of the broth while it is simmering, because that removes some of the flavor. Instead, pour the cooked broth through a fine-mesh sieve at the end.

Old Hen Broth

GALLINA VECCHIA FA' BUON BRODO

MAKES 5 QUARTS

1 (4- to 6-pound) stewing hen, liver, hearts, and gizzard removed; wings tips tucked behind the breasts

2 celery stalks, leaves still attached

2 carrots

2 medium white onions, halved

1 bunch fresh flat-leaf parsley

¼ teaspoon (8 to 10) whole Tellicherry black peppercorns

q.b. fine sea salt

• Place the pasta insert in a large pot. Put the hen, celery, carrots, onions, parsley, and peppercorns in the insert. Fill the pot with enough water to cover the ingredients by about 2 inches. Bring to a boil, then reduce the heat to maintain a simmer and cook, uncovered, until the broth has reduced by one-third, about 2½ hours. (Do not skim the foam or the fat that rises to the top.) Take a taste—if you're satisfied with the flavors, season with salt and turn off the heat. If not, simmer for 30 minutes more and taste again.

• When the broth is done, carefully lift the insert and allow the broth to drain into the pot. Put the insert into a large bowl so any remaining broth isn't wasted and set aside until cool enough to handle. Discard the vegetables. Using your fingers, remove the meat from the hen carcass and set aside for another use.

• Pour the broth through a fine-mesh sieve into a large container. Cover and refrigerate until the fat rises and congeals at the top. Use a spoon to remove the fat from the surface and discard. Store in the refrigerator for up to 1 week or in the freezer for up to 3 months.

While beef broth can be made with a variety of cuts—oxtails, marrowbones, or knuckles—English-cut short ribs are my meat of choice. Unlike flank-cut short ribs, English-cut are sliced into 2-inch pieces along the bone with the meat sitting on top. I roast the bones until they are brown on all sides before adding them to the stockpot. Cook with Carnaroli rice for *Risotto con Radicchio* (page 180) or serve over cooked pasta.

Once the broth has finished cooking, remove the meat and serve it over crostini topped with a spoonful of *Salsa Verde* (page 50). Or combine the shredded meat with an egg and a bit of flour, shape it into a small meatball, and dust with bread crumbs before frying in olive oil.

Beef Broth with Short Ribs

BRODO DI COSTATA DI MANZO

MAKES 2½ QUARTS

2 pounds (1 kg) English-cut short ribs, cut into 2-inch pieces

2 celery stalks, leaves attached

2 carrots

2 medium white onions, halved

1 bunch fresh flat-leaf parsley

¼ teaspoon (8 to 10) whole Tellicherry black peppercorns

q.b. coarse sea salt and crushed Tellicherry black peppercorns

- Preheat the oven to 450°F (230°C).

- Arrange the short ribs in a single layer on a rimmed baking sheet or in a baking dish. Roast, turning the ribs occasionally, until they are brown on all sides, 30 to 40 minutes.

- Place the pasta insert in a large pasta pot. Put the ribs, celery, carrots, onions, parsley, and peppercorns in the insert. Fill the pot with enough water to cover the ingredients by about 2 inches. Bring to a boil, then reduce the heat to maintain a simmer and cook, uncovered, until the broth has reduced by half, about 3 hours. (Do not skim the foam or the fat that rises to the top.)

- When the broth is done, carefully lift the insert, allowing the broth to drain into the pot. Put the insert in a large bowl so any remaining broth isn't wasted and set aside until cool enough to handle. Discard the vegetables. Using your fingers, remove the meat from the bones and set aside for another use.

- Season with salt and pepper and pour the broth through a fine-mesh sieve into a large container. Cover and refrigerate until the fat rises and congeals at the top. Use a spoon to remove the fat from the surface and discard. Store in the refrigerator for up to 1 week or in the freezer for up to 3 months.

Throughout Italy, empty water bottles are filled with this quick, all-purpose vegetable broth. Made with scallions, parsley, and basil (although any greens that aren't quite lively enough for a salad can easily fill in), Italians use *Brodetto* in all sorts of ways: as a drink, to cook pasta, to stir into soups and stews, or to steam or boil vegetables.

I once made this broth while visiting my good friend and food blogger Elizabeth Minchilli at her farmhouse in Umbria. On a whim, we threw in some tomato leaves from her vegetable garden, which imparted a deep "green" flavor to the broth. If you grow your own tomatoes, give it a try. Or ask farmers at your local market if they have any to spare.

Quick Vegetable Broth

BRODETTO

MAKES 6 CUPS

1 bunch scallions

1 large bunch fresh flat-leaf parsley

1 large bunch basil

2 garlic cloves

1 large tomato

1 small sprig tomato leaves (optional)

20 cherry tomatoes

q.b. fine sea salt

• Put the scallions, herbs, garlic, and 6 cups (1.5 L | 1360 g) water in a large saucepan. Cut the large tomato in half and squeeze the juice into the pot, then add the tomato and tomato leaves (if using) to the saucepan. Bring to a simmer, cover, and cook for 10 minutes. Using a slotted spoon, remove and discard the herbs, garlic, and tomato leaves. Add the cherry tomatoes and cook the *Brodetto* for 2 minutes more. Turn off the heat. Season with salt. Strain through a fine-mesh sieve into a saucepan to use immediately, or pour the broth into clean mineral water bottles and store them in the refrigerator for up to 1 week or in the freezer for up to 3 months.

Mashed potatoes may not be the first thing you think to keep in your ready to use repertoire, but I make a batch of buttery, Parmesan cheese–strewn mashed potatoes almost every week and am always wishing I had made just a little bit more. Using medium-waxy potatoes like Yukon Golds yields a creamier end result, and making sure to mix them just enough to be smooth but not so much as to overly break up the potato starches and make them gummy is key in creating a creamy end product.

Put them to use in one of the two *Gatò di Patate* that start on page 222, or drizzle with a medium to robust extra-virgin olive oil and serve as a side with Fried and Baked Green Tomatoes with Grapes (page 276).

Mashed Potatoes

PURÈ DI PATATE

MAKES ABOUT 8 CUPS

4 pounds (1.8 kg) Yukon Gold potatoes (about 24 medium potatoes), unpeeled, diced into 4 to 6 pieces

2 tablespoons coarse sea salt

8 tablespoons (115 g) unsalted butter, diced

1 cup (250 ml | 240 g) whole milk

1 cup (120 g) finely grated Parmigiano-Reggiano cheese

A generous grating of nutmeg

q.b. fine sea salt and crushed Tellicherry black peppercorns

• Put the potatoes in a large stockpot and add enough water to cover them by 2 inches. Bring to a boil, salt the water with 2 tablespoons of the coarse sea salt, and stir to combine. Reduce the heat to maintain a simmer and cook until the potatoes can easily be pierced with a knife, about 15 minutes. Drain the potatoes and peel them as soon as you can handle them.

• Return the peeled potatoes to the pan and use a potato masher to mash just until no chunks remain. Add the butter, milk, cheese, and nutmeg. Place over medium heat and use a wooden spoon to vigorously stir the potatoes until the butter and milk have been almost completely incorporated and the potatoes are somewhat dry and fluffy, about 5 minutes. Season with fine sea salt and pepper.

• Use immediately, or store tightly covered in the refrigerator for up to 1 week.

It is so wonderful to have al dente cooked rice in a container in the fridge. Just like having farro or beans ready to be sautéed, a container of Carnaroli rice is great to have on hand to sauté in melted butter with a generous grating of Parmigiano-Reggiano, and a generous crack of pepper or nutmeg at the end. Or mix with peas and other seasonal vegetables or make The Contessa's delicious Rice Salad (page 186).

Boiled White Rice

RISO IN BIANCO

MAKES ABOUT 2 CUPS

1 tablespoon unsalted butter

q.b. coarse sea salt

1 cup (250 g) Carnaroli rice

q.b. mild extra-virgin olive oil (optional)

• Line a baking sheet with paper towels. Fill a medium pasta pot (with a colander insert if you have one; imagine you are cooking spaghetti) with water and add the butter and a generous amount of salt. Bring to a boil. Once the water is boiling, add the rice. Cover the pot and wait until the water comes back to a boil. Using a wooden spoon, stir the rice every now and then to prevent it from lumping and cook until the rice is almost al dente, 10 to 15 minutes. Remove the colander insert (or drain the rice in a fine-mesh sieve) and run the rice quickly under cold running water to wash off any excess starch. Pour the rice over the prepared baking sheet and use your hands to spread it out. Let cool.

• Pour into a bowl and drizzle with olive oil (or melted butter) and mix just to combine. Store in an airtight container in the refrigerator for up to 5 days.

Simply Sautéed, or Roasted Vegetables

**VERDURE A SALTATE "ZAK-ZAK"
O SEMPLICEMENTE ARROSTITE**

Saltate "Zak-Zak"

When sautéing vegetables, pour at least ½ cup (125 ml | 115 g) cooking extra-virgin olive oil into a large skillet with a lid and add 2 lightly crushed garlic cloves. (I leave them whole so the clove is so evident that it can be removed if someone does not want to eat garlic.) Add 1 teaspoon red pepper flakes and a pinch of fine sea salt, and cook over medium-low heat until the garlic starts to turn golden, 2 to 3 minutes. Add the vegetable stems, first, cover the pan and cook for a few minutes, then add the rest of the vegetable and cook until just tender. Season with another pinch of salt and a drizzle of robust extra-virgin olive oil at the table. I particularly love to make a mixture of different colored chard with a handful of spinach, parsley, or basil mixed in right at the end. It's all about the textures: crunchy stems and velvety, just-sautéed greens with a nice spicy kick in every mouthful.

Semplicemente Arrostite

Over the years, I discovered that the key to roasting vegetables is a garlic and aromatic herb bed and cutting the vegetables irregularly to give the final roast different variations of texture. Drizzle a baking dish with a generous layer of cooking extra-virgin olive oil and add as many crushed garlic cloves with the skin on and aromatics as you wish (such as rosemary, sage, bay leaf, thyme, and/or whole black peppercorns.) Cut the vegetables into cubes, toss them gently in the oil and aromatics, and season with fine sea salt. Roast in a preheated 400°F (200°C) oven, tossing them occasionally until tender. Serve hot, right out of the oven, or at room temperature with a sprinkle of rinsed capers or dry Sicilian oregano blossoms.

Nothing gives me more pleasure than taking half a day off to make my *Ragù Toscano*. I had the fortune to spend a lot of time in the kitchens of two very important chefs in Tuscany: my "guru," Carlo Cioni from Ristorante Da Delfina in Artimino, and Fabio Picchi in the kitchens of Cibreo in Florence. Plenty of time—and plenty of *ragù*—into knowing these chefs, I realized that this basic, quintessential Tuscan dish has numerous interpretations and variations. Fabio uses copious amounts of high-quality extra-virgin olive oil, while Carlo observes a more parsimonious use of "liquid gold," doling it out carefully and judiciously.

It's not just them. There are actually fourteen different types of *ragù* officially registered with L'Accademmia Italiana della Cucina, including variations from Bologna and Toscana in the north to Bari and Naples in the south. Cooks in the Emilia-Romagna region add butter and/or cream, while Tuscans (myself included) use only high-quality extra-virgin olive oil. Everyone will agree that a true Italian *ragù* is a meat-based sauce with tomato as a flavoring, not the other way around.

After spending years tasting and preparing *ragù* by both Carlo's and Fabio's (and plenty of other's) methods, I feel I have finally mastered my version of the recipe. My *ragù* takes plenty of time, patience, and dedication to the task—which to me feels like a full therapy session. The result of all the chopping, watching, stirring, tasting, and tweaking is a *ragù* with incredible depth and complexity and a dark, nutty, almost *amaro* (bitter) flavor.

I always make more than I plan to serve, inviting my friends over for *pappardelle col ragù* and thinking of the different variations I will make with the leftovers: Tuscan-Style Lasagna

Tuscan *Ragù*, My Way
IL MIO RAGÙ ALLA TOSCANA

(page 167), *arancini* (fried rice balls), or a *timballo* topped with creamy mashed potatoes, much like shepherd's pie. I always save a bit for a favorite snack of mine: a slice of toasted bread, a heaping spoonful of *ragù*, and melted stracchino (a soft, creamy cow's-milk cheese) on top.

This is one of those recipes where the best of the best all come together: Your ingredients— particularly the extra-virgin olive oil and the meat—need to be of the highest quality; a quality saucepan will help you in simmering at a perfect point without burning the *ragù*; a great glass of wine (I'd go with a white wine from the Bolgheri coast of Tuscany, but that's me) will calm any nerves you may have. A sharp knife comes in handy, too. There is a noticeable difference when you make a *ragù* starting with a *soffritto* that was made in a food processor and one that was chopped patiently and happily with a very good, very sharp knife.

To make sure the *ragù* develops a superior homogenous texture and flavor without sticking to the pan, I employ a combination of factors (which, as with all good things in life, you'll get better at the more you practice it). One, watch and listen to the simmering, sticking close by to stir as often as possible. Two, learn to adjust the flame so the *ragù* cooks at a constant, even simmer.

The *ragù* freezes very well; I freeze it in single portions so if I am eating alone, I have enough for me and don't waste a drop of precious *ragù*. To defrost, take the *ragù* out of the freezer in the morning and it should be at least partially thawed by the evening. If it is not completely defrosted, you can submerge the *ragù* (still in its storage container) in a bowl of hot water to speed things along. I strongly recommend never to microwave it, since it dries the *ragù* out and it loses its magic.

>>>

3 cups (700 ml | 700 g) *Soffritto* (page 40)

2 pounds (900 g) lean ground beef (90% lean or more), broken apart with your fingers

1 cup (250 ml | 250 g) dry red wine, such as Chianti

2 cups (567 g) peeled and diced canned or fresh San Marzano tomatoes

1 tablespoon *estratto di pomodoro* (tomato paste)

q.b. fine sea salt and crushed Tellicherry black peppercorns

2 bay leaves

2 sprigs rosemary

2 fresh sage leaves

q.b. freshly grated Parmigiano-Reggiano cheese

Robust extra-virgin olive oil, to finish

- In a large pan or Dutch oven, warm the *soffritto* over high heat. Once it is hot, add the meat a little bit at a time, grinding it between your fingers as you add it to the pan. Use a metal spoon to continue breaking it apart so it doesn't clump together and end up looking like meatballs. Cook, stirring continuously, until the *soffritto* and the meat are mixed together and the meat is browned, about 5 minutes. The meat should feel loose and fluffy when mixed vigorously.

- While stirring, pour the wine over the meat and cook until it has evaporated completely, about 10 minutes. Add the diced tomatoes and mix well, then add the *estratto* and stir until the sauce returns to a simmer, about 3 minutes. Reduce the heat to the lowest possible temperature and season with about 1 tablespoon of sea salt and a pinch of pepper. (It is better to put some, but not too much, so you can correct for the seasonings once the sauce is finished. But if you don't add any salt while cooking, the final *ragù* will lose some of its gutsy notes.) Continue to stir the *ragù* constantly (this is very important to ending up with a perfectly even *ragù*).

- Add the bay leaves, rosemary, and sage and cook, stirring and tasting very frequently, until the ragù is very fine in texture, dark in color, and grainy (not too soupy or saucy) with a very nutty, complex flavor, about 30 minutes. Taste and adjust the seasoning.

- To store in the fridge, transfer the *ragù* to a storage container and pour a thin layer of the same extra-virgin olive oil you used in the *soffritto* over the top to create a sealing layer (this will keep the *ragù* from drying out), then cover the container with its lid. The *ragù* will keep in the refrigerator for about 1 month.

A NOTE ABOUT SERVING:

• Serve this *ragù* over your favorite pasta—
especially one that will "trap" the *ragù* and take
it along into your mouth, such as pappardelle,
penne, rigatoni, or *pasta al ceppo*. Remember:
Eat pasta with sauce, not oversauced pasta.
Visually you should have a plate with 75
percent pasta and 25 percent *ragù*, not the
other way around.

• When cooking your pasta, pour a few cups of
the hot water into a pasta serving bowl to warm
the bowl. Drain and discard the water and put
a few tablespoons of the *ragù* at the bottom
of the bowl. Drain the pasta and quickly drop
it into the serving bowl, topping it with a few

more tablespoons of *ragù*. Mix gently to avoid
breaking the pasta and coat it evenly with the
ragù. Grate a generous amount of Parmigiano-
Reggiano over the top and if you like, drizzle
with a little pour of top-quality Tuscan finishing
olive oil. Enjoy it with a wonderful glass of
Chianti Classico (suggestions follow).

TO DRINK:

A great plate of *pasta col ragù* deserves a very
dry, simple Chianti Classico from some of my
favorite producers such as Castello di Monsanto,
Monteraponi, or Badia a Coltibuono.

To Begin With
PER INCOMINCIARE

My favorite antipasto is simple:

thin slices of rustic bread smeared with sweet butter and topped with a whole oil-packed anchovy. I usually have a plate of these on the table when guests arrive, along with one or two more room-temperature small bites, a few slices of salumi, and *Cipolline Agrodolce* (page 302). Other times, I assemble a platter with a wedge or two of cheese, pickled vegetables, sun-dried tomatoes, and small squares of fresh focaccia—purchased on the way home.

The tradition of antipasto or "before the meal" harkens back to medieval Italy, when diners would mingle over small bites of food before sitting down to eat. The aim was to spark the appetite with finger foods rather than fill diners up. That said, for casual entertaining—especially during warm weather—I like to make four to six antipasti and serve them as a full lunch or dinner. Otherwise, the amount of antipasti served varies on the occasion. If I am hosting a four-course meal (which is rare—usually to pair with special wines or to celebrate a holiday) I serve one antipasto. If I'm planning a meal with pasta or risotto as the second course, I'll prepare two or three antipasti. Regardless of the amount offered, if it's more than one dish, serve antipasti at a leisurely pace, rather than all at once.

Some of the simplest antipasti are bruschetta and crostini: small pieces of bread topped with chopped vegetables, a piece of cheese, or a slice of salumi. The main difference is this: Bruschetta are toasted or grilled, rubbed with garlic, and drizzled with olive oil before adding (typically raw) toppings. Crostini, which means "little crusts," are also toasted but tend to be the base for cooked toppings like liver spreads, cooked beans, or caponata. Then there's the ever-enticing *fettunta* (literally, "soaked slice") from Toscano: a thick slice of bread grilled on both sides and rubbed all over with garlic before being drenched in freshly pressed olive oil, or *olio nuovo*. I've included one of my favorite variations for *Fettunta col Cavolo Nero* (Fettunta with Kale) but serving it plain isn't a rare occurrence in my— or other Florentine—kitchens.

Crostini e Fettunta

Some of my favorite crostini are made by Patrizio, the private chef at Tenuta di Capezzana, in Carmignano, Tuscany. He shares my belief that the kitchen should be a convivial place, and thus there are always plenty of smiles and laughter around his stove. He also is the man lucky enough to get to cook with the sought-after, bright green and vibrant in both color and flavor olio nuovo produced each year on the property. One of the (many) ways he opens his kitchen—and his heart—to the lucky guests around his table is through his inventive yet simple crostini. Patrizio serves a mix of them on a big platter—a great way to allow guests to choose their favorites and open everyone's palates and stomachs for the meal to come. The short recipes included here are a jumping-off point; feel free to come up with your own house recipes. Really, almost anything you put on a slice of well-toasted bread will be instant crostini and, I imagine, an instant hit.

Crostini di Fegatini

SERVES 6 TO 8

• In a small skillet, combine ¼ cup (60 ml | 56 g) robust extra-virgin olive oil, ¼ cup (56 g) chopped red onion, and 2 peeled garlic cloves. Cook until very tender, about 10 minutes. Add ¾ pound (330 g) cleaned chicken livers to the pan and cook, stirring occasionally, over low heat until the livers are very soft and cooked through, about 20 minutes. Pour in 2 tablespoons (30 ml | 28 g) *vin santo* and stir to combine. Add 1 anchovy and 2 tablespoons (28 g) rinsed, salt-packed capers. Remove the pan from the heat and coarsely chop (add olive oil as needed—the final mixture should be smooth and creamy). Serve over toasted slices of Tuscan bread with more olive oil drizzled on top.

Crostini della Miseria

SERVES 6 TO 8

• Cut the crusts off two small pieces (36 g) dried, old Italian bread and tear it into small cubes. Place in a small bowl and add ¼ cup (60 ml | 56 g) dry white wine (such as Trebbiano). Set aside to soak for 5 minutes, then use your fingers to squeeze out excess moisture and add to a food processor. Add ¼ cup (45 g) rinsed, salt-packed capers and 2 tablespoons (30 ml | 28 g) robust extra-virgin olive oil and blend until coarsely ground. Transfer to a dish and fold in 2 teaspoons plus 1 tablespoon finely chopped fresh flat-leaf parsley and ¼ cup (112 g) robust extra-virgin olive oil. Season with salt and stir in ½ tablespoon (28 g) *estratto di pomodoro* (tomato paste)—(or enough to make the mixture orange). Spread the mixture over slices of toasted Tuscan bread.

Crostini di Melanzana

SERVES 6 TO 8

- Preheat oven to 350°F (180°C). Finely chop the leaves from 2 rosemary sprigs, 2 sage sprigs, 1 garlic clove, 1 tablespoon (11 g) coarse sea salt, and 1 teaspoon (2 g) crushed Tellicherry black peppercorns to make the *sale aromatico*. Use a sharp paring knife to make four medium U-shaped incisions into the sides of a large eggplant (600 g) and stuff each of the incisions with the *sale aromatico*. Drizzle the eggplant with robust extra-virgin olive oil and wrap in aluminum foil. Bake until the eggplant is very soft, about 1¼ hours. Remove the eggplant from the oven and set aside to cool. Coarsely chop the eggplant and transfer to a fine-mesh strainer. Use the back of a spoon to press out excess moisture from the eggplant and discard. Transfer the eggplant to a bowl and mix in 1 finely chopped garlic clove, 1 tablespoon (1 g) finely chopped fresh flat-leaf parsley, 5 tablespoons (85 g) robust extra-virgin olive oil, and season with salt and pepper. Spread the eggplant mixture over slices of toasted Tuscan bread.

Fettunta col Cavolo Nero

SERVES 6 TO 8

- Bring a large pot of salted water to a boil. Add one large bunch (200 g) stemmed *cavalo nero* (Tuscan kale). Reduce the heat to maintain a simmer and cook until very soft, 20 to 30 minutes. Remove with a slotted spoon, reserving the cooking water. Coarsely chop the kale. Toast 8 slices Tuscan bread and rub with the cut side of a garlic clove. Dip briefly in the kale cooking water and place on a plate. Drizzle with robust extra-virgin olive oil (*olio nuovo* if you can find it) and season with fine sea salt. Top each with the kale and drizzle with a squeeze of fresh lemon juice and more olive oil, then season with salt and pepper. Serve immediately.

During lunch at La Bilancia near Loreto Aprutino, I noticed that some customers were eating cooked greens topped with white beans, a dish listed on the menu as misticanza. To a Florentine like me, misticanza is a raw salad of lettuces, greens, and herbs. In Abruzzo, misticanza means "cooked" in local dialect and refers to a dish of blanched seasonal greens, sautéed in olive oil with garlic and onions, and gently tossed with local tondini del Tavo—perfectly round beans grown in the region.

One of my favorite things about Italy is that two completely different dishes can have the same name in different regions. When I serve *Misticanza di Firenze* as a first course to my Italian friends, I always get a few bewildered looks (salad is a decidedly second course in Italy) alongside raves. When I serve *Misticanza Abruzzese*, I just get the raves.

Misticanza, Two Ways
MISTICANZA DUE MODI

Eating salad as a first course is one of the many gifts I received from living in Northern California. But *Misticanza di Firenze* is more than a green salad. The idea is to combine as many seasonal greens and herbs as possible so each bite offers a different blend of greens. In Firenze, depending on the time of year, *misticanza* can have as many as sixteen varieties of greens, such as arugula, basil, borage, celery leaves, chicory, dandelion, chard, escarole, mâche, romaine, chives, kale, spinach, fennel, parsley, lovage, mint, watercress, and/or small turnip, beet, and radish tops. For a first course, use about 2 loosely packed cups per person—or more to your liking.

Florentine Mixed Winter Greens Salad
LA MISTICANZA DI SCOLTELLATO DI FIRENZE

• Once all your greens are thoroughly washed and dried, place them in a large serving bowl. Using a small serrated knife and a small chef's knife, shred the greens by crossing the knives in the bowl as if you are sharpening them. Once the greens are cut, drizzle in red wine vinegar and robust extra-virgin olive oil in a ratio of 2:3 and season with salt and pepper. Using your hands, toss the salad well to coat every piece. It's best to eat the salad with your fingers so you can taste all the many greens. Yes, you can even lick your fingers.

TO DRINK:
An Il Benefizio Pomino Bianco from the Frescobaldi family. The crisp white wine will stand up to vinegar and all those bitter green flavors.

Mixed Winter Greens and Beans

MISTICANZA ABRUZZESE

SERVES 4

3 pounds (1.35 kg) seasonal greens
 and fresh herbs (such as chicory,
 spinach, chard and kale stems and
 leaves, romaine, escarole, arugula,
 fresh flat-leaf parsley, basil,
 and chives)

¼ cup (60 ml | 55 g) robust
 extra-virgin olive oil

1 medium yellow onion, finely
 chopped

3 garlic cloves, finely chopped

1 cup (200 g) cooked *tondini del Tavo*
 or other white beans (see
 page 29)

q.b. fine sea salt

½ cup (14 g) chopped *cruschi*
 (see page 26), to finish

• Bring a large pot of salted water to a boil. Add the greens and herbs, in batches if necessary, and boil until bright green and tender, about 5 minutes. Drain the greens through a fine-mesh sieve and set aside to cool for a few minutes. When the greens are cool enough to handle, squeeze out any excess water and coarsely chop.

• In a large skillet, combine the olive oil, garlic, and onion and sauté over medium heat until the onion is tender, 4 to 5 minutes. Stir in the greens and cooked beans and warm through. Season with salt and transfer to a serving platter. Sprinkle with *cruschi* and serve warm or at room temperature.

TO DRINK:
A fresh and lively Ilico Montepulciano d'Abruzzo from Dino Illuminati.

Agrumato is citrus-infused oil created by simultaneously crushing whole fresh citrus with freshly harvested olives. The flavor is intensely pure and much more nuanced than the more common infusion method. In Abruzzo, olive farmers traditionally make citrus oils for family and friends (not for sale or cooking) to be used as a condiment on grilled fish, seafood, and vegetables. To make your own lemon oil, combine 1 cup cooking extra-virgin olive oil and a quarter lemon in a saucepan. Bring the oil to a simmer, turn off the heat, and allow the lemon to infuse the oil. When cool, strain into a jar or bottle. Store at room temperature for up to a week.

I like to highlight the simple beauty of *agrumato* by pairing it with fresh, in-season asparagus. The bright, slightly acidic citrus oil highlights the green vegetable and cuts through the fat of crisped prosciutto. During the autumn and winter, use the same method with Treviso radicchio (a red bitter green similar to endive).

Broiled Asparagus, My Way

ASPARAGI A "MODO MIO"

SERVES 4

2 bunches (700 g) asparagus

Extra-virgin olive oil with lemon (*agrumato*)

q.b. fine sea salt

¼ cup (57 g) cubed prosciutto (marinated in olive oil if you can find it)

2 large hard-boiled eggs, coarsely chopped

Parmigiano-Reggiano cheese, or shaving

q.b. crushed Tellicherry black peppercorns

• Preheat the broiler.

• Put the asparagus on a rimmed baking sheet and drizzle with lemon olive oil. Use your hands to rub the stalks all over with oil and season with salt. Place under the broiler and broil, turning the asparagus occasionally until all sides are charred and the asparagus is tender, 10 to 12 minutes. Remove from the oven and set aside to cool.

• Meanwhile, in a nonstick medium skillet, cook the prosciutto over medium heat until crisp, about 5 minutes.

• Divide the asparagus among four plates and top each with some of the chopped hard-boiled egg, prosciutto, and a drizzle of lemon olive oil. Using a vegetable peeler, shave a few Parmigiano-Reggiano slices over each serving, and season with salt and pepper.

TO DRINK:
A bright white wine from the Alto Adige such as Terlaner Pinot Bianco from Cantina Terlano, or Praepositus Kerner from Abbazia di Novacella.

Mina Schiralli's kitchen in Bari, the capital of southern Italy's Puglia region, is the kitchen everyone dreams of when they think of an Italian *nonna*'s house. It's warm and functional and always full of food, half-empty dishes, laughter, and small, happy children underfoot. Mina is what everyone dreams of when they think of an Italian *nonna*: small in stature, wielding a big smile and a hug that you are sure to feel in your bones, and a force behind (and in front and to the side of) the stove.

When Mina makes focaccia, she uses the recipe another *nonna*—her mother—gifted her on the day Mina was married, forty years ago. She hasn't changed the recipe at all, and there's no fancy technique or equipment needed to make it. The opposite, in fact. She uses a large, old, slightly misshapen pan, and she wraps the rising dough in a fleece blanket, and sets it on the bed in the nearby bedroom "so it rises like a baby." The only ingredient that needs extra-special care to ensure your focaccia is as life-altering as Mina's is good, robust extra-virgin olive oil. Lots and lots . . . and lots of good, robust extra-virgin olive oil. Mina uses the Crudo extra-virgin olive oil produced by her husband, Rafaelle, and sons Gaetano and Guiseppe (or Pino, as he's known to family and friends), and its spicy, rich tones make her focaccia all the better.

Focaccia with Extra-Virgin Olive Oil

FOCACCIA DI OLIO D'OLIVA

MAKES ONE 9 x 13-INCH FOCACCIA

6½ cups (850 g) all-purpose flour

1 medium russet potato, peeled, boiled, and grated

1 tablespoon plus ½ tsp fine sea salt

1 tablespoon (12 g) fresh yeast

3 cups (700 ml | 700 g) lukewarm water

7 tablespoons (110 ml | 99 g) robust extra-virgin olive oil

½ cup (75 g) large cherry tomatoes, halved

1 teaspoon Sicilian oregano blossoms

¼ cup (45 g) Tremiti or Castelventrano olives

q.b. coarse finishing salt

• Put the flour in a large bowl and use your hands to create a well in the center. Add the grated potato, 1 tablespoon of the salt, and the yeast (making sure it doesn't touch the salt until the water is added). Slowly pour in the water, a little at a time, using your hands to mix until a soft, runny dough forms. Knead the dough until it is smooth and doesn't stick to your hands (it should feel almost like it slides off your fingers), about 10 minutes. (You can also do this in a stand mixer fitted with a hook attachment.)

• Pour 3 tablespoons (45 ml | 42.5 g) of the oil onto a 9 x 13-inch baking dish. Pour the dough into the center of the pan. Wet your hands with a little bit of water and gently press the dough into the pan and spread it to the edges. Cover with a towel and set aside in a warm, draft-free space until doubled in size, about 1 hour.

>>>

• Meanwhile, in a medium bowl, combine the
tomatoes, 2 tablespoons (30 ml | 28 g) of the olive
oil, ½ teaspoon of the sea salt, and the oregano
blossoms. Set aside to marinate.

• When the dough has risen, preheat the oven to
425°F (220°C).

• Remove the towel and drizzle the top of the
focaccia with the remaining 2 tablespoons (30 ml |
28 g) olive oil. Gently press the tomatoes facedown
into the dough. Add the olives. (The dough should
start to swallow the tomatoes and olives—Mina
would tell you this is "the moment you know the
dough has risen enough.")

• Sprinkle with coarse salt and immediately transfer the pan to the oven and bake until the focaccia is deeply browned, 35 to 40 minutes. Set aside to cool slightly, then cut the focaccia into squares and set on a paper towel–lined plate to catch any extra oil. Serve warm or at room temperature. Focaccia will keep in an airtight container at room temperature for up to 3 days.

Segare

The Italian verb *segare* means "to saw" (as in, cutting wood). The success of the following four *segato* recipes relies heavily on cutting (sawing) the ingredients into equal-size pieces as well as using equal amounts of each. Just as equal measures of diced onions, carrots, and celery are essential to *Soffritto* (page 40) or dicing the potatoes and green beans to the size of *trofie* for Trofie with Basil Pesto and Green Beans (page 147), the following recipes require the ingredients to be sliced to the same thickness. Each mouthful results in equal bites of every flavor and texture. If you have good knife skills, by all means use them, but an inexpensive Japanese mandoline slicer is a worthwhile piece of kitchen equipment and becomes especially useful when making *segato*.

Shaved Fennel, Porcini, and Pecorino

SEGATO DI FINOCCHIO, FUNGHI E PECORINO DI PIENZA

SERVES 4

2 fennel bulbs, trimmed and sliced into ⅛-inch pieces

4 porcini mushrooms, sliced into ⅛-inch pieces

One 4-ounce (113 g) piece aged pecorino, sliced into ⅛-inch pieces

¼ cup robust extra-virgin olive oil

Juice of ½ lemon

¼ cup fresh flat-leaf parsley leaves, torn

¼ cup fresh mint leaves, torn

q.b. coarse sea salt and crushed Tellicherry black peppercorns

• Arrange the sliced fennel, mushrooms, and pecorino on four plates. Drizzle each with olive oil and lemon juice and top with parsley and mint leaves. Season with salt and pepper just before serving.

TO DRINK:
Since fennel makes most wines taste the same, drink a simple, fruity red wine such as a Mona Nera Tenuta di Capezzana.

Blood Orange, Lemon, and Red Onion Salad

INSALATA DI TAROCCHI, LIMONI E CIPOLLA

SERVES 4

1 cup (250 ml | 240 g) white wine vinegar

Coarse sea salt

1 small red onion, sliced into ¼-inch slices and separated

3 blood oranges, peeled and sliced into ¼-inch slices

1 lemon, peeled and sliced into ¼-inch slices

¼ cup (50 g) Taggiasca olives, pitted and halved

¼ cup (5 g) fresh flat-leaf parsley leaves, torn

Robust extra-virgin olive oil, to finish

• Line a plate with paper towels and set aside. Bring 2 cups water to a boil in a medium pot. Add the vinegar and a pinch of salt. Add the onion slices and blanch for 30 seconds. Using a pair of tongs or a slotted spoon, transfer the onions to the paper towel–lined plate and dry thoroughly. Arrange the orange and lemon slices and the blanched onions in an overlapping pattern on a platter. Scatter the olive halves over the top. Drizzle with olive oil, sprinkle with the parsley, and serve.

TO DRINK:

A fruity white wine from Sicily, such as a Regaleali Bianco from Tasca d'Almerita.

Lattice of Zucchini and Toasted Pistachio

SEGATO DI ZUCCHINE E PISTACCHI TOSTATE

SERVES 4

3 tablespoons (45 ml | 45 g) white wine vinegar

6 fresh flat-leaf parsley sprigs, stems and
  leaves separated

4 basil sprigs, stems and leaves separated

6 fresh chives

Coarse sea salt

4 small (4- to 6-inch) zucchini, sliced lengthwise into ⅛-inch-thick slices on a mandoline

6 tablespoons (90 ml | 80 g) robust extra-virgin olive oil

q.b. coarse sea salt and crushed Tellicherry black peppercorns

½ cup (45 g) unsalted pistachios, toasted

• Line a baking sheet or platter with paper towels and set aside. In a large straight-sided skillet, combine 1 tablespoon (15 ml | 15 g) of the vinegar, the parsley stems, basil stems, and chives. Fill the skillet three-quarters full with water and season with salt. Bring to a boil. Carefully add the zucchini slices one by one to the boiling water and blanch for 1 minute (the zucchini soften and brighten in color). Using a spatula, so the zucchini doesn't break, carefully transfer the blanched zucchini to the paper towels and dry thoroughly on both sides. (The zucchini can be prepared up to this point and kept at room temperature or in the refrigerator for up to 6 hours.)

• In a small bowl, whisk together the remaining 2 tablespoons (30 ml | 30 g) vinegar with the olive oil. Season with salt and pepper.

• Weave the zucchini slices into lattice designs on four plates and spoon the dressing over the top. Sprinkle each dish with the basil and parsley leaves and pistachios.

TO DRINK:
A velvety, young, and mineral Etna Rosso "Rosso di Verzella" from Cantina Bennati in Sicily.

Roast Beets, Gorgonzola, and Black Walnuts

SEGATO DI BIETOLE, GORGONZOLA E NOCI

SERVES 6

6 medium beets, cleaned and tops trimmed

½ cup (75 g) chopped black walnuts, warmed

½ cup (70 g) crumbly mountain Gorgonzola cheese, crumbled

⅓ cup (80 ml | 75 g) robust extra-virgin olive oil

1 tablespoon (16 g) true balsamic vinegar

q.b. fine sea salt and crushed Tellicherry black peppercorns

• Preheat the oven to 400°F (200°C).

• Wrap each beet in aluminum foil and place on a baking sheet. Bake until the beets are tender when pierced with a fork, about 1 hour. Set aside to cool for 8 to 10 minutes. When the beets are cool enough to handle, remove the foil and slip off and discard the skins. Cut each beet into 6 slices and put them in a large bowl.

• In a small skillet, toast the walnuts over medium heat, stirring often, until warmed through, about 5 minutes. Add the walnuts, gorgonzola, olive oil, and vinegar to the bowl with the beets, and season with salt and pepper. Serve immediately.

TO DRINK:
A Barbera d'Asti "Montebruna" from Braida. The cherry and mixed berry flavors will pair beautifully with the earthy beets and spicy Gorgonzola.

Say this recipe title around a Florentine speaker and you'll likely get a look of shock and a hearty laugh: *carciofi 'ritti* translates to "artichokes with a hard-on" in Florentine. It's a lighthearted way to introduce a dish that is one of my favorite ways to prepare an artichoke.

Starting in spring through the close of summer, towers of large artichokes known as *mamme* (or "mothers") in every shade of purple and green are piled in front of restaurants and in outdoor markets. If possible, seek out artichokes that still have a longer (2- to 3-inch) stem attached. Work quickly and keep a bowl of acidulated water nearby to help prevent the artichokes from turning black.

I always pair wine with food (or food with wine), but when planning a dinner centered around fine wines, I skip an artichoke course. The hardy members of the thistle family contain a sizeable amount of tannins (the bittering substance found in wine and black teas), which can overwhelm your palate and keep you from tasting the nuanced flavor of quality wine. Instead, pair with water or sparkling wine.

Artichokes with a Hard-On

CARCIOFI 'RITTI

SERVES 4

1 lemon, peeled with a vegetable peeler and halved

4 large (globe) artichokes

Robust extra-virgin olive oil

1 garlic clove, crushed

2 fresh or dried bay leaves

2 tablespoons fresh mint leaves, torn

2 tablespoons fresh flat-leaf parsley leaves

q.b. fine sea salt and crushed Tellicherry black peppercorns

TO DRINK:
Water or sparkling wine, such as Prosecco from Mionetto. (Or any simple wine, since you won't be able to taste it anyway!)

• Squeeze the juice of the peeled lemon into a large bowl of water. Remove and discard the tough outer leaves of the artichokes until the yellow part of each artichoke is exposed. With a serrated knife, cut about one-third off the top of each artichoke. Using a knife or a vegetable peeler, peel the tough, woody outer stem. As you work, put the artichokes in the bowl of lemon water.

• Put the artichokes top-down in a medium pot or Dutch oven. Add enough olive oil to come halfway up the sides of the artichokes, about ½ cup, then pour in enough water to cover the artichokes completely. Scatter the lemon peel, garlic, bay leaves, mint, and parsley around the artichokes and bring to a boil. Reduce the heat to low and cover the pot. Let the artichokes steam until the artichokes are almost tender when pierced with a knife, about 15 minutes. Transfer the artichokes to serving bowls and strain the broth through a fine-mesh sieve. Season with salt and pepper and ladle ½ cup (125 ml | 125 g) of the broth into bowls. Serve at room temperature. Alternatively, refrigerate the artichokes for up to 2 days and served chilled.

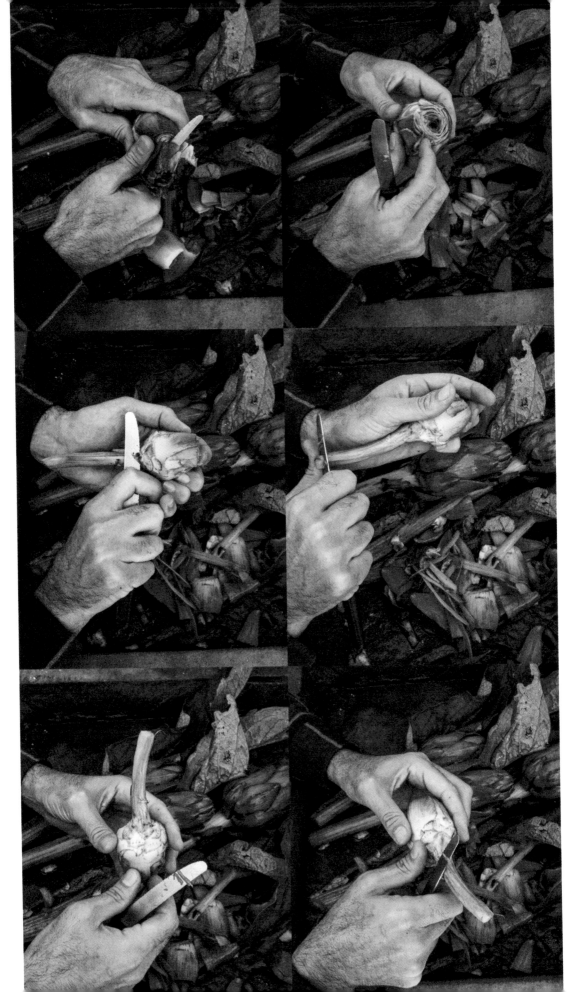

I first had this at Ristorante S. Pietro with Lucia, my good friend and co-owner of the incredible anchovy producer IASA. Chef Franco Tammaro made this simple, clean soup for us on a cold, dreary March evening in Cetara. It's incredible how something so simple can stir so many emotions—you taste both the earth and the sea in just one spoonful. Now when I make it, it brings me back to the chilly night and the warmth of both Lucia's spirit and the saline broth.

Farro Soup

ZUPPA DI FARRO

SERVES 4

2 cups (312 g) cooked farro
(see page 193), cooking water
reserved

Robust extra-virgin olive oil

Splash of *colatura d'alici*
(anchovy essence)

Pinch of fine sea salt

Pinch of Sicilian oregano blossoms

• Divide the farro among four warm soup bowls. Top with just enough hot farro cooking water to cover the farro. Drizzle with olive oil and *colatura*. Sprinkle with sea salt and crushed oregano blossoms and serve immediately.

TO DRINK:
A Sangiovese-based wine, with earthy tones, such as Il Poggio from my friend Laura Bianchi at Castello di Monsanto.

About twenty-five years ago, when I started teaching cooking in Toscano at Capezzana in Carmignano and Da Delfina in Artimino, no one knew what *cavolo nero* (also called black, Tuscan, or dinosaur kale) was. Nowadays, it is ubiquitous and available all year long, but half a century ago, you never ate *cavolo nero* until after the first frost. These *tortini*, based on those made by Carlo at Da Delfina with wild nettles, are wonderful to serve as an appetizer. The beauty of this dish is the combination of bitter *tortino* with the sweet *salsina* made with tomatoes and cannellini bean purée. Serve alongside toasted Italian bread to sop up all the flavors.

Kale Custards with Cannellini Cream

TORTINI DI CAVOLO NERO CON SALSINA DI FAGIOLI

MAKES 4

CUSTARDS

4 tablespoons (32 g) grated Parmigiano-Reggiano cheese

2 tablespoons (18 g) bread crumbs

1 tablespoon (14 g) unsalted butter, at room temperature

1 pound (450 g) *cavolo nero* (Tuscan kale), cleaned and deribbed

2 large eggs

q.b. fine sea salt and freshly ground Tellicherry black peppercorns

>>>

• Preheat the oven to 350°F (180°C).

• ***To make the custards:*** In a small bowl, combine 2 tablespoons (16 g) of the Parmesan with the bread crumbs. Thoroughly butter four 4-ounce ramekins, then coat each with the cheese–bread crumb mixture.

• Bring a large pot of salted water to a boil. Add the kale, cover the pot with a lid, reduce the heat slightly, and boil until the kale is tender and bright green, 4 to 5 minutes. Drain through a colander and set aside to cool slightly. Once the kale is cool enough to handle, squeeze out any excess moisture and coarsely chop.

• In a medium bowl, combine the chopped kale, eggs, and the remaining 2 tablespoons (16 g) cheese. Divide the mixture among the prepared ramekins and place in a large baking dish. Place the dish in the oven and carefully add enough boiling water to come two-thirds up the sides of the ramekins. Bake until the custards are set, but jiggle slightly when shaken, about 20 minutes. Carefully remove the ramekins from the hot water and set aside to cool.

>>>

SAUCE

1 tablespoon (15 ml | 14 g) mild extra-virgin olive oil

1 tablespoon (15 g) finely chopped yellow onion

¼ cup (60 ml | 55 g) *Salsa di Pomodoro* (page 42)

1 cup (200 g) cooked cannellini beans (see page 11)

q.b. fine sea salt and freshly ground Tellicherry black peppercorns

• ***Meanwhile, to make the sauce:*** In a medium saucepan, heat the tomato sauce and the beans with some of their cooking liquid over a medium flame. Bring to a soft simmer for just a minute. Place a fine mesh sieve over a bowl, add the bean and tomato mixture, and using the back of a tablespoon, press the bean mixture through the colander to purée. Add the olive oil and taste for seasoning.

• Turn the custards out into warmed pasta bowls, giving each a gentle shake to release from the molds. To serve, place some of the bean purée next to each custard. Serve with some crusty toasted Italian bread. To eat, spread some of the custard on the toast and top with some of the puréed bean sauce.

TO DRINK:

A typical flavor of the area such as an earthy "Barco Reale" from Tenuta di Capezzana.

This recipe—elegant, chic, and delicious as it is written—is also a stellar jumping-off point. Add a teaspoon of sautéed ground sausage or Tuscan *Ragù, My Way* (page 63) in the middle of each, as if it were an *arancino*. Use spinach leaves, kale leaves, or beet tops in place of the chard. Substitute leftover risotto for the rice. If *olio nuovo* isn't in season, serve with a spoonful of tomato sauce, bean sauce, or *ragù*. Serve as an appetizer when made in a medium ramekin or as a main dish when using a larger one. Whichever way you make them, *sformatini* always make dinner guests very happy—and make you look as if you worked all day for it.

Carnaroli Rice Custards Wrapped in Chard Leaves

SFORMATINI DI CARNAROLI AVVOLTI IN FOGLIE DI BIETOLE I

MAKES 4

1 tablespoon (14 g) unsalted butter

4 young, tender, medium-size chard leaves (look for those with green stems, not white), washed and dried

1 cup (250 ml | 250 g) *Brodetto* (page 56)

3 whole eggs

1¼ cups (100 g) grated Parmigiano-Reggiano cheese

q.b. fine sea salt and crushed Tellicherry black peppercorns

1 cup (190 g) cooked (al dente) Carnaroli rice (see page 59)

1 small scallion, thinly sliced

2 tablespoons (30 ml | 30 g) cooking extra-virgin olive oil

A few fresh flat-leaf parsley leaves

A few fresh basil leaves

Olio nuovo, for finishing

• Generously butter four 3½-inch 4-ounce ramekins.

• Using your fingers, carefully separate the chard leaves from the stems, trying to keep the leaves intact so they will fully cover the bottom and sides of the ramekin. Set the stems aside.

• Line a baking sheet with paper towels and set aside. In a medium-size skillet, bring the *brodetto* to a boil over medium-high heat. Add the chard leaves and blanch until soft, about 90 seconds. Use a spatula to carefully transfer the leaves to the paper towel–lined baking sheet and set aside to dry slightly.

• Very carefully place the heart of one leaf in the center of each ramekin, and, using your index finger, press the leaf gently along the bottom and sides of the ramekin.

• In a medium bowl, whisk together the eggs and 1 cup of the cheese. Season with salt and pepper, then, using a spatula, fold in the rice.

• Preheat the oven to 350°F (180°C).

>>>

- Using a soup spoon, fill the ramekins two-thirds of the way with the rice mixture. Fold the ends of the chard leaves over the rice and top each with a tablespoon of the cheese. Cover each ramekin tightly with aluminum foil and place the ramekins in a baking dish. Place the dish in the oven and carefully fill the dish with boiling water until it reaches halfway up the sides of the ramekins. Bake for 20 minutes, then carefully, wearing oven mitts, remove the foil. Bake until the cheese is golden, about 10 minutes more. Remove the baking dish from the oven and transfer the ramekins to a wire rack. Let cool for 5 minutes, then gently run a butter knife around the edges of the ramekins. Place a salad bowl on top of each ramekin and with a gentle *colpo* (dry hit) flip the ramekin onto the dish to remove the *sformatino* (the chard leaves should be beautifully encasing the final *sformatini*).

- Sprinkle with fresh basil and drizzle with *olio nuovo* and serve immediately.

TO DRINK:
A Grignolino del Monferrato Casalese 2015 from the Vicara winery (who are the cousins of Contessa Rosetta Clara at Principato di Lucedio).

Bagna Caôda (which means "hot bath") is a warm, garlicky dip that comes from Piemonte on the border of France and Switzerland. It is served communally—much like fondue—alongside raw and blanched vegetables for dipping. Too often, *Bagna Caôda* can have an unpleasant harsh or metallic taste and an unappealing gray color. To counteract this, Cesare Giaccone, the chef/owner of the eponymous restaurant in Albaretto della Torre, a small village in Piemonte, stirs a cup of local Barolo into his *Bagna Caôda*. The wine rids the dip of any salty, bitter flavors and results in a nutty and complex dip. In addition to raw and blanched vegetables, dress cubed and cooked potatoes with *Bagna Caôda* or serve it as a side to roasted meats.

Hot Bath

BAGNA CAÔDA

SERVES 6

1 cup (250 ml | 226 g) whole milk

4 heads garlic, separated, peeled, halved, and green germs removed

1 cup (250 ml | 230 g) medium extra-virgin olive oil

¼ cup (95 g) anchovies packed in extra-virgin olive oil

¼ teaspoon salted capers, rinsed

1 cup (250 ml | 250 g) Barolo wine

Assortment of cleaned sliced vegetables such as bell peppers, fennel, carrots, broccoli and cauliflower florets, radishes, snap peas, asparagus, beets, green beans, and/or endive

• In a small saucepan, bring the milk to a simmer over medium-high heat. Add the garlic cloves and simmer for 1 minute. Strain through a fine-mesh sieve and rinse the garlic well with water.

• In a medium saucepan, heat the olive oil over medium heat until warmed through. Add the garlic and cook until it is soft and creamy and can be crushed with the back of a spoon, about 30 minutes. Stir in the anchovies and capers and heat through, stirring frequently, so the dip doesn't separate. Pour in the wine and stir to combine. Serve the *bagna caôda* straight from the pan or pour it into a warm bowl and surround with the vegetables for dipping.

TO DRINK:
A Barbera d'Alba from Giacomo Bologna or Barbaresco from Produttori del Barbaresco.

When English wine merchants started to travel to Toscana in the Renaissance to buy a year's worth or more of red wine, crafty wine merchants would offer their customers a piece of *finocchio* (fennel) to cleanse their palates between tasting wines. Fennel—like artichokes—contains tannins that can make one wine taste imperceptible from another. The wine merchants would then sell inferior wines at a higher price to patrons, who were duped into thinking they were buying the very best. As a result of this bait-and-switch tactic, *infinnochiare* is the Italian expression that means to trick or take someone for a ride.

Finocchi Infinocchiati combines fennel with earthy red Chianti (no need to use your best bottle!) as a nod to these devious merchants of the past. The result is no trick, however. Be sure to season the caraway blend that is sprinkled on top well; it adds both crunch and seasoning while elevating the elegant flavor of the dark-red braised greens.

Fennel Braised in Chianti

FINOCCHI INFINOCCHIATI

SERVES 4

1 tablespoon (14 g) unsalted butter, at room temperature

4 medium fennel bulbs, bottoms trimmed, quartered lengthwise

1 cup (250 ml | 250 g) Chianti or dry red wine

q.b. coarse sea salt and freshly ground Tellicherry black peppercorns

1 teaspoon (3 g) caraway seeds

1 tablespoon (10 g) bread crumbs

1 tablespoon (10 g) almond meal

Robust extra-virgin olive oil, to finish

• Preheat the oven to 350°F (180°C). Butter a 9 x 13-inch baking dish.

• Arrange the fennel quarters in the prepared baking dish. In a liquid measuring cup, combine the Chianti and 1 cup (250 ml | 250 g) water. Pour the wine-water mixture into the pan until it comes halfway up the sides of the pan. Season with salt and pepper, then cover the dish tightly with aluminum foil and bake until the fennel is slightly translucent and a small knife slides easily in and out, about 45 minutes.

• In a small bowl, mix together the caraway seeds, bread crumbs, and almond meal. Season generously with salt. Divide the fennel among four plates, sprinkle with the caraway blend, and drizzle with olive oil. Serve immediately.

TO DRINK:
This is a very tough dish to pair with a red wine, but any simple Chianti Classico, young and fruity, would do.

I don't know a kid of any age that doesn't like *Pizza Senza Crosta*, a bit of a cross between fondue, mozzarella sticks, and pizza. First, you heat rich tomato sauce in a large pot and add big wedges of mozzarella. When the mozzarella starts to melt, it's time to serve. The pan is brought directly to the table and set alongside a basket of cut-up focaccia or ciabatta. Bowls of toppings—olives! anchovies! *Cruschi!* (page 26)—are littered around the table, and everyone digs in, spooning sauce over bread, trying to snag the gooey chunks of cheese and toppings. It's a double-dipping safe zone that I'm always excited to be a part of.

Pizza Without Crust

PIZZA SENZA CROSTA

SERVES 6 TO 8

2 cups (500 ml | 500 g)
 Salsa di Pomodoro (page 42)

q.b. coarse sea salt and crushed
 Tellicherry black peppercorns

2 or 3 basil sprigs, plus more to finish

1 ball (225 g) *mozzarella di bufala*,
 sliced into 12 equal pieces

Focaccia, ciabatta, or rustic Italian
 bread, cut or torn into pieces

Bowls of olives, anchovies,
 pepperoncini, or *cruschi*,
 for serving

• In a large straight-sided skillet, warm the tomato sauce over medium-low heat. When the sauce begins to bubble, season with salt and pepper and stir in the basil and mozzarella slices. Cover and heat until the mozzarella is partially melted (you want some stringy pieces), about 8 minutes. Remove the pan from the heat and scatter additional basil over the top. Serve immediately with bread and condiments.

TO DRINK:
A sparkling Franciacorta Bellavista.

MATERA, BASILICATA. CAPER BUSHES GROW OUT OF WALL CREVICES.
(ABOVE, PAGES 112–113)

Cooking tender octopus at home can feel like a daunting task. And there are hundreds of old wives' tales to swear by: Slap it forty times against a wooden table, rub it with a radish, add a wine cork to the pot. The real secret to a tender final dish is to simmer the octopus slowly in water before quickly grilling (and to add the wine cork—it has no scientific explanation, but I swear it works!). I like to counterbalance the bittersweet char of the tender octopus with plenty of salt (olives and salted capers) and acid (lemon juice) and toss it with potatoes and olive oil. It makes for an unforgettable (and beautiful) potato salad that none of your diners will be able to get enough of!

Grilled Octopus and Potato Salad with Capers and Olives

POLPO, PATATE, CAPPERI E OLIVE

SERVES 4

2 (2-pound | 900-g) octopuses, beaks removed (your fishmonger can do this for you)

q.b. coarse sea salt

7 large (400 g) fingerling potatoes, peeled and sliced on an angle into 1-inch pieces

½ cup (125 ml | 115 g) robust extra-virgin olive oil

⅓ cup (40 g) pitted Taggiasca olives

1 tablespoon (12 g) salted capers, rinsed and drained

2 lemons, sliced into wedges

• Bring a large pot of water to a boil. Add the whole octopuses and simmer until very tender when pierced with a knife, about 40 minutes. Remove the octopuses from the water, pat dry, and slice the tentacles into 1-inch-long pieces.

• Put the potatoes in a large pot of salted water and bring to a boil. Cook until tender, 8 to 10 minutes. Drain the potatoes, pat dry, and transfer to a large bowl.

• Heat an outdoor grill to medium-high or heat an indoor grill pan over medium-high heat. Grill the octopus tentacles until they are brown and crisp on all sides, about 10 minutes total. Slice the tentacles on an angle into 1-inch pieces. Add the grilled octopus, olive oil, olives, and capers to the bowl with the potatoes. Toss well and serve with lemon wedges.

TO DRINK:
A delicious Ligurian white Colli di Luni Vermentino "Il Maggiore" from Ottaviano Lambruschi. It has an almost salty minerality.

In 1962, my fantastic friend Lucia di Mauro's family on the Amalfi coast was the first to put tuna in a glass jar. Lucia's grandfather thought it would be beautiful to see the fillets marinating in the olive oil. It was a big hit, and since then, many companies across the world started to put the fish in jars rather than cans.

Ventresca is the most prized, precious part of the tuna, the belly. It is tender, tasty, and so incredibly *not* fishy that many people prefer this to any other part of the fish. This is my favorite way to serve it, either as a plate among many antipasti or as a simple one-meal dish alongside some toasted Focaccia with Extra-Virgin Olive Oil (page 83). Taste the dish as you're mixing it together: It should taste like the sea, with a nice bright acidity at the end from the lemon juice, and each bite should have a bit of everything.

Tuna Belly with Beans

VENTRESCA CON FAGIOLI

SERVES 4 TO 6

1 (185-g | 6½-ounce) jar *ventresca di tonno* (tuna belly)

1 cup (170 g) cooked beans (see page 11)

2 tablespoons (30 ml | 56½ g) mild extra-virgin olive oil

1 tablespoons (15 ml | 28 g) fresh lemon juice

½ bunch fresh flat-leaf parsley, torn

q.b. crushed Tellicherry black pepper

½ teaspoon *colatura di alici* (anchovy essence)

• In a large bowl, use your hands to mix the tuna and cooked beans, tossing gently to keep the beans from breaking. Add the olive oil, lemon juice, and parsley and season with pepper. Taste, then add the *colatura* and taste again. Correct the seasonings as needed and serve.

TO DRINK:
"Vitamenia Rosato," a very unusual Rosato wine from Patrizia Malanga in Vigne di Raito, right above Cetara.

This is one of those dishes that I only make when I can invite my friends to stand in the kitchen with me and eat it as I make it—with crisp Vermentino from Sardinia not far from hand. The more types of seafood, the better, and don't be afraid to substitute whatever looks freshest at the market. The real secret is simply to not add too many pieces at once to the frying oil. You want to make sure the temperature of the oil remains even during cooking so the fish remains light and crisp. Sometimes I batter and fry a few very thin lemon slices for a jolt of bitter, acidic flavor between bites of seafood.

Mixed Fried Seafood

FRITTINI DI FRUTTI DI MARE E LIMONI

SERVES 6 TO 8

1 cup (135 g) all-purpose flour

1 teaspoon fine sea salt, plus more as needed

1¼ cups (300 ml | 300 g) cold San Pellegrino

8 cups (1.9 L | 750 g) mild extra-virgin olive oil

½ pound (225 g) large shrimp, peeled and deveined, tails left on

½ pound (225 g) sardines or whiting

6 pounds (2.7 kg) squid, cleaned and cut into rings, tentacles kept whole (about 2½ pounds cleaned)

1 lemon, cut into wedges

• Line a baking sheet with paper towels, newspaper, or brown paper and set a wire rack on top.

• In a large bowl, whisk together the flour and salt. Whisk in the San Pellegrino (don't worry about getting it smooth; a few lumps are okay).

• Attach a deep-fry thermometer to the side of a large pot. Pour in enough olive oil to come 4 inches up the sides of the pan. Heat over medium-high heat until the thermometer registers 350°F (180°C).

• Dip the shrimp into the batter, allowing the excess to drip back into bowl. Add the shrimp individually to the hot oil. Fry, turning occasionally to cook evenly and gently, until golden and crisp, 1 to 2 minutes. Using a spider or slotted spoon, transfer the shrimp to the wire rack and season with salt. Repeat with the sardines and squid, making sure the cooking oil comes back to temperature between the batches.

• Transfer the fried seafood to a large platter and serve with lemon wedges.

TO DRINK:
A crisp Vermentino from Sardinia from Contini.

I always serve this dish to my American friends during Thanksgiving as either an appetizer or as dessert, instead of pumpkin pie. Just like Turkey Breast Cooked in Milk with Herbs (page 282), I make sure they get the ingredients they're looking for in a traditional meal . . . but with an Italian twist! The key to this dish is using very high-quality traditional balsamic vinegar from Modena. This thick, sweet vinegar with a subtle acid finish is one of the most magical and unique food products in the world. This is the time to splurge on a bottle of the best. Enjoy the balsamic with these poached pumpkins, drizzled over chunks of Parmigiano-Reggiano, with fresh strawberries, or simply by the spoonful.

Poached Baby Pumpkins with Traditional Balsamic Vinegar

ZUCCA CON ACETO BALSAMICO TRADIZIONALE DI MODENA

SERVES 4

2 teaspoons (9 g) Demerara sugar

½ teaspoon sea salt

2 star anise pods

2 sprigs mint, plus chopped fresh mint leaves to finish

Juice of 1 lemon (reserve the juiced rinds)

Juice of 1 orange (reserve the juiced rinds)

8 whole Tellicherry black peppercorns

4 miniature pumpkins, pumpkins halved and seeded

Balsamico Tradizionale di Modena DOP, to finish

• Bring a large pot of water to a simmer. Add the sugar, salt, star anise, mint sprigs, lemon and orange juice and the juiced rinds, and the peppercorns. Add the pumpkin bottoms and tops. Simmer gently so the pumpkin bottoms do not break, cooking just until the flesh is tender when pierced with a knife, 15 to 20 minutes for the bottoms and 10 for the tops. Drain and pat the pumpkin pieces dry. Place the pumpkin bottoms on four plates and drizzle generously with the balsamic vinegar. Sprinkle with fresh mint and top with the pumpkin tops. Serve warm.

TO DRINK:
A lively Lambrusco from the hills of Modena.

At Masseria Mirogallo, a beautiful family-run farm in Lucania, this recipe is often made for a quick, filling lunch. *Spaccatelle*, derived from *spaccare*, means "to break, smash, or divide," and is the key to this simple dish. Cut whole peeled tomatoes in half, discard the seeds, and scatter on a plate with garlic, olive oil, salt, and capers. Eat with fresh semolina bread. That's it! So satisfying and so simple!

Broken Fresh Tomato Halves

SPACCATELLE DI POMODORI

SERVES 1

1 small garlic clove, thinly sliced

2 cups whole peeled tomatoes, halved and deseeded

¼ cup robust extra-virgin olive oil

Pinch of fine sea salt

6 to 8 salted capers, rinsed and drained

Fresh semolina bread, for serving

• Put the thinly sliced garlic in a shallow bowl. Top with the tomatoes and drizzle with olive oil. Season with salt and sprinkle the capers over the top. Serve immediately with fresh bread.

TO DRINK:

A rich and succulent wine from Basilicata, such as Aglianico del Vulture "Gricos" by Grifalco della Lucania.

This is one of my favorite dishes in the world . . . with an ingredient that seems to turn people away in droves. However, the moment I put a platter of it in front of friends, preferably in the summer during an al fresco lunch, people love it! It seems to be simply a matter of preconceived notions! Serve it as a *pietanza* (main course) along with Mashed (page 57) or Steamed Potatoes with Red Onions and Capers (page 305). If you have leftovers, sandwich slices between Focaccia with Extra-Virgin Olive Oil (page 83) with a smear of *Salsa Verde* (page 50).

Boiled Veal Tongue with Green Sauce

LINGUA CON SALSA VERDE

SERVES 8 TO 10

1 (2-pound | 900-g) beef tongue, rinsed

1 medium onion, quartered

2 carrots, each cut into 4 pieces

2 celery stalks, each cut into 4 pieces

1 bunch fresh flat-leaf parsley

2 fresh or dried bay leaves

3 or 4 juniper berries

2 whole cloves

10 whole Tellicherry black peppercorns

½ cup (125 ml | 150 g) Salsa Verde (page 000)

½ cup (125 ml | 115 g) medium extra-virgin olive oil

TO DRINK:
A red wine such as a Rosso di Montalcino from Casanova di Neri.

• In a large Dutch oven, combine the tongue, onion, carrots, celery, parsley, and bay leaves. Add enough cold water to cover the tongue by about 2 inches. Bring to a boil over medium-high heat. Using a slotted spoon, skim off and discard any scum from the cooking liquid. Add the juniper berries, cloves, and peppercorns and reduce the heat to maintain a simmer. Cook, partially covered, until the tongue is tender when pierced with a knife at the thickest part, 1½ to 2½ hours. Add more water to the pan as needed to keep the tongue covered in liquid.

• Transfer the tongue from the poaching liquid to a large bowl and set aside to cool slightly; discard the poaching liquid. As soon as the tongue is cool enough to handle (some people wear rubber gloves), use a knife to make an incision into the skin and, using your fingers, peel off and discard all the skin. Scrape off any bumps and trim off the gristle and fat on the underside.

• Put the peeled tongue in a deep dish. Cover with plastic wrap and press down to remove any excess water. Discard the excess water and set aside to cool completely. Thinly slice the tongue crosswise and refrigerate until chilled. Whisk the olive oil into the *salsa verde*. Spread half the *salsa verde* over a large serving platter. Arrange the tongue slices on top and spread the remaining salsa verde over the tongue.

4

Now, for a First Course

ORA PER PRIMO

Like quality olive oil and wine,

the best pasta starts with the best ingredients. Quality pasta depends on how the wheat is grown and milled, how the dough is made and shaped, how the pasta is dried, and finally how it tastes once it is cooked and combined with a sauce.

Many Italians (and others) eat pasta every day—sometimes twice a day—especially now that top-quality dried pasta is readily available. In fact, many brands of dried pasta are so good that homemade fresh pasta is made only on special occasions. Here are a few things to keep in mind to become a knowledgeable pasta consumer:

- Artisanal pasta producers purchase quality 100% durum semolina with a high protein content and a higher price from farmers who grow the wheat under specific conditions.
- Artisanal pasta makers use bronze dies to create different shapes of pasta. The dies cost more and break down more frequently, but the result is pasta with a sandpaperlike surface that allows sauces to cling to the rougher edges. While industrial pasta makers use bronze dies as well, theirs are lined with a smooth Teflon coating so the pasta is extruded at a much faster rate and production yields are much higher.
- When you cook artisanal pasta, most of the starch stays in the pasta rather than leaching out into the cooking water. Without the rougher edges and less starch, sauce tends to pool in the bowl rather than coat each pasta strand.

- **MY FAVORITE** Italian producers are Rustichella d'Abruzzo in Abruzzo, Benedetto Cavalieri in Puglia, and Martelli in Toscana, but I encourage you to seek out and discover your own favorites! Remember, when choosing a good pasta brand, make sure it is artisanal. The texture and flavor matter—it's very important that your pasta has flavor, not just be simply flour and water.

How to Cook Pasta

Once you have quality pasta, you need to know how to cook it. Cooking pasta requires your full attention and should be eaten as soon as possible after cooking.

- Determine how many people you will be serving so you can figure out how much pasta to cook. Cook 70 to 80 g per person for a *primi*; if pasta will be served as the main course, cook 125 g per person.
- For each pound (450 g) of pasta, bring a large pot of water to a boil. Add a generous amount of coarse sea salt, about 2 tablespoons. It may seem like a lot, but the water should be briny and taste of the sea.
- When cooking spaghetti or other longer pastas, gently drop the pasta into the boiling water. Instead of stirring or pressing down on the pasta, let it soften and submerge itself in the water. Once the pasta is submerged, give it a stir so it doesn't stick on the bottom.
- Different shapes require different amounts of time to cook. Rigatoni and penne will take more time than spaghetti and linguine. While most packages give cooking times for each pasta, the best way to know when your pasta is done is to taste it. After 4 minutes or so, remove a strand or two with tongs, look at it, and taste it. When it's al dente, the pasta should be the same color throughout, not white in the middle. If it's not done, continue to cook and taste until the pasta is al dente. Err on the side of

undercooking the pasta, as it will continue to cook when combined with the sauce.

• When the pasta is almost done, scoop out a cup or two of the pasta cooking water and reserve for the sauce, if needed. Once drained, toss the pasta and the sauce together to combine. If the sauce seems dry, add a little bit of the reserved cooking water to thin it out.

• Pasta should be served in warm bowls to prevent it from cooling off. Just before the pasta is finished cooking, remove 2 cups of the pasta cooking water and divide it among the serving bowls to heat them while combining the sauce and the pasta in the cooking pot. The bowls can also be warmed at a low temperature in the oven. Pour out the water before plating the pasta.

• By this time, everyone should be seated at the table. Pasta waits for no one! Set the skillet on a trivet on the table, divide the pasta among the warmed bowls, and pass the cheese, when called for.

Leftover pasta can be added to soups or made into a frittata (page 281), so don't hesitate to make the entire package at once. Serve in wedges as a side dish to grilled meats or topped with a fried egg for a quick lunch.

Every Saturday in Florence I make my rounds—the market, the butcher, the wine store—before heading home to make *Spaghetti alla Carbonara. Carbonara* means "charcoal burner," and legend has it that this hearty dish was first prepared for charcoal workers. The key to such a simple dish is in the ingredients: fresh, room-temperature eggs, sharp Pecorino Romano, and especially salty *guanciale* (cured pork jowl).

Spaghetti with Egg, Pecorino Romano, and Guanciale

SPAGHETTI ALLA CARBONARA

**SERVES 6 AS A *PRIMI*,
4 AS A *SECONDI***

2 tablespoons (34 g) coarse sea salt

1 pound (453 g) durum wheat semolina spaghetti

2 pieces (50 g) guanciale or pancetta, cut into ½-inch cubes

2 large eggs, at room temperature

1 cup (60 g) grated Pecorino Romano cheese, plus more to finish

q.b. crushed Tellicherry black peppercorns

• Bring a large pot of salted water to a boil. Gently add the pasta, letting it soften and submerge itself in the water. Once the pasta is submerged, give it a stir so it doesn't stick on the bottom. After 4 minutes, taste a strand of pasta for doneness. Continue to taste a strand until the spaghetti is al dente, about 10 minutes.

• While the pasta is cooking, heat a large skillet over medium heat. Add the guanciale and cook until translucent, not browned, about 2 minutes. In a large serving bowl, whisk together the eggs, grated cheese, and peppercorns until smooth and creamy. When the spaghetti is al dente, drain it through a colander and add the pasta to the bowl, tossing well to coat the strands of pasta evenly. Stir in the guanciale and divide among warm pasta bowls. Serve immediately with additional cheese.

TO DRINK:
Since I always make this dish at home (or only have it at Da Nazzareno), I always drink it with a nice glass of Castello di Nipozzano from my family friend the Marchesi de' Frescobaldi.

When teaching this recipe, I tell my students that if they can master this dish, they are well on their way to becoming pasta experts. It may seem like a simple dish to prepare, but precise timing and attention to detail are essential to its success. Having eaten hundreds of versions of this Roman classic in restaurants and in the homes of friends, I finally came up with a method that guarantees a perfect *Cacio e Pepe*. Use artisanal pasta; the strongest, most pungent pecorino you can find (my favorite is Sini Fulvi, a Roman producer), and sea salt and Tellicherry black peppercorns crushed in a mortar with a pestle. Have the ingredients measured, prepped, and ready to go from the skillet to warm bowls.

Spaghetti with Pecorino Romano and Black Pepper

SPAGHETTI CACIO E PEPE

**SERVES 6 AS A *PRIMI*,
4 AS A *SECONDI***

q.b. coarse sea salt

1 pound (453 g) durum wheat
   semolina spaghetti

2 cups (120 g) grated Pecorino
   Romano cheese, plus more for
   serving

1 tablespoon crushed Tellicherry
   black peppercorns, plus more
   if needed

TO DRINK:
A gutsy wine to stand up to
the sharp pecorino, such as a
Taurasi from Mastroberadrino
or a red from Feudi di San
Gregorio.

• Bring a large pot of salted water to a boil. Gently add the pasta, letting it soften and submerge itself in the water. Once the pasta is submerged, give it a stir so it doesn't stick on the bottom. After 4 minutes, taste a strand of pasta for doneness. Continue to taste a strand until the spaghetti is almost al dente, about 10 minutes. Remove 2 cups (500 ml | 500 g) of the cooking water and reserve. (At this point, everyone should be seated at the table.)

• Drain the pasta in a colander and return it to the pot. Immediately add a handful of the cheese to the warm spaghetti. Using tongs, gently lift and toss the spaghetti to coat it with the cheese as it melts. Turn the heat to medium-low, add about ½ cup of the cooking water, and continue to mix, adding the cheese and a little more water as necessary until the spaghetti is evenly coated and creamy.

• Sprinkle the pepper over the top and toss just until there are black flecks dotting the spaghetti. Taste and season with salt and pepper as necessary. Bring the pot directly to the table and serve immediately in warm pasta bowls with extra cheese and pepper on the side.

Salina is one of the larger of the eight Aeolian Islands, right off the northeastern tip of Sicily. Another of the islands is nearby Stromboli, which is home to one of Italy's three active volcanoes! From Salina, you can actually see lava spewing high into the night sky over Stromboli. It's quite a spectacle.

It is in Salina that Antonino Caravaglio grows the capers, caper berries, and caper shoots for Manicaretti. Salina became famous when it was used as the location for the award-winning movie *Il Postino* (*The Postman*), and the beautiful house where the movie was filmed is located not too far from Antonino's caper fields. This simple, delicious bucatini recipe with tuna and capers—which I first had there—is now one of the four basic pastas I teach at my cooking classes.

Bucatini with Tuna, Olives, Capers, and Lemon

BUCATINI COME IN SALINA

SERVES 4

1 pound (340 g) durum wheat semolina bucatini

1 cup (250 ml | 230 g) mild extra-virgin olive oil

1 pound (450 g) sushi-grade ahi tuna, cut into ¼-inch-thick slices

q.b. coarse sea salt and crushed Tellicherry black peppercorns

3 garlic cloves, coarsely chopped

1 cup (140 g) Taggiasca olives, pitted and coarsely chopped

2 tablespoons (18 g) salted capers, rinsed

1 lemon, quartered and sliced thin

Torn fresh flat-leaf parsley and basil leaves, to finish

• Bring a large pot of salted water to a boil. Gently add the pasta, letting it soften and submerge itself in the water. Once the pasta is submerged, give it a stir so it doesn't stick on the bottom. After 4 minutes, taste a strand of pasta for doneness. Continue to taste a strand until the bucatini is almost al dente, about 9 minutes.

• While the pasta is cooking, heat a large skillet over medium heat. Add the olive oil and tuna and season with salt and pepper. Stirring carefully, so the tuna doesn't break apart, add the garlic, olives, capers, and lemon slices and cook until the tuna is an opaque light pink color, about 2 minutes. When the bucatini is al dente, drain it through a colander and add the pasta to the tuna mixture. Using tongs, toss well and season with salt and pepper.

• Bring the skillet directly to the table and serve immediately in warm pasta bowls garnished with parsley and basil leaves.

TO DRINK:
A dry Malvasia from Antonino Caravaglio, of course!

Orecchiette, or "little ears," is the signature pasta of Puglia. Small and round, they have little pockets that catch sauce. My friend Rossella Florio, who comes from San Severo in northern Puglia, says her family ate orecchiette many times a week, prepared with eggplant, fava beans, onions, and broccoli rabe. This is my take on that typical dish. To flavor the broth the pasta cooks in, I boil the broccoli rabe stems first, then the leaves and florets. It's an easy way to extract additional flavor without adding another ingredient.

Orecchiette with Sausage and Broccoli Rabe, My Way

ORECCHIETTE ALLA PUGLIESE A "MODO MIO"

SERVES 6 AS A *PRIMI*, 4 AS A ONE-DISH MEAL

q.b. coarse sea salt

1 large bunch broccoli rabe, stems, leaves, and florets separated

1 pound (453 g) durum wheat semolina orecchiette

½ cup (125 ml | 115 g) robust extra-virgin olive oil, plus more for drizzling

2 garlic cloves, crushed

2 (½-pound | 226 g) spicy Italian sausages, casings removed

q.b. red pepper flakes

TO DRINK:
A Primitivo or Negroamaro Notarpanaro from Taurino in Puglia.

• Bring a large pot of salted water to a boil. Add the broccoli rabe stems and boil for 15 minutes. Using tongs, remove the stems and discard. Add the leaves to the pot, boil for 5 minutes, then add the florets and cook until tender and bright green, about 3 minutes more. Use a slotted spoon to transfer the leaves and florets to a colander and set aside to drain.

• Add the pasta to the boiling *brodetto* (broth) and cook until al dente, 8 to 10 minutes. (The pasta will continue to cook with the sauce.) Drain, reserving 2 cups (500 ml | 500 g) of the cooking water.

• While the pasta is cooking, in a large skillet, heat the olive oil over medium heat. Add the garlic and the sausage and cook, stirring frequently to break up the meat, until it is browned and cooked through, about 7 minutes. Stir in a pinch of red pepper flakes and season with salt.

• Remove and discard the garlic and add the pasta and the broccoli rabe leaves and florets to the skillet, stirring well to heat through. If the pasta and sauce are too dry, add some of the reserved cooking water. Bring the skillet to the table and serve in warm bowls.

Nicolina Sergiacomo Peduzzi

The Woman Behind the Pasta

From the first day I met the Peduzzi family—the makers behind Rustichella d'Abruzzo pasta—they have treated me like a family member: Stefania and Giancarlo, and Gianluigi and Maria have treated me like a brother, their five children like an uncle, and the matriarch—Nicolina Sergiacomo Peduzzi—like a son.

The Peduzzis share many meals together, but every family member (unless they're traveling) sits down at two p.m. every Sunday for a three- to four-hour lunch. The menu follows a format: the first course is pasta (spaghetti with tomato sauce or white *ragú* or gnocchi with butter and sage); the second is pork, lamb, or beef with a side of broccoli rabe or cooked greens; dessert is small pastries or

cookies from the *pasticceria* down the street and plentiful cups of espresso. No subject is off-limits, and each member of the family will tell you that this lunch is the highlight of the week. "The more I travel, the more I realize how lucky I am to work and live with my family," Nicolina's daughter, Stefania, says. "I have cooked and eaten our pasta all over the world, and it never tastes as good as when we eat it in my mother's kitchen. Our pasta is our family. Our family is our pasta. Even when we argue, we keep our discussions within the family. *I panni sporchi si lavano in casa* (dirty clothes should be washed at home)."

I've spent many Sunday lunches (and plenty of other meals) around Nicolina's table, but the dish that stands out in my mind when I think of that strong, beautiful family is the first pasta dish she made for me (and one she still prepares when I come "home").

Spaghetti alla Nicolina (recipe follows) is composed of just four ingredients, and they all must be of the best quality you can find: zucchini, Pecorino Romano, olive oil, and, of course, spaghetti. The zucchini is sliced to various thicknesses and caramelized—almost charred—in a good amount of olive oil before being tossed with cooked spaghetti and plenty of sharp Pecorino Romano. *Il tutto è più della somma delle singole parti* ("The whole is greater than the sum of its parts").

Spaghetti with Zucchini and Pecorino Romano

SPAGHETTI ALLA NICOLINA

SERVES 4 TO 6

8 medium zucchini, sliced into rounds of different thicknesses (between ¼ to ½ inch thick)

q.b. coarse sea salt

1 cup (250 ml | 230 g) medium extra-virgin olive oil

q.b. crushed Tellicherry black peppercorns

1 pound (450 g) durum wheat semolina spaghetti

1 cup (140 g) grated Pecorino Romano cheese

TO DRINK:
Nicolina usually serves a bottle of Montepulciano d'Abruzzo from Cantina Zaccagnini with this dish.

- Layer the zucchini slices in a colander, seasoning each layer with a generous pinch of salt. Set aside to rest for 30 minutes, then rinse and dry the zucchini.

- In a large skillet, heat the olive oil over medium heat. Add a quarter of the sliced zucchini, but do not stir. Every 2 to 3 minutes, add another quarter of the zucchini. Once all the zucchini has been added, cook, gently stirring the zucchini every few minutes until the zucchini slices range in color from light gold to dark golden brown, and in texture from soft to crisp, 20 to 25 minutes. Season with pepper.

- While the zucchini is cooking, bring a large pot of salted water to a boil. Gently add the pasta, letting it soften and submerge itself in the water. Once the pasta is submerged, give it a stir so it doesn't stick on the bottom. After 4 minutes, taste a strand of pasta for doneness. Continue to taste a strand until the spaghetti is almost al dente, about 10 minutes.

- Drain the spaghetti in a colander and immediately add to the zucchini. Sprinkle with cheese and, using tongs, gently lift and toss the spaghetti to mix well. Season with salt and pepper. Bring the skillet to the table and serve immediately in warm pasta bowls.

Ceci, the Italian word for "chickpeas," are another staple that I like to cook weekly and keep in my fridge to use in soups, salads, and stews. Like beans, dried chickpeas that have been soaked and cooked are infinitely more flavorful than canned ones. One cup dried chickpeas will yield 3 cups cooked (about twice the amount you need for this recipe). Use any extra ones in salads, eat them as a snack, or blend with garlic and olive oil for a dip. This soup is also a good way to use up those pasta odds and ends in the pantry—you know, the two ounces of broken lasagna, 1-inch pieces of spaghetti, or that handful of bow ties you don't know what to do with.

Chickpea, Tomato, and Broken Pasta Soup

SPAGHETTI A PEZZI CON POMODORO E CECI IN BRODETTO

SERVES 4

1 cup (185 g) dried chickpeas

6 cups (1.4 L | 1.4 kg) *Brodetto* (page 56)

½ pound (225 g) durum wheat semolina spaghetti

1 pint (225 g) cherry tomatoes, halved

8 fresh basil leaves, torn

Robust extra-virgin olive oil, to finish

• Place the chickpeas in a medium bowl and cover with 3 inches (about 4 horizontal fingers) of water. Set aside to soak overnight at room temperature.

• Drain the chickpeas and place in a large saucepan. Add enough water to cover the chickpeas by 3 inches (about 4 horizontal fingers). Bring to a boil over high heat, then reduce the heat to maintain a simmer and cook until the chickpeas are tender, 45 minutes to 1½ hours. Drain the chickpeas and set aside.

• In a medium saucepan, bring 3 cups (750 ml | 750 g) of the *brodetto* to a boil. Break the spaghetti into 1- and ½-inch-long pieces as you add the pasta to the *brodetto* and cook until al dente, depending on the type of pasta(s) used.

• Drain the pasta through a fine-mesh sieve, reserving the *brodetto*, and set aside. Add the remaining 3 cups (750 ml | 750 g) *brodetto* and the chickpeas and heat over medium heat until the chickpeas are warmed through.

• To serve, divide the pasta and chickpeas among four soup bowls. Sprinkle with the cherry tomatoes and ladle the hot *brodetto* over the top. Garnish with basil and olive oil and serve.

TO DRINK:
A young Sagrantino di Montefalco from Arnaldo Caprai in Umbria.

Liguria, the home of pesto, is also home to *trofie*, a short, thin pasta made by rubbing and rolling a piece of dough. The success of the classic regional combination of *trofie* with pesto, potatoes, and string beans relies on proportions. Preparing an equal amount of pasta and vegetables and making sure the potatoes and string beans are cut to the same size as the *trofie* (about 1 inch in length) results in a dish that has superlative texture and flavor in each mouthful. The picture here shows the ideal proportions (to scale)!

Trofie with Basil Pesto and Green Beans

TROFIE CON TANTO VERDE

SERVES 4

1⅓ pounds (600 g) Yukon Gold potatoes, peeled and cut into ½-inch cubes

½ pound (225 g) green beans, trimmed and cut into ½-inch pieces

½ pound (225 g) *trofie* pasta

6 tablespoons (30 g) Arugula and Herb Pesto (page 43)

¼ cup fresh basil leaves

Mild extra-virgin olive oil, to finish

• Bring a large pot of salted water to a boil. Add the potatoes and boil until they are cooked through but still firm, about 5 minutes. Using a slotted spoon, transfer the potatoes to a large bowl. Add the beans to the same water and blanch until crisp, 2 to 3 minutes. Transfer the beans to the bowl with the potatoes, then add the *trofie* to the boiling water and cook until just slightly underdone, about 8 minutes (start testing the pasta after 5 minutes so you don't overcook it). Return the potatoes and the beans to the boiling water. Cook until the pasta is al dente, about 2 more minutes. Remove 2 cups (500ml | 500g) of the cooking water and preserve. Drain the pasta-potato mixture.

• Put the pesto in a large serving bowl. Dilute with 4 tablespoons of the reserved water and stir together. Transfer the drained pasta mixture to the serving bowl and toss gently with the pesto. Top with basil and olive oil just before serving.

TO DRINK:
Pair a crisp white wine from Liguria, such as Riviera Ligure di Ponente Pigato "Bon in da Bon" BioVio or a light red that you love.

The Italian flag is commonly referred to as the *tricolore* ("three colors"), and I often make this pasta as part of our *Festa della Reppubblica* national holiday on June 2. (I also make the same dish using *Riso in Bianco* (page 59) in place of the *paccheri* for my friend Donatella de Peverelli, who cannot eat wheat!) The colors of the dish are beautiful—perfect for the Day of the Republic—and the strings of the mozzarella make it seem almost as if you are eating a pizza Margherita.

Paccheri with Tomatoes, Mozzarella, and Basil

PACCHERRI TRICOLORE

**SERVES 6 AS *PRIMI*,
4 AS A *SECONDI***

1 pound (450 g) *paccheri* pasta

¼ cup (60 ml | 113 g) medium
extra-virgin olive oil

1 teaspoon *estratto di pomodoro*
(tomato paste)

2 scallions, thinly sliced

1½ cups (275 g) cherry tomatoes,
halved

½ pound (225 g) *mozzarella di
bufala*, cut into large cubes

q.b. fine sea salt and crushed
Tellicherry black peppercorns

Fresh basil leaves, torn,
for serving

- Bring a large pot of salted water to a boil. Gently add the pasta, letting it soften and submerge itself in the water. Once the pasta is submerged, give it a stir so it doesn't stick on the bottom. After 5 minutes, taste a piece of pasta for doneness. Continue to taste a strand until the pasta is almost al dente, 8 to 10 minutes.

- While the pasta is cooking, in a large skillet, heat the olive oil over medium heat. Add the *estratto*, stirring well so it melts into the oil, about 1 minute. Add the scallions and tomatoes and cook, stirring occasionally, until soft, about 4 minutes.

- Drain the pasta through a colander and immediately add it to the skillet. Add the mozzarella cubes and, using a pair of tongs, gently lift and toss the pasta until well combined. Season with salt and pepper. Divide among warm bowls. Top with torn basil leaves before serving.

TO DRINK:
A red wine with a nice lively acidity, such as the Campi Flegrei "Agnanum" made with Piedirosso grapes, cuts through the tomato and mozzarella.

This is the simplest, greenest, quickest dish to make. It's more of a tonic than anything else—a base of green *brodetto* filled with whatever is in season, cut into pieces of the same size: peas, asparagus, zucchini, fava beans, leeks, scallions, parsley, spinach, basil . . . the list goes on! I like a little bit of everything, and it is fun when you mix and match whatever you have in your farmers' market or garden. If I'm making this soup in the autumn or winter (with, say, *cavolo nero*, savoy cabbage, green cabbage, leeks, and chard), I simple omit the basil and spinach and let it cook longer, and serve the more rustic variety hotter. The only "rule" is to not cut everything to the same size before boiling until tender in the *brodetto*. It's all about the textures and surprising bites with every spoonful. Finish with a drizzle of robust extra-virgin olive oil (use bright green *olio nuovo* if it's in season.) I also like to keep the minestrone entirely unseasoned—you will see that the natural minerals of the vegetables add a natural salinity—taste and correct at the end or place some sea salt and pepper on the table.

Very Fresh Green Vegetable Minestrone

MINESTRONE DI PRIMAVERA FRESCHISSIMO

SERVES 8 TO 10

6 cups (1.4 L | 1440 g) *Brodetto* (page 56)

2 small scallions, chopped into ½- or ¼-inch pieces

2 baby leeks, chopped into ½- or ¼-inch pieces

1 new green garlic (or ramps, when in season), finely chopped

3 medium zucchini or 6 tender baby ones (if you can find ones that have the blossom attached, even better), chopped into ½- or ¼-inch pieces

3 celery stalks, leaves included, chopped into ½- or ¼-inch pieces

3 cups (45 g) small baby spinach, torn into uneven pieces

3 cups (45 g) small tender chard leaves, torn into uneven pieces

1 cup (15 g) fresh flat-leaf parsley leaves, torn into uneven pieces

1 cup (15 g) fresh basil leaves, torn into uneven pieces

Robust extra-virgin olive oil, to finish

Focaccia, for serving

q.b. fine sea salt and crushed Tellicherry black peppercorns

• In a large stockpot, combine the *brodetto*, scallions, leeks, green garlic, zucchini, celery, baby spinach, chard, parsley, and basil. (If you want to add more of one green or another, go for it.) Cover the pot and bring to a boil over high heat. Reduce the heat to maintain a simmer and cook, still covered, until tender, about 20 minutes. Set aside to rest for 10 minutes. Serve warm with olive oil, focaccia, salt, and pepper.

TO DRINK:

A crisp white wine from the Val d'Aosta such as Les Cretes. The minerality and acidity of the wine will brighten the green notes of the minestrone even more.

After a long flight I crave this comforting soup—which is a good reason to keep containers of Old Hen Broth (page 54) in the freezer (if you can't get to my favorite place to rest my weary traveler's body, Cammillo in Firenze). Lightly beaten eggs and Parmigiano-Reggiano are gently poured on top of the piping hot soup, resulting in a floating crepe. Once the crepe is firm, use scissors to cut it up into *stracci*, or torn pieces, and breath a sigh of relief—you're home.

Egg and Parmigiano-Reggiano Dumplings in Broth

STRACCIATELLA ALLA ROMANA

SERVES 4

6 cups (1.4 L | 1440 g) Old Hen Broth (page 54)

2 large eggs

1 cup (80 g) grated Parmigiano-Reggiano cheese, plus more to finish

½ teaspoon freshly grated lemon zest (from about ½ lemon)

A few gratings of fresh nutmeg

q.b. coarse sea salt and crushed Tellicherry black peppercorns

• Bring the broth to a boil in a medium saucepan. In a medium bowl, whisk together the eggs, cheese, lemon zest, and nutmeg. Season with salt and pepper. Gently pour the egg-cheese mixture into the boiling broth. Once the crepe floats to the surface, reduce the heat to medium. When the crepe is firm, use a pair of scissors to cut it into small pieces. Ladle into warm bowls and serve with additional cheese, if desired.

TO DRINK:
Just enjoy the soup and feel better.

Marcella Hazan included the late Countess Lisa Contini Bonacossi of Villa Capezzana's recipe for *acqua cotta* ("cooked water") in her *Essentials of Classic Italian Cooking*, calling the countess "one of the most gifted Tuscan cooks." The original recipe includes cabbage, kale, cannellini beans, and a bouillon cube. This version, from Villa Capezzana's chef, Patrizio, takes plenty of cues from the benchmark original but uses chicken broth in lieu of the bouillon cube and keeps the vegetables to a simple yet aromatic mix of onions, celery, and tomatoes before ladling the whole of it over day-old bread—just enough "to make the bread wet."

"Cooked Water" with Vegetables, Day-Old Bread, and Poached Eggs

ACQUA COTTA ALLA MAREMMANA

SERVES 4

4 cups (1000 ml | 680 g) whole peeled tomatoes, run through a food mill or food processor

1 cup (250 ml | 230 g) mild extra-virgin olive oil

4 medium red onions, cut into quarters and sliced

6 celery stalks, coarsely chopped

6 cups (1400 ml | 1400 g) Old Hen Broth (page 54)

4 slices stale day-old rustic Italian bread, cubed

4 large eggs, poached (see Note)

TO DRINK:
A very fruity Morellino di Scansano from Tenuta di Belguardo from the Mazzei family.

• In a medium pan, heat the tomatoes over medium heat until warmed through. Keep warm.

• In a large straight-sided skillet, combine the oil and onions and sauté over medium heat until the onions are soft but not colored, about 10 minutes. Add the celery and cook until tender, about 10 minutes. Stir in the tomatoes and broth and bring to a boil. Cover the pan, reduce the heat to low, and cook until all the vegetables are very soft, about 1 hour.

• Divide the bread among four bowls and spoon the *acqua cotta* over the top. Top with a poached egg.

NOTE: *To poach the eggs, bring a medium pot of water to a simmer. Working with 2 eggs at a time, gently crack the eggs into separate small bowls or ramekins. Use a slotted spoon to gently stir the pot of simmering water and carefully slide one of the eggs into the water. A few seconds later, slide the second egg in. Give the water another gentle stir. Poach until the whites are set but yolks are still runny, 3 to 5 minutes. Use a slotted spoon to transfer the eggs to paper towels and repeat with the other 2 eggs.*

Springtime marks the arrival of zucchini and their beautiful blossoms. This warrants a true celebration at dinner tables across Florence. My favorite way of serving them is this recipe—which is perfect as an appetizer with just one blossom, or a primo with two, or as a *pietanza* (main dish) when served alongside a nice spoonful of *ragù*. Use blossoms that are long and similar in length, and make sure you use the sweetest cherry tomatoes you can find. The ricotta stuffing is fluffy and light and makes the dish seem almost like a pasta-free cannelloni! If you have extra caramelized tomatoes (or do as I do and just make extra), spoon them over toasted bread, toss with pasta, or use as a topping for grilled fish.

Baked Zucchini Blossoms with Sheep's-Milk Ricotta and Caramelized Cherry Tomatoes

FIORI DI ZUCCHINE RIPIENE CON RICOTTA E SUGHETTO DI POMODORINI

SERVES 4

CHERRY TOMATOES

3 tablespoons (41 g) mild extra-virgin olive oil

4 cups (600 g) cherry tomatoes

3 garlic cloves, halved

q.b. sea salt and crushed Tellicherry black peppercorns

>>>

• **To make the cherry tomatoes**: Preheat the oven to 250°F (120°C).

• In a large ovenproof skillet, combine the olive oil, tomatoes, and garlic. Season with salt and pepper and bring to a simmer over medium heat. Transfer the skillet to the oven and bake until the tomatoes are wrinkly and caramelized, about 2 hours. Remove the pan from the oven and set aside to cool. (I like to keep the tomatoes in the skillet that I cook them in until I can gently move them into a serving bowl; this method makes them less likely to fall apart.)

• Meanwhile, to make the zucchini blossoms: Line a baking sheet with parchment paper and drizzle with the olive oil.

• In a medium bowl, whisk the ricotta and eggs until the mixture is light and fluffy. Stir in the zucchini, basil, parsley, and nutmeg, then cover the bowl and refrigerate for 1 hour.

>>>

ZUCCHINI BLOSSOMS

1 tablespoon (15 ml | (13 g) extra-virgin olive oil

1 cup (250 g) fresh ricotta

2 large eggs

2 medium zucchini, diced

6 fresh basil leaves, torn

¼ cup fresh flat-leaf parsley sprigs

A few gratings of nutmeg

8 to 10 large zucchini blossoms

2 tablespoons (4 g) grated Parmigiano-Reggiano cheese, plus more to serve

• After you've removed the tomatoes from the oven, increase the oven temperature to 350°F (180°C).

• Gently open the petals on each zucchini blossom and inspect the inside for any dirt or insects. Rinse the blossoms gently with water and let them dry on paper towels. Using a knife, make a small slice down one side of each blossom and remove the pistil by pinching it off. Fill each blossom with 1 to 2 tablespoons of the chilled cheese-zucchini mixture. Place them in a single layer on the prepared baking sheet, carefully spreading the sliced blossoms into fans. Dust them with grated Parmigiano-Reggiano.

• Place a large baking dish on the lower rack of the oven. Fill it three-quarters full with hot water (this will ensure a warm, steamy environment so the zucchini blossoms won't dry out while baking). Place the baking sheet on the upper rack and bake until the zucchini blossoms are firm to the touch when gently poked with your finger, about 30 minutes.

• Gently transfer the baked zucchini blossoms to a serving platter and sprinkle with more Parmigiano-Reggiano and a bit of salt and pepper. Serve immediately with the cherry tomatoes.

TO DRINK:
A fruity Sicilian red, such as Tenuta delle Terre Nere from Mount Etna.

In the autumn, when the leaves on trees start turning brown and the new, bright green olive oil starts to flow, I crave hearty, *amaro* (bitter) greens such as cavolo nero, broccoli rabe, savoy cabbage, romanesco broccoli, and *radicchio tardivo*. It's as if my body, like a tree, is telling me to build up a *serbatoio* ("reserve") of nutrients and chlorophyll to get me through the dark and dreary winter. I make this version during the latter part of the year, but come spring, substitute peas, asparagus, fava beans, and basil. In late summer, add fresh green beans and some arugula pesto. Whatever the season, toss the vegetables with a chewy, meaty pasta such as torchio, rigatoni, or penne rigate.

The Greenest Pasta

PASTA COL PESTO VERDISSIMO

SERVES 4

q.b. coarse sea salt

2 large bunches fresh flat-leaf parsley, plus more to finish

1 large bunch *cavolo nero* (Tuscan kale), stems and leaves separated

1 large leek, halved lengthwise

2 cups (20 g) mixed greens such as lettuce, arugula, and spinach

½ cup (125 ml | 115 g) robust extra-virgin olive oil or *olio nuovo*, plus more to finish

1 garlic clove, thinly sliced

q.b. crushed Tellicherry black peppercorns

2 cups (250 g) pasta, such as penne rigate

2 tablespoons (24 g) Italian pine nuts, toasted and chopped

>>>

• Bring a large pot of water to a boil, season heavily with salt, and add the parsley, kale stems, leek, and greens. Bring the water back to a boil, then reduce the heat to maintain a simmer and cook for 30 minutes, until the greens are tender and the broth is slightly green in appearance.

• Using tongs, transfer the stems and greens to a colander and set aside to cool slightly. When cool enough to handle, squeeze out the excess water. Finely chop and set aside.

• In the same water, blanch the kale leaves for 30 seconds. Transfer the kale leaves to the colander, reserving the cooking water for the pasta. Once the leaves are cool enough to handle, squeeze out the excess water, finely chop, and set aside.

• In a large skillet, combine the olive oil and garlic. Season with salt and cook gently over low heat until the garlic is slightly golden, 2 to 3 minutes. Add the chopped kale, parsley, and greens and cook until you hear the greens almost cracking and start to get a little color, 4 to 5 minutes. Season with salt and pepper and set aside.

>>>

2 strips of lemon zest (removed with a vegetable peeler), each about 1-inch long

q.b. freshly grated Parmigiano-Reggiano cheese

TO DRINK:
An earthy Chianti, such as Castello di Monsanto or a Sangiovese-based Montevertine.

• Bring the cooking water back to a boil and add the pasta. Cook until the pasta is al dente. Remove about 2 cups (500 ml | 500 g) of the pasta water, then drain the pasta and add it directly to the skillet with the kale. Turn the heat to high and stir in the pine nuts and lemon zest and mix well over high heat. Add some of the reserved pasta water, season with salt and pepper, and heat until warmed through, about 5 minutes (the resulting pasta should almost be soupy in consistency). Transfer to four warm bowls and drizzle generously with *olio nuovo*. Sprinkle with freshly torn parsley and grated Parmesan and serve immediately.

The *famiglia* Titone from just outside of Trapani in western Sicily is one of the most authentic families I have the honor of knowing. They are third-generation (soon to be fourth!) pharmacists and the owners of the first organic olive farm in Sicily, the Azienda Agricola Titone. To me, their farm is the ultimate example of integrity, sustainability, and the 0-km approach to saving our planet. The olive groves, the land, the farm, the animals, and the immaculate *frantoio* all come together to produce one of the most delicious olive oils, which keeps winning awards all over the world.

This recipe, given to me by my friend Antonella, was her late mother Maria's, and is an excellent example of the "fusion cuisine" that comes out of port cities like Trapani. In this case, Genoese merchants brought their *aligata Ligure*, a sauce made with garlic, anchovies, and walnuts, and Sicilian merchants then made a few local changes, substituting almonds for walnuts and adding tomatoes. The traditional recipe also calls for 1 clove of garlic per serving, but if you wish to have a milder sauce, reduce it to 2 cloves for the entire dish.

The most authentic shape to serve this gutsy pesto is with *busiate*, which are long, twisted, rough, and thin and made with a whole meal durum wheat flour called *tumminia*. The nutty, sweet flour almost has a flavor of cinnamon and nutmeg to it, and when the pasta is cooking, the whole kitchen will smell as if you are making bread or toast. The most authentic *busiate* comes from a young miller named Filippo Drago and is worth seeking out. Find it online or in specialty food shops around the United States, or order directly from the importer, the very charismatic Beatrice Ughi from Gustiamo Imports (gustiamo.com).

If you can't find *busiate*, Antonella suggests using *fusilli col buco*, bucatini, or linguine. But remember: In this case, less is more when it comes to dressing the pasta. It's all about the pasta, not the sauce!

Busiate Pasta with Almond and Tomato Pesto

BUSIATE COL PESTO ALLA TRAPANESE

SERVES 4

1 cup Almond and Tomato Pesto (page 45)

1 pound (450 g) *busiate* Trapanesi pasta

2 teaspoons grated Pecorino Siciliano (Pecorino Romano or a very dry aged caciocavallo can be substituted)

• Bring a large pot of salted water to a boil. Gently add the pasta, letting it soften and submerge itself in the water. Once the pasta is submerged, give it a stir so it doesn't stick on the bottom. After 4 minutes, taste a strand of pasta for doneness. Continue to taste a strand until the *busiate* is al dente, about 10 minutes. Reserve 1 cup (250 ml | 250 g) of the cooking water. Drain the pasta in a colander.

• Put 1 tablespoon of the pesto in a large pasta bowl and, using a fork, whisk in 2 tablespoons of the reserved starchy cooking water. Transfer the *busiate* to the pasta bowl and add the rest of the pesto. Toss to combine, making sure the pasta is coated evenly throughout. Sprinkle with the cheese and serve immediately.

TO DRINK:

A succulent Carricante Buonora Tascante 2015 from the Tasca d'Almerita family, who are also among the most authentic Sicilian families I know. Anna Tasca Lanza, author of *The Heart of Sicily* and many other wonderful books put Sicily *on* the food map, and her beautiful daughter, Fabrizia Lanza, has a wonderful cooking school at the winery (annatascalanza.com) and is the author of *Coming Home to Sicily.*

Abruzzo is known for its sheep's-milk cheeses. With its flock of 350 sheep, Fratelli Del Proposto produces some of the finest ricotta and aged pecorino in the region, and Antonietta de Zio, the chef at La Bilancia restaurant, just down the road from the farm, makes these light and airy dumplings with cheese. Search out fresh ricotta where you are—the flavors should be mineral, grassy, and almost barnyard in flavor. Eat a bit as fresh as you can get it then wait a few days to make these dumplings. Antonietta says this recipe is best made with ricotta that is a few days old. Serve as a side dish or as a vegetarian main course.

Antonietta's Ricotta Dumplings in Tomato Sauce from La Bilancia

POLPETTE DI RICOTTA DI ANTONIETTA

SERVES 8 TO 10
(MAKES 18 TO 20 *POLPETTE*)

1 cup (223 g) sheep's-milk ricotta cheese

¼ cup (15 g) chopped fresh flat-leaf parsley leaves

1 cup (150 g) Grana Padana cheese, grated

3 large eggs

Fine sea salt

¾ cup (100 g) bread crumbs

3 cups (700 ml | 650 g) cooking extra-virgin olive oil

2 cups (500 ml | 540 g) *Salsa di Pomodoro* (page 42), warmed

TO DRINK:
A ruby red, with a more intense rose color than a rosé, such as a Villa Gemma Cerasuolo d'Abruzzo from Masciarelli.

• Line a large plate with paper towels.

• In a large bowl, mix together the ricotta and parsley. Add the grated cheese and eggs, season with salt, and mix well. Stir in the bread crumbs. Moisten your hands with a bit of olive oil and scoop out a heaping tablespoon of the mixture. Using a circular motion, shape it into an oblong croquette. Continue with the remaining mixture.

• Fill a deep medium saucepan with olive oil to a depth of 2 to 3 inches. Heat the oil over medium-high heat. When the oil is hot, add the *polpette* three or four at a time and fry until golden, turning the *polpette* so they brown evenly on all sides, 3 to 4 minutes per batch. Transfer the fried *polpette* to the paper towel–lined plate.

• Warm the tomato sauce in a large skillet. Add the *polpette* to the sauce and cook until they are softened and have absorbed some of the sauce, about 10 minutes. Serve hot.

"L'Ultimo Vero Toscano"

Carlo Cioni—Da Delfina, Artimino, Toscana

Carlo Cioni, owner and chef of Da Delfina, taught me how to be fearlessly *autentico*. He calls himself *l'ultimo vero uomo in Toscana*, "the last true man left in Tuscany." Having spent his entire life atop Artimino, he has a certain *Citizen Kane* attitude about him, yet when you catch him looking out over the glorious view and the ever-changing light of the landscape all around his restaurant, you can see his facial expression shift and soften.

There are many roads to take to go to Artimino, but my favorite way is to follow the Arno upstream and make a left turn into a potentially dangerous one-car tunnel

beneath the railroad track from Florence to Pisa. You then come to a pre–First World War single-lane bridge to cross over the Arno, and finally a very steep and winding one-lane road through beautiful vineyards and centuries-old olive groves to the top of the hill. This is where you'll find Da Delfina. On clear days, you can see as far south as the Monte Amiata, the entire Chianti Classico hills, and the towers of San Gimignano. Wherever you look, you feel like you are floating inside a Renaissance painting.

When you walk inside the former farmhouse, it feels, very simply, like home. The roaring fire of Carlo's spit and grill, all the old copper *pentole* hanging on the walls, and the perfumes coming from the immaculate kitchen conspire to make you hungry as soon as you step in the door.

Once you've survived the drive and taken in the landscape, the experience truly starts when Carlo comes to the table with the Italian-only menus. No matter which of the simple, rustic dishes you choose, Carlo will have final approval of your choice. We've had many heated debates over my order and Carlo always wins . . . and don't tell him, but he is always right. Put yourself in his very capable hands, order some local Carmignano wine, and bring a hearty appetite.

I first visited Da Delfina with my mother on a very dark, cold night. After eating Carlo's famous *ribollita*, I made another reservation two days later and kept on coming back until I had eaten his entire menu in less than a week. Carlo is more than a keeper of Tuscan traditions, and Da Delfina is more than a farmhouse. To me, Carlo is a truly authentic Italian cook, mentor, guru—he's my pope, and Da Delfina, my Vatican.

Che pasticcio (what a mess)! This recipe from Da Delfina in Toscana is hardly a mess, it's pure perfection! In Tuscany, especially in the countryside, a baked pasta dish is rarely labeled *lasagna.* Rather, it is *pasticcio* (or *pasta impasticciata* or *strascicata*). For me, there is only one *pasticcio* in the world, served by Carlo Cioni at his Ristorante Da Delfina. To me, Carlo defines the meaning of authenticity and sustainability, and he is determined to share, keep alive, and pass on his Tuscan heritage. He is my mentor, guru, and, many times, the father I never had.

He reigns as the custodian of all authentic recipes from Toscana, and his *pasticcio* is the recipe of all recipes! He makes the pasta dough so (so, so) thin that it is almost transparent. The bright yellow-orange color comes from the farm eggs he uses, and when you bite into its soft, supple texture, you feel like you are biting into little layers of clouds. Carlo doesn't make his *pasticcio* with meat and *salsa colla* as I do here; instead, he makes it with wild nettles in the spring and artichokes in the autumn.

I strongly encourage you to travel to Tuscany to eat Carlo's pasta. Even after twenty-five years of making my version, it's never quite as good as Carlo's!

If you can't devote the whole day to pasta-making, there are some quality store-bought fresh pasta sheets or dry egg pasta sheets in specialty food stores around the world. (But please, skip the standard dried lasagna noodles—they are made of durum wheat semolina and water and give the dish a totally different flavor.) If you are using store-bought, cook them until about halfway to al dente in boiling salted water, then lay them on olive oil–rubbed parchment paper. Remember they are going in the oven at the end!

Tuscan-Style Lasagna (But is it really?)

PASTICCIO TOSCANO

SERVES 4

SFOGLIE

4 cups (500 g) "00" flour (Sources page 352), plus more as needed

10 large eggs

1 teaspoon mild extra-virgin olive oil

q.b. fine sea salt

>>>

• **To make the sfoglie:** Mound the flour on a clean work surface and make a large well in the center. Crack the eggs into the well and add the olive oil and a pinch of sea salt. With the help of a fork, carefully whisk the eggs as if you were making scrambled eggs. Gradually start to whisk a bit of the flour into the egg mixture. Draw little amounts at a time until the mixture starts to feel somewhat solid, and then clean the fork with your fingers, dust some of the flour on your clean hands, and start to work it all together with your hands. Knead the dough until you see your hands becoming dry (if necessary, add a little bit more flour, or, if it becomes too dry and tough, sprinkle in a bit of water and continue to knead). Knead until smooth and dry, about 10 minutes.

>>>

SALSA COLLA
(or *Besciamella*)

3 tablespoons (40 g) unsalted butter

4 tablespoons (40 g) "00" flour

2 cups (500 ml | 500 g) whole milk, cold

q.b. freshly grated nutmeg

q.b. fine sea salt

TO FINISH
6 tablespoons (80 g) unsalted butter

q.b. grated Parmigiano-Reggiano cheese

2 cups (500 ml | 453 g) Tuscan *Ragù*, My Way (page 63), at room temperature

• Place the dough in a glass bowl, cover with a linen cloth, and set aside to rest for 30 minutes.

• Break the dough into 4 equal pieces and roll one ball at a time into a flattened rectangular shape. Pull it though the pasta machine until you achieve the thinnest possible sheet, about ⅛-inch thick. Cut the edges of the pasta to be exactly the same rectangular or square shape as the mold you will be using for the lasagna and lay them between linen cloths. Set aside to dry in a cool, dry place until you are ready to continue.

• *To make the* salsa colla: Have all the ingredients ready and measured before even thinking about making this salsa. (While you're at it, turn the phone off and enjoy!)

• In a medium saucepan with tall sides, melt the butter over medium heat. Wait until the little bubbles subside and reduce and most of the watery part of the butter has evaporated, 8 to 10 minutes. Using a tea strainer or small fine-mesh sieve, start dusting the flour over the butter and, with the help of a whisk, stir vigorously until it all blends and starts to stick together, about 3 minutes. Gradually pour in the cold milk, whisking vigorously. Season with nutmeg and salt. Once the milk starts to steam, turn off the heat—the sauce should be very liquid and runny.

• Preheat the oven to 375°F (190°C). Place a baking dish filled halfway with water on the bottom rack. Generously butter a 10 x 6-inch baking pan and dust with Parmigiano-Reggiano.

• Drizzle 3 tablespoons of the *salsa colla* and 3 table-spoons of the *ragù* over the bottom of the prepared baking dish. (Imagine you are Jackson Pollock—it should be just a sprinkle here, a dollop there). Lay one piece of the *sfoglia* on top of and repeat, then, using your hand, spread them irregularly, with a little pressure downward and making sure you make it all

even, spreading the sauces to the edges. Repeat the layering until you run out of *sfoglia* (you should come about two-thirds of the way up the dish). Cover the last layer with a generous amount of the *salsa colla* and a few sprinkles of *ragù*. Dot the top with butter.

• Cover the dish with aluminum foil and place in the middle rack of the oven. Bake for 20 minutes, then remove the foil and the water bath and bake until the top is evenly golden and crusty, about 15 minutes. (You can even turn the broiler on for just a minute right before removing.) Remove the dish from the oven and set aside to cool slightly. *Pasticcio* should be eaten warm, not piping hot.

• Cut into squares and serve.

TO DRINK:
A delicious bottle of Brunello di Montalcino "Tenuta Nuova" from my friend Giacomo Neri, winemaker and owner of Casanova di Neri in Montalcino. He's my guru when it comes to being an autentico wine producer.

A GOLDEN CARNAROLI RICE FIELD AT PRINCIPATO DI LUCEDIO READY TO BE HARVESTED.

taly is Europe's largest rice producer, accounting for 5 percent of the world's total rice production. The fertile Po Valley in northern Italy, watered by pristine cold water from the melting snowcaps of the Alps, has sustained this important agricultural product for more than five centuries. The Moors brought rice to Sicily, where it became an important crop long before Genoese and Venetian merchants spread the grain throughout Italy and France, later propagating it to all the continents during the age of European colonization and expansion after the fifteenth century.

Between the cities of Milano and Torino lies the province of Vercelli, where it is said that the very first rice in Italy was initially planted in the fields of a Cistercian monastery known today as Lucedio. The monks developed a small system of canals from nearby streams of the Po River to flood the fields and protect the rice during the planting and growing seasons. Over the centuries, the entire Vercelli province experienced a gradual landscape transformation to become one of the most highly specialized rice-growing areas of the world. As time passed and the monastery declined, Lucedio was taken over by a succession of feudal lords. The original church of Santa Maria di Lucedio and the medieval structures saw such a huge

Italian Rice
RISO ITALIANO

expansion in size that the estate became a *principato* (principality), with close ties to the kingdom of Savoy. Surrounded by rice fields, at one time the principality housed more than four thousand inhabitants who did the backbreaking manual planting and harvesting of the rice.

In 1937, Count Paolo Cavalli d'Olivola from Torino bought the estate, increasing the property to more than 1,000 acres of rice fields and creating Italy's largest rice estate. Today, his daughter Contessa Rosetta Clara Cavalli d'Olivola, oversees the estate and the farming of the rice fields with utmost care. When I first met her in 1987, we decided to develop and grow a "Grand Cru single plantation" estate rice. The Principato di Lucedio brand was born—a true single-paddy, harvest-dated rice. Now the fresh, single-varietal rice grown by the contessa is packed in signature cloth bags and is available on market shelves and many menus across the United States.

At the Principato di Lucedio, careful attention is given to each step of the rice-growing process to ensure a sustainable and pristine growing environment. Young rice shoots are planted at the end of April. The fields are then flooded to protect the rice plants from fluctuating temperatures, an eventual late-spring frost, or any other adverse environmental conditions. In midsummer, golden clusters of rice kernels form on each stalk. Careful monitoring is crucial to prevent the rice from developing infestation or disease. During the hot summer days, the kernels develop to plump perfection and the rice stalks begin to bend from the weight. The fields are drained in late August and the rice is harvested in mid-September before the first autumn rains. Then the rice is left to dry for two months in the ancient barns and buildings of the *principato*. Countess Rosetta Clara keeps the rice in its protective husk until orders are received to guarantee a fresher product. The rice kernels are first milled using a rice huller to remove the outer husks of the grain which is called the "chaff." At this point, the product is brown rice. The milling is then continued, removing the rest of the husk and the germ (bran), resulting in white rice.

Italy grows the variety of rice known as *Japonica* (Japanese) variety (*Oryza sativa var. japonica*), a short-grain variety characterized by its unique starch content, stickiness, and texture. This barrel-shaped rice is different than long-grain rice, which is usually boiled or steamed. Italian rice is classified into four categories by the length and width and amylopectin starch content: *superfino*, *fino*, *semifino*, and *orginario*. *Superfino* rice is the one most frequently used for making risotto in Italy, with Arborio the variety popular outside of Italy. I, along with many chefs, prefer the Carnaroli variety, which was catalogued in the 1950s. Among the *semifino* is Vialone Nano, a variety widely planted in the Veneto.

Carnaroli Considered the king of Italian rice, Carnaroli kernels are the longest and thickest of the *superfino* rice. This long, oval grain contains the highest concentration of starch, which creates a superior texture when making risotto. Because of its thickness, the rice remains al dente even after cooking, making it the preferred choice of many chefs for making risotto.

Arborio A *superfino*-classified rice, named after the nearby commune of Arborio in the province of Vercelli. Arborio rice's kernels are shorter than those of Carnaroli, with a burnished, uniformly opaque creamy color and a solid white center. Arborio has a high starch content that is slowly released during the cooking process, creating a lush blanket of creamy starch that coats each kernel. Arborio is often used to make *risotto alla Milanese* and rice pudding (page 339).

Vialone Nano A *semifino* variety widely planted in an area south of Verona that has a shorter, rounder grain with an almost pearl-like shape. Use it when making Venetian-style seafood risotto with squid ink or mixed shellfish. This pebbly rice is also great for making rice salad (page 186) and paella.

Keep in Mind: When purchasing Italian rice, check the "best by" date. Some producers sell "aged" rice, arguing that it remains more al dente when cooked, but there's no reason to eat an "old" or "aged" grain of any kind. As with most things food-related, the fresher, the better. Whichever rice you use, store it in a cool, dry place.

Risotto, Three Ways

RISOTTO TRE MODI

The more often you make risotto, the easier (and tastier!) it will be. The recipes that follow for basic, *con radicchio* (with radicchio), and *verdissimo* (green) risotto are just jumping-off points for the varieties of risotto that will be at your fingertips once you master the technique. The cooking always remains the same: Aromatic vegetables are sautéed in olive oil until soft. Once the rice is added, the grains are stirred and toasted until the rice begins to pop—like popcorn. Hot, simmering broth is added to the rice by the ladleful, always stirring over an even heat and waiting to add more until absorbed into the starchy rice, repeating as much as needed until the rice is creamy and cooked through.

The most important elements you should keep in mind when making a risotto are:

- Cook the rice in a large saucepan (copper, if possible, for even distribution of heat).
- Remove the risotto from the flame before it is al dente, since it will continue to cook off the heat because it is hot.
- Finish the risotto with plenty of stock so that it is *all'onda* (wavy), not solid like mashed potatoes.
- Stir in optional additions at the end: saffron threads, Barolo wine, herbs, cooked vegetables, porcini mushrooms, gorgonzola, cooked sausage, or any leftover meat or fish, cut into small cubes.
- Seat your guests before serving risotto. Like pasta, risotto should never be kept waiting.
- I always make a large amount of risotto so there's enough left over for *arancini* (rice balls), risotto cakes (add an egg or two, some bread crumbs, and grated cheese and fry), or to just enjoy for lunch the next day.

Basic Risotto

RISOTTO IN BIANCO

SERVES 4 TO 6

8 cups (2000 ml | 1800 g) water or broth, such as Old Hen Broth (page 54), Beef Broth with Short Ribs (page 55), or *Brodetto* (page 56)

4 tablespoons (56 g) unsalted butter

1 small white onion, finely chopped

q.b. fine sea salt

1 cup (250 ml | 250 g) dry white wine

2 cups (500 g) Arborio, Carnaroli, or Vialone nano rice

q.b. crushed Tellicherry black peppercorns

• In a medium saucepan, warm the water or broth to a gentle simmer.

• In a large saucepan or Dutch oven, melt the butter over medium heat. Once the butter has melted, add the onion and season with salt. Cook until the onion is translucent, about 5 minutes. Stir in the rice and increase the heat to high. Cook, mixing vigorously, until the rice starts making a popping sound, like popcorn, about 5 minutes. Pour in the wine and stir to combine. Allow the wine to evaporate, about 3 minutes, then stir in four ladles of the warm water or broth and stir to combine. Reduce the heat to low and cook until the liquid has been absorbed, about 5 minutes. Continue adding the broth, a ladle at a time, allowing the rice to slowly absorb each addition of the broth before adding the next so its starches are slowly released. Once the risotto is almost al dente, about 20 minutes, season with salt and pepper. Mix in any optional ingredients and stir in an additional two ladlefuls of the broth. Turn off the heat. The rice should be *all'onda*, or wavy, when the pan is gently shaken. The rice will continue to absorb some of the liquid once divided among warm bowls.

TO DRINK:

No wine suggestion, but if you put shaved truffles on the risotto, you should open a wonderful bottle of an older vintage Barolo from Bruno Giacosa.

Beautiful *radicchio tardivo di Treviso* is now an IGP product, meaning it can only have that name if it's farmed in Treviso—located on the foothills of the Alps right outside Venice. It has somewhat the same texture as Belgian endive, but with a very rich, naturally beautiful bitter flavor. You can eat it raw, grill it, sauté it, and use it in any way you can imagine. Here is one of my favorite *risotti* for the wintertime. If you have some in house, sprinkle a few pieces of crispy pancetta over the top for another layer of flavor.

Risotto with Radicchio

RISOTTO CON RADICCHIO

SERVES 6

5½ cups (1.3 L| 300 g) **Old Hen Broth (page 54) or Beef Broth with Short Ribs (page 55)**

½ cup (125 ml | 115 g) **medium extra-virgin olive oil**

1 medium **white onion, finely chopped**

2 cups (200 g) **Carnaroli rice**

½ cup (125 ml | 125 g) **dry red wine**

q.b. **coarse sea salt and crushed Tellicherry black peppercorns**

1 large **radicchio (*di Chioggia* or *di Treviso* if you can find it), thinly sliced**

q.b. **freshly grated Parmigiano-Reggiano cheese**

• In a medium saucepan, bring the broth to a simmer over medium heat.

• In a Dutch oven, combine the olive oil and onion and sauté over medium heat until the onion is transparent, about 5 minutes. Stir in the rice and toast, stirring regularly, until the rice starts popping (it will sound like popcorn), about 5 minutes.

• Pour in the wine and cook until evaporated, 3 to 4 minutes. Add a few ladles of stock (about 1 cup | 250 ml | 250 g) and season with salt and pepper. Stir the rice slowly and cook until most of the broth has been absorbed, about 5 minutes. Continue stirring and adding broth, another ½ cup (125 ml | 125 g) at a time, just so the broth forms a thin layer over the simmering rice. If the rice begins to stick, turn down the heat, and cook until most of the broth has been absorbed and the rice is almost al dente, 20 to 25 minutes.

• Stir in the radicchio and cook until the rice is al dente, about 5 minutes more, adding just enough of the broth to make sure the risotto is *all'onda*, or wavy. Divide the risotto among six warm bowls and top with Parmigiano-Reggiano.

TO DRINK:
A beautiful bottle of "Bricco dell'Uccellone" from Braida, one of my favorite wines of Piemonte.

The Greenest Risotto

RISOTTO VERDISSIMO

SERVES 6 TO 8

GREEN BROTH

2 large (230 g) bunches flat-leaf parsley

1 large (315 g) bunch kale

2 cups (113 g) leftover greens, such as arugula, lettuce, or chard leaves

1 large leek (210 g), halved lengthwise and cleaned well

RISOTTO

½ cup (125 ml | 115 g) robust extra-virgin olive oil

1 leek, halved lengthwise, cleaned well, and thinly sliced

q.b. fine sea salt

2¼ cups (500 g) Carnaroli rice

½ cup (125 ml | 125 g) dry white wine

q.b. crushed Tellicherry black peppercorns

1 large bunch kale, coarsely chopped

Olio nuovo, if available, or robust extra-virgin olive oil, for drizzling

A few fresh mint or fresh flat-leaf parsley leaves, torn (optional)

- *To make the green broth:* In a large stockpot, combine the parsley, kale, greens, and leek halves. Pour in 4 cups (1 L | 907 g) water and bring to a boil over high heat. Once you reach a boil, reduce the heat to maintain a simmer and cook for 30 minutes, or until it smells like a fresh meadow. Strain the broth through a fine-mesh sieve and discard the vegetables. The broth can be made a day ahead and refrigerated. Reheat it before using.

- *To make the risotto:* In a Dutch oven, combine the olive oil and leek and place over medium heat. Season with a pinch of salt and cook until the leeks are wilted, but not brown, about 5 minutes. Add the rice and stir it well so each grain is coated with the oil. Sauté until it makes a cracking or popping sound, like popcorn, about 5 minutes. Pour in the wine and cook, stirring, until the wine has evaporated, 2 minutes. While stirring continuously, add two or three ladles of the hot green broth and cook until the liquid has been absorbed. Continue adding the broth, a ladle at a time, allowing the rice to slowly absorb each addition of the broth before adding the next so its starches are slowly released. Once the risotto is almost al dente, 15 to 18 minutes, season with salt and pepper and stir in the kale. Stir in an additional two ladlefuls of the broth and turn off the heat. The rice should be *all'onda*, or wavy, when the pan is gently shaken. The rice will continue to absorb some of the liquid once divided among six to eight warm bowls.

- Serve immediately with *olio nuovo* and a sprinkle of mint or parsley, if desired.

TO DRINK:

A Barbera d'Alba from Odero or Valpolicella from Allegrini.

Contessa Rosetta Clara makes this for me when I visit her at the Principato di Lucedio in Piemonte, although she's the first to admit that she only makes it when I'm in town! It's too bad; the recipe—written originally as a hearty breakfast for farmers to sustain them through a long day—combines sausages, rice, and beans and is one of my favorites (especially made with the contessa's incredible Carnaroli rice)! Many recipes will say you want the spoon to stand up in the rice, but here you want it to be much looser (it will thicken up dramatically as it cools). Carla Farchetti, one of the chefs in the *principato's* kitchen, offers up this tip to decide how much rice to make: "Count the number of people and make ½ cup per person . . . plus two fistfuls extra."

Soupy Rice from Vercelli

PANISSA DEL VERCELLESE

SERVES 6 TO 8

2 tablespoons (30 ml | 27 g) cooking extra-virgin olive oil

1 small yellow onion, chopped

½ pound (250 g) ground Italian sausage

2¼ cups (500 g) Carnaroli rice

1 cup (240 ml) dry, dark red wine, preferably Barbera

2 cups (340 g) cooked cranberry beans, cooking liquid reserved

⅔ cup (90 g) grated Parmigiano-Reggiano cheese

q.b. fine sea salt and crushed Tellicherry black peppercorns

• In a large Dutch oven, heat the olive oil over medium-high heat. Add the onion and cook, stirring occasionally, until it is transparent, 2 to 3 minutes. Add the sausage to the pan and use a wooden spoon to break it apart. Cook until lightly browned all around, about 3 minutes. Add the rice and wine and stir to combine. Pour in enough of the bean broth and beans to cover the rice and sausage mixture and bring to a boil. Cook, stirring frequently and adding bean broth and beans as needed to keep the rice covered, until the rice is al dente, about 15 minutes. Stir in the cheese and season with salt and pepper. Serve warm.

TO DRINK:

A Grignolino from Piemonte. This old wine used to be regarded as more important than Barbera, but has suffered from a bad reputation in recent years. The green, bright, tart red is back again and is ideal for cutting through the creaminess of the dish.

When Contessa Rosetta Clara Cavalli d'Olivola started making rice salad for her family, they didn't understand why. When she was born, the only rice in her mother's kitchen was for risotto, and in Piemonte at the time the cuisine focused on meat and dairy—not fresh vegetables (in fact, fresh vegetables were only eaten by the lower classes). But Rosetta Clara persisted, tossing in whatever fresh vegetables were in season and dicing them fine enough to be the same size as the cooked granules of rice. Quickly her family came around to the idea, then friends began requesting the dish on hot summer afternoons.

The Contessa's Rice Salad

INSALATA DI RISO DELLA CONTESSA

SERVES 4 TO 6

2 cups (450 g) Carnaroli rice

1 cup (200 g) zucchini, very finely diced

1 cup (250 g) tomatoes, very finely diced

½ cup (100 g) black olives, very finely diced

½ cup (100 g) green olives, very finely diced

1 cup (140 g) celery, very finely diced

1 cup (200 g) yellow bell peppers, very finely diced

1 cup (150 g) carrots, very finely diced

1 cup (140 g) Parmigiano-Reggiano cheese, very finely diced

Juice of 1 lemon

2 tablespoons (30 g) mayonnaise (see Note)

2 tablespoons (30 g) Dijon mustard

3 tablespoons (45 ml | 41 g) robust extra-virgin olive oil

1 cup (200 g) tuna packed in olive oil

q.b. fine sea salt and crushed Tellicherry black peppercorns

• Put the rice in a medium pot and add enough water to cover by 2 inches. Season with salt. Bring to a boil, then reduce the heat to maintain a simmer and cook until the rice is al dente, 7 to 9 minutes. Drain the rice through a fine-mesh sieve and transfer to a large bowl. Set aside to cool completely.

• Once the rice is cooled, add the zucchini, tomatoes, black and green olives, celery, bell peppers, carrots, and cheese, mixing just to combine.

• In a small bowl, whisk together the mayonnaise, mustard, and olive oil. Pour over the rice-vegetable mixture and toss just to combine. Stir in the tuna and season with salt and black pepper.

• Serve at room temperature.

TO DRINK:
We always drink a Capichera Bianco with rice salad. It is deliciously crisp and very fruity, as if it has tropical fruit aromas and flavors.

NOTE: To make the mayonnaise, in a medium bowl, combine 1 egg yolk, 2 teaspoons fresh lemon juice, and ¼ teaspoon Dijon mustard. Season with fine sea salt and whisk vigorously for 30 seconds. While whisking continuously, gradually add ¾ cup (185 ml | 171 g) olive or canola oil in a slow, thin stream until thickened and light in color, 6 to 8 minutes. Makes about 1 cup.

I don't think there is any recipe more fun or one that takes me back to the 1960s as the rendition that Carmen Rummo made for us at Principato di Lucedio under the watchful eye of Contessa Rosetta Clara. This dish originates from the era during which Napoli and Palermo were part of the Bourbon Kingdom of the Two Sicilies. The *sartù* in the name is a poor Italian translation of *sur tout* (in French, "above all"). While there are many reasons for the "above all" addition to the title, these are the two that seem most authentic:

1. The rice is above and all around the various treasures inside the ring or crown.
2. The dish is so above all other dishes because it is so incredibly complicated. The work that goes into it makes it even more delicious.

I personally like to believe both of them!

Stuffed Rice Crown

CORONA DI RISO DETTO SARTÙ

SERVES 6 TO 8

MEATBALLS

½ small bread roll, torn into pieces

4 tablespoons (60 ml | 60 g) whole milk

⅓ pound (150 g) ground beef (80 to 90% lean)

⅓ pound (150 g) ground pork sausage

1 large egg

1 small garlic clove, finely chopped

2 teaspoons finely chopped fresh flat-leaf parsley

q.b. sea salt and crushed Tellicherry black peppercorns

½ cup (125 ml | 115 g) cooking extra-virgin olive oil

PEAS

½ tablespoon (7 g) unsalted butter

1 small scallion, thinly sliced

1 tablespoon (15 g) finely chopped pancetta

>>>

• **To make the meatballs:** In a small bowl, combine the bread pieces and milk. Set aside for 5 minutes. Remove the bread and squeeze out the excess milk; discard the milk. Put the bread in a large bowl and add the ground beef, sausage, egg, garlic, and parsley. Season with salt and pepper. Measure out ½ teaspoon and roll into ½-inch balls.

• Add enough of the cooking olive oil to a large, straight-sided sauté pan to come ¼ inch up the side of the pan and place over medium-high heat. Once the oil is hot, add the meatballs in batches and sauté until browned and cooked through, 10 to 15 minutes.

• **To make the peas:** In a medium sauté pan, combine the butter, scallion, and pancetta and sauté over medium heat until the pancetta is crisp, about 5 minutes. Add the peas and white wine and bring to a boil. Boil until the liquid evaporates, about 2 minutes, season with salt and pepper, and set aside to cool.

>>>

¾ cup (113 g) frozen peas

½ cup (125 ml | 125 g) dry white wine

q.b. fine sea salt and crushed Tellicherry black peppercorns

ARTICHOKES

1 tablespoon (15 ml | 12 g) mild extra-virgin olive oil

1 garlic clove, peeled and left whole

1 cup (175 g) coarsely chopped marinated artichoke hearts

2 tablespoons (12 g) finely chopped fresh flat-leaf parsley

q.b. fine sea salt and freshly crushed Tellicherry black peppercorns

TOMATO SAUCE

3 cups (750 ml | 810 g) *passata di pomodoro*

1 garlic clove, peeled and left whole

TO ASSEMBLE

2 tablespoons (28 g) unsalted butter

¼ cup (35 g) finely ground bread crumbs

2 cups (500 g) Carnaroli or Arborio rice, cooked, cooled, and tossed with 1 tablespoon mild extra-virgin olive oil (page 59)

1 hard-boiled egg, thinly sliced

1 large egg

2 tablespoons grated Parmigiano-Reggiano cheese

1 tablespoon finely chopped fresh flat-leaf parsley

q.b. fine sea salt

6 hard-boiled quail eggs, halved

- *To make the artichokes:* In a medium sauté pan, combine the olive oil, garlic, and artichoke hearts and sauté until the hearts are warmed through, about 3 minutes. Stir in the parsley and season with salt and pepper. Set aside to cool.

- *To make the tomato sauce:* In a medium sauté pan, combine the *passata di pomodoro* and garlic and bring to a simmer. Simmer for 5 minutes to reduce the sauce slightly, then add the meatballs and cook until the meatballs are warmed through. Set aside.

- *To assemble:* Preheat the oven to 350°F (180°C).

- Heavily butter a 9½-inch ring mold and sprinkle evenly with 2 tablespoons of the bread crumbs. Spoon 2½ cups of the rice into the mold (the rice should come about ½ inch up the side of the mold). Add the peas in one layer, then the artichokes. Spoon a third of the meatballs and tomato sauce over the artichokes. Top with the hard-boiled egg slices.

- In a medium bowl, toss the remaining rice with the egg, cheese, and parsley and season with salt. Add ½ cup of the meatball and sauce mixture to the rice and stir to combine. Spoon the rice mixture into the mold and use the back of a spoon to press it into the pan. Sprinkle with 2 tablespoons of the bread crumbs, pressing the bread crumbs in slightly with your fingers.

- Bake until the top is golden, about 1 hour. Set aside to cool, then unmold onto a serving platter. Spoon the remaining meatball and tomato sauce mixture into the center of the crown and decorate with quail eggs. Serve at room temperature.

TO DRINK:

Such an incredible dish deserves to be served with one of the most important wines of Campania, the "Montevetrano" made by the wonderful Silvia Imparato. This wine is on a class of its own.

Farro Is Farro

Farro is an ancient grain that has been found at archeological sites from Neolithic Egypt to Turkey to early Bronze Age Mesopotamia. Ancient rabbinic literature cites farro as one of the five grains that can be used to make matzoh during Passover. The ancient Romans cultivated the grain in the Italian peninsula where it became known as *far* or *gran far*, which was milled into puls to make a dish similar to today's polenta.

With the advent of intensive modern wheat agriculture after the World Wars, farro lost its popularity, but during the last twenty years, the grain has gone through a renaissance because it grows easily and is packed with nutrition. The nutritional virtues of farro have long been revered in Italy. Farro is rich in fiber, magnesium, and vitamins A, B, C, and E. Protein content is high, so when it is combined with beans or legumes, farro forms a complete protein.

In Italy today, farro is cultivated in a small area around the foothills on both sides of the central Apennines, mainly in Toscano, Umbria, Marche, and Abruzzo. Farro thrives on well-draining stony or rocky hillsides from 600 to 1,000 feet above sea level. Planted in October and harvested in June, farro survives under poor conditions, without the use of fertilizers or pesticides.

You may find many people telling you that farro is called emmer or eikorn, but that is not correct. Farro is farro! In Italy, *farro* is the overarching term used for einkorn, emmer, and spelt (also known as *farro piccolo*, *farro medio*, and *farro grande*),

each a subspecies of the genus *Triticum* (wheat) and each with a different genetic makeup. Farro, essentially, is an unhybridized ancestor of modern wheat. (Barley, by the way, is of a different genus altogether, and neither a species nor a subspecies of wheat.)

• **Farro Grande: Spelt** (*Tristicum aestivum spelta*) is a subspecies of *Triticum aestivum*, which includes common bread wheat (*Triticum aestivum aestivum*).

• **Farro Piccolo: Einkorn** (*Triticum monococcum monococcum*) is a subspecies of *Triticum monococcum*.

• **Farro Medio: Emmer** (*Triticum turgidum dioccum*) is a subspecies of *Triticum turgidum*, which includes durum wheat. It is the primary farro grain planted in Italy (Abruzzo included), and it is considered to be of a higher quality for cooking than spelt or einkorn.

To cook farro, put 1 cup (190 g) uncooked farro in a small bowl, cover with cold water, and set aside to soak for 20 to 25 minutes. Drain the water, rinse the farro well, and transfer to a medium saucepan. Pour in enough fresh water to cover the farro. Bring to a boil over medium-high heat. Reduce the heat to low and simmer, uncovered, until the farro is al dente, 10 to 15 minutes.

Immediately drain and rinse the farro with cold running water to stop the cooking process. Toss with mild olive oil to prevent the grains from sticking together. Use right away or store in an airtight container in the refrigerator for up to 1 week. Makes 2 cups.

Cooking farro ahead of time is always a great idea. It can be refrigerated or stored in the freezer. It can be stirred into soups and salads, tossed with olive oil–packed tuna as a filling for Roasted Red Peppers with Farro or Tuna (page 196), or made into this simple, savory *torta*, kind of like a quiche without a crust. Serve it in small slices as an antipasto, larger slices with a bright green salad for a satisfying main course, or top with Tuscan *Ragù*, My Way (page 63) for a one-dish meal.

No zucchini? Sauté some chopped mushrooms, kale, onions, or other vegetables instead. Shredded zucchini flowers, torn mint, or snipped chives can be used in place of basil and parsley. To make sure the *torta* comes out easily (and ensure a golden, extra-flavorful crust) thoroughly butter the baking pan and dust with grated Parmigiano-Reggiano on the bottom and sides.

Farro and Zucchini Torta

TORTA DI FARRO E ZUCCHINE

SERVES 8 TO 12

Unsalted butter, for the pan

¾ cup (84 g) finely grated Parmigiano-Reggiano cheese, plus more to finish

2 tablespoons (30 ml | 30 g) mild extra-virgin olive oil

2 small zucchini, thinly sliced into ¼-inch rounds

6 large eggs, beaten

2 cups (312 g) cooked farro (see page 193)

1 cup (250 g) fresh ricotta

½ cup fresh basil leaves, torn

½ cup fresh flat-leaf parsley leaves, torn

q.b. sea salt and crushed Tellicherry black peppercorns

· Preheat the oven to 350°F (180°C). Using a paper towel or pastry brush, generously butter a 10-inch springform pan. Dust the sides and bottom of the pan with ¼ cup (28 g) of the Parmigiano-Reggiano.

· In a medium skillet, heat the olive oil over medium heat until warm. Add the zucchini and sauté until lightly brown, 5 to 7 minutes. Set aside to cool slightly.

· Meanwhile, beat the eggs well in a bowl. Add the farro, ricotta, zucchini, and the remaining ½ cup (56 g) Parmigiano-Reggiano. Add the basil and parsley and season with salt and pepper. Pour the mixture into the prepared springform pan and cover the top with a sprinkle of Parmigiano-Reggiano. Bake until golden and firm and a paring knife inserted into the center comes out clean, 30 to 35 minutes. Let cool to room temperature before slicing and serving.

TO DRINK:

A Vermentino from the Tuscan coast, such as Solosole from Poggio al Tesoro.

I have been serving this room-temperature dish as a summer lunch (along with a nice *Misticanza*, page 76) for as long as I can remember. Half a pepper, faceup, with a few spoonfuls of the farro and tuna filling suffices as a first course, or serve a whole pepper al fresco as a main dish during hot summer nights. It's also beautiful to line a cupcake or *sformatino* mold with roasted red peppers as done with the chard leaves on page 103, and then stuff and very firmly pack the farro and tuna inside. Perfect to serve along with grilled fish.

Roasted Red Peppers with Farro and Tuna

PEPERONI RIPIENI DI FARRO E TONNO

SERVES 8 AS APPETIZER, 4 AS A MAIN COURSE

2 cups (312 g) cooked farro (see page 193)

1 (4-ounce) can tuna packed in olive oil, drained

1 small scallion, thinly sliced

½ cup (80 g) pitted and coarsely chopped Taggiasca or picholine olives

Zest and juice of ¼ lemon

½ cup (125 ml | 115 g) robust extra-virgin olive oil, plus more as needed

q.b. fine sea salt and crushed Tellicherry black peppercorns

Splash of *colatura di alici* (anchovy essence)

4 large red peppers

3 tablespoons fresh flat-leaf parsley leaves, torn by hand

• In a large bowl, combine the farro, tuna, scallions, olives, lemon zest, lemon juice, and olive oil. Season with salt and black pepper. Add a small splash of *colatura* and set aside to rest at room temperature for at least 2 to 3 hours (the mixture can also be made ahead and kept in the refrigerator overnight).

• Meanwhile, prepare the peppers. If using an open flame, char the peppers until blackened on all sides. Otherwise, preheat the oven to 375°F (190°C). Rub the peppers with a few tablespoons olive oil, place on a baking sheet, and roast until tender and soft, about 45 minutes.

• When cool enough to handle, use your fingers to peel off as much of the blackened skin as possible while keeping the peppers intact. Remove the stems from the peppers and, using a paper towel, remove and discard as many of the seeds as possible. Place on a plate and set aside.

• When ready to serve, fill the peppers with the farro-tuna mixture, drizzle with olive oil and sprinkle with the parsley. Serve at room temperature.

TO DRINK:
A crisp Ligurian white, such as Albarola by Lunae Bosoni.

In the Garfagnana, the valley in the Apennines above the beautiful city of Lucca, this hearty soup is a staple. It was there that I heard the word *farro* for the first time almost thirty years ago, and there that I first had this soup (which is now a staple in my cool-weather kitchen). It's so easy to make when you have all the ingredients ready in your fridge: deep and dark *Soffritto* (page 40), rich Old Hen Broth (page 54), parcooked farro—cooked halfway and still very crunchy—and slow-cooked beans in their broth (see page 11). I value texture in my meals and wrote this recipe so the farro and beans in this potage are more al dente than they are in most soups served nowadays. For a truly authentic rendition of this very Tuscan *minestra*, let it cook longer and serve only when all the textures are similar on every spoonful.

Farro Soup with Black Kale

ZUPPA DI FARRO CON CAVOLO NERO

SERVES 4 TO 6

6 cups (1.5 L | 1500 g) Old Hen Broth (page 54)

2 cups (280 g) cooked beans (page 11), plus 1 cup (250 ml | 250 g) bean cooking liquid

2 tablespoons (30 ml | 27 g) medium extra-virgin olive oil

2 tablespoons (45 g) *Soffritto* (page 40)

3 cups (420 g) cooked farro (see page 193)

3 fresh sage leaves, coarsely chopped

½ bunch *cavolo nero* (Tuscan kale), stemmed, leaves thinly sliced

q.b. sea salt and crushed Tellicherry peppercorns

q.b. robust extra-virgin olive oil

· In a large bowl, combine 1 cup (250 ml | 250 g) of the Old Hen Broth with the bean cooking liquid. Set a food mill on top of the bowl and pass through 1 cup (140 g) of the beans. Mix well to combine and set aside.

· In a large Dutch oven, combine the olive oil and *soffritto* and cook over medium heat, stirring, until warmed through. Add the farro and stir, toasting it for about 30 seconds, then add the bean puree and broth. Add the remaining 5 cups (1.25 L | 1134 g) Old Hen Broth and bring to a roaring boil. Add the remaining 1 cup (140 g) beans and reduce the heat to medium-low. Stir in the sage and kale and season with a small pinch each of salt and pepper. (Be careful of adding too much—it is better to add more at the table when the soup is finished rather than run the risk of oversalting.) Cover the pot and cook for 10 minutes. Remove from the heat, stir the soup, and set aside to rest for 5 minutes. The consistency should be runny as a risotto when freshly made, rather than dense and thick.

· Serve in warmed soup bowls and drizzle with a very generous amount of grassy, spicy robust olive oil.

TO DRINK:
A fruity, medium-body red from the Lucca area, such as the Palistorti Rosso from Tenuta di Valgiano.

Fregola Sarda

Throughout the centuries, Sardinia, like its sister island Sicily was invaded by Romans, Spaniards, Arabs, and others, all of whom left behind many culinary influences. For instance, *fregola sarda*, a rough, pearl-shaped pasta, was brought to Sardinia by Ligurian immigrants from a colony in Tunisia, and thus shares many similarities with the couscous of North Africa. Like couscous, the Sardinia pasta is made by hand-rubbing together semolina flour, water, and a bit of saffron into small balls. Once toasted, the tiny, irregular nuggets range in color from beige to dark brown.

Traditionally, *fregola sarda* is served in light fish soups, but the chewy pasta provides a blank canvas for endless combinations. Toss with a few spoonfuls of Caponata (page 313) for an antipasto, serve instead of polenta or orzo with a zesty winter stew like *Peposo* (page 225), pair with lamb sausage, or chop vegetables into a small dice and toss with the cooked pasta. Manicaretti now imports and distributes *fregola sarda* across the United States, and one of our biggest buyers is Blue Apron, a nationwide delivery service that provides ingredients and recipes for their customers to cook at home. It gives me such joy to see this irregular-shaped, saffron-imbued little pasta getting such deserved attention.

· **Cook fregola sarda like you would any pasta:** Bring a large pot of salted water to a boil. Add the *fregola sarda* and cook, stirring occasionally, until al dente, about 15 minutes. Drain and transfer to a large bowl. Serve warm or at room temperature.

Along with spaghetti, *fregola sarda* is one of my favorite pasta shapes because of its incredible versatility. It's very important in this particular recipe, as with the recipe for *Spaghetti a Pezzi con Pomodoro e Ceci in Brodetto* (page 144), that you remember that the pasta—*fregola sarda* in this case—is one of many ingredients, and try not to overload the dish with it. It's all about proportion, texture, and taste.

Fregola Sarda with Shrimp, Peas, and Asparagus

FREGOLA SARDA CON SCAMPI, PISELLI, E ASPARAGI

**SERVES 4
(ABOUT 6 CUPS TOTAL)**

4 cups (1 L | 960 g) *Brodetto* (page 56)

1 teaspoon saffron threads

½ cup (80 g) *fregola sarda*

8 to 10 asparagus stalks, trimmed and sliced into ¼-inch rounds

½ cup (75 g) fresh peas

¾ cup (227 g) small (20-count) shrimp, peeled, deveined, and cut into ¼-inch pieces

q.b. coarse sea salt and crushed Tellicherry black peppercorns

Fresh basil and flat-leaf parsley, finely chopped

Robust extra-virgin olive oil

• In a large pot, reheat the *brodetto*. Ladle ½ cup of the *brodetto* into a small bowl and add the saffron threads. Set aside.

• Bring a medium pot of salted water to a boil. Add the *fregola sarda* and boil until al dente, 12 to 15 minutes. Drain the *fregola sarda* through a fine-mesh sieve but do not rinse.

• Add the asparagus to the simmering *brodetto* and cook until green color is brightened, 3 to 4 minutes. Add the peas and the saffron water along with the threads and cook for 3 to 4 minutes more, until brighter green. Add the diced shrimp and cook until the shrimp develop color and turn from gray and translucent to pink and opaque. This happens quickly, 3 to 4 minutes. Stir in the *fregola sarda* and season with salt and pepper.

• To serve, ladle into four warm bowls, sprinkle with herbs, and drizzle with olive oil. Serve immediately.

TO DRINK:
A crisp and lively white wine with a bit of a backbone from Sardinia, such as the Vermentino di Sardinia "Stellato" by Pala.

The first time I tried *fregola sarda* was, aptly, in Contessa Rosetta Clara's summer Sardinian home. I've been lucky enough to spend many summers in Sardinia and each has been full of moments where I felt I was living in a dream. The light, the water, the desertlike vegetation along those big granite boulders dotting the coast, and the small coves make it unlike any other spot on the Mediterranean.

One of the places I've stayed—the incredible Cala di Volpe hotel—served cold *fregola sarda* salad each day in a variety of combinations and pairings. I loved the salad so much that I would always buy some to take home. Later on, the Peduzzi family of Rustichella d'Abruzzo and I brought *fregola sarda* to the United States through Manicaretti for the first time, and soon everyone on this side of the world fell in love with it, too.

You might not use all the *fregola sarda* you've cooked for this recipe if you wish to have the dish be more about the shrimp and zucchini than the pasta. As I've said before, we eat pasta with sauce in Italy, not the other way around! So if there are any *avanzi*, just toss with more olive oil and keep in an airtight container to use as you would rice or leftover pasta.

Just like at Cala di Volpe, I'm always making different variations of this salad: Try zucchini with clams or mussels or cherry tomatoes and tuna or make up your own. My only suggestion: Do as they do in Sardinia, and keep it simple.

Cold Fregola Sarda Salad

INSALATA DI FREGOLA SARDA

SERVES 6
AS A FIRST COURSE

½ cup plus 1 tablespoon (125 ml | 115 g) mild extra-virgin olive oil (preferably from Sardinia, Sicily, or Liguria)

1 cup (175 g) *fregola sarda*

1 small onion, very finely chopped

2 medium zucchini, cut into ⅛-inch dice

2 cups (450 g) small raw rock shrimp

q.b. fine sea salt and crushed Tellicherry black peppercorns

Juice of ½ lemon

¼ cup (5 g) fresh basil leaves, torn

TO DRINK:

A crispy, citrusy white wine from Sardinia (one you want to drink a couple of glasses of and then go back to the beach), such as a Vermentino from Sella & Mosca.

• Lightly oil a rimmed baking sheet with 1 tablespoon olive oil. Bring a medium pot of salted water to a boil. Add the *fregola sarda* and cook until just before it is al dente, about 11 minutes. Quickly drain through a fine-mesh sieve and spread evenly on the oiled baking sheet. Set aside to cool to room temperature.

• In a large skillet, heat 1 tablespoon of olive oil over medium heat. Add the onion and cook, stirring occasionally, until transparent, about 5 minutes. Add the zucchini and cook until the zucchini is tender, about 5 minutes. Add the shrimp and cook, tossing until they just turn opaque, about 90 seconds. Season with salt and transfer the shrimp-zucchini mixture to a serving bowl.

• Add the *fregola sarda* one handful at a time, using your hands to mix well. Add the remaining olive oil as you go along. Season with salt, pepper, and lemon juice. Fold in the basil leaves and mix well, always with your hands. Serve at room temperature.

You Need Cornmeal to Make Polenta

C'E BISOGNO DELLA FARINA DI GRANO TURCO PER FARE LA POLENTA

"Polenta" derives from the Latin word *puls*. During Ancient Rome, polenta was made by slowly cooking crushed, stone-ground farro (*Triticum dicoccum*) with milk, cheese, or lamb meat. Puls was known throughout Italy, and the Roman writer Apicio wrote about *puls punica*, a sweet recipe made with farro *puls*, cheese, honey, and eggs.

Corn (*grano Turco* or "Turkish Grain" in Italian), a New World crop, made its appearance in the Italian peninsula in the 1550s thanks to the merchants of the Republic of Venezia, who introduced it to the lagoon area of Polesine (today's Rovigo) and the fertile Valsugana northwest of Venezia. After successfully growing there, corn plantations spread rapidly west throughout the entire Po Valley and eastwards to Friuli.

At first, the fresh corn was boiled or grilled on the cobs, but the corn grew so abundantly and prolifically that that farmers began to hang it under barn roofs to dry. After being ground, it was mixed with water over fire and quickly became a creamy, comforting substitute for *puls*.

Cornmeal for polenta is made from different varieties of corn that are crushed into fine, medium, and coarse grinds and used for various cooking purposes from region to region in Italy.

- **Bramata:** Coarse in texture and deep yellow in color, *bramata* cornmeal creates the rough, thick polenta that most people are familiar with. Once the corn ears are dried and shucked, the kernels with hulls and germs are stone ground twice, first on a coarse setting, then a fine. Immediately after *bramata* polenta is made, pour it onto a wooden board or into soup bowls and serve immediately, topped with a favorite sauce, cheese, or meat.
- **Bramata Bianca:** Also a coarse polenta, *bramata bianca* is made from vitreous white corn. Served both soft and hard, popular from Venezia to the Trieste coastline, it is often topped with a *ragù* of squid and its black ink.
- **Fioretto:** A soft, finer version of *bramata* polenta, *fioretto* is bright golden yellow and has sweet notes of fresh corn. To make *fioretto*, corncobs from the Bergamo plains (north of Milan) are husked and dried in temperature-controlled rooms. The kernels are then stone ground to a fine meal with the hull and germ, imparting a deeper flavor and more nutrition to the polenta.
- **Taragna:** A blend of coarse cornmeal and buckwheat, *taragna* is sometimes called *polenta nera* (black polenta). Popular in the Brescia and Bergamo areas of northern Italy (closer to the Swiss and Austrian borders), *taragna polenta* is cooked to a thin consistency and served with cubes of Fontina, Taleggio, or Castelmagno cheese or topped with sausages and kale or a hearty pork *ragù*.

A wide copper pot is the best heat conductor for cooking polenta, but a Dutch oven or large saucepan will work, too. Vacuum-packed polenta has a longer shelf life. Keep in mind that once the bag is opened, it should be used as soon as possible to avoid turning rancid or attracting insects.

- ***To cook polenta,*** bring 2 cups water to a boil in a large (preferably copper) pot. Add a good pinch of salt, stir the water with a whisk, and very slowly pour 1 cup polenta into the whirling water, whisking continuously to avoid lumps. Once all the polenta has been added, reduce the heat to low and cook until the grains are soft, 20 to 30 minutes. Stir often with a wooden spoon, scraping along the bottom of the pot to stop the polenta from sticking, which, of course, it will. (In Italy people love the *crosticina* and save it to be eaten when the pot gets cold, and you eat it as a gift for the person who stirred all the times. It's like eating a chip!)

Cook more polenta than you need for one meal and pour leftovers into a baking dish. Refrigerate until firm to be sliced and grilled or fried during the coming days.

Making polenta is like making risotto. It's soothing, therapeutic, and you always make more than you need. It's like making bread, thinking of all the things you can serve it with, or pasta, thinking what sauce to serve atop. And once it's made you can do so many things with it: sauté, deep-fry, bake, or grill. Contrary to belief and the directions on most packages, when making polenta I start to whisk the polenta into the water right before the water starts to boil. Once it starts to boil, you have higher chances of the polenta lumping together, and you end up with big dumplings, or *grumi* as they are called in Italy. If you start to add the polenta when the water is almost to a boil, the lumps never happen. Trust me, I've done it a thousand times! Not to worry! Make sure you are using high-quality *farina di grano Turco* and, for this particular dish, use *bramata*, the coarsely ground meal.

Polenta Gratin

POLENTA AL FORNO

SERVES 6 TO 8

2 tablespoons (28 g) unsalted butter

1 cup (140 g) grated Parmigiano-Reggiano cheese

1 pound (450 g) *bramata* (coarsely ground Italian cornmeal)

q.b. fine sea salt

1 cup (140 g) shredded aged Castelmagno cheese

½ cup (70 g) mountain Gorgonzola, cut into ¼-inch cubes

· Butter a medium baking dish with 1 tablespoon of the butter and dust with 2 tablespoons of the Parmigiano-Reggiano.

· In a large pot (copper if you have one), heat the water. When it is close to a boil, start to pour in the polenta, whisking continuously. Once all the polenta is in, reduce the heat to low and simmer, stirring continuously with a wooden spoon and scraping along the bottom of the pot to avoid sticking, until the grains are soft, about 25 minutes. Stir in the remaining 1 tablespoon butter and season with salt.

· Preheat the oven to 400°F (200°C).

· Spoon the cooked polenta into the prepared baking dish, using the back of the spoon to even out the layer. Sprinkle the polenta with the Castelmagno and then dot with Gorgonzola. Dust the top evenly with the remaining Parmigiano-Reggiano. Bake until the cheeses have melted and the top is golden, 8 to 10 minutes. Set aside to cool slightly (or to room temperature) before serving.

TO DRINK:

A robust, gutsy Amarone della Valpolicella Classico 2012 from Allegrini. The huge backbone and dark fruit sweetness are a perfect complement to the savory polenta crust.

MATERA, BASILICATA, ONE OF THE OLDEST CITIES IN ITALY, AND A WORLD HERITAGE SITE FOR UNESCO.
YOU MUST TRY TO VISIT IT!

This is a recipe straight from my heart. Whenever I make it, it takes me back to my childhood. Even now, whenever I have small children over for dinner, this is one of the dishes that I make: They eat it with a spoon, sit so quietly, and always, always ask for more. When my mother would make it, she would make it either savory—as in this recipe for gnocchi—or sweet, serving the warm semolina to us in bowls with a generous swirl of honey and a sprinkle of cinnamon and nutmeg. It was pure heaven!

Roman-Style Semolina Rounds with Butter and Parmigiano-Reggiano

GNOCCHI DI SEMOLINO ALLA ROMANA

SERVES 8/
MAKES 36 GNOCCHI

12 tablespoons (160 g) unsalted butter

4 cups (1 L | 1000 g) whole milk

2 cups (500 ml | 500 g) still mineral water

2 cups (375 g) coarsely ground Italian semolina

2 large egg yolks

½ cup (40 g) grated Parmigiano-Reggiano

q.b. freshly grated nutmeg

q.b. coarse sea salt and crushed Tellicherry black peppercorns

• In a large saucepan, combine the milk, water, and 9 tablespoons of the butter and heat over medium heat. Once you see the mixture start to steam, whisk vigorously and pour in the semolina in a very thin stream until all of it is added. Cook, stirring often with a stainless-steel spoon, for 10 minutes. Stir in the egg yolks, 1 tablespoon of the Parmigiano-Reggiano, and nutmeg to taste. Cook, mixing often and vigorously, for 5 minutes more, until the dough comes together and is smooth.

• Pour a bit of cold water into a large baking dish, and spread the semolina evenly over the dish—it should be about ½-inch thick. Cover the semolina with a sheet of plastic wrap and set aside to cool. Chill in the refrigerator until the semolina is cold, about 1 hour.

• Preheat the oven to 475°F (245°C). Generously butter a round or oval baking dish and dust with 3 tablespoons Parmigiano-Reggiano, pepper, and nutmeg.

· Use a thin-lipped espresso cup or a fine-rimmed small glass about 2 inches wide to cut the semolina into rounds (almost as if you were making sugar cookies). Sprinkle ¼ cup Parmigiano-Reggiano on a small plate. Dip each of the rounds in the cheese before placing in the prepared baking dish (use some of the cuttings between the rounds to prop up the rounds behind them, so that they stick up at a 25-degree angle and are not totally flat against the bottom of the dish. They have to be somewhat layered, like fish scales, so they all fit in the dish). Dot each of the rounds with a bit of the remaining butter and dust with additional cheese. Season with pepper and nutmeg. Bake until the gnocchi start to sizzle and turn golden, 5 to 6 minutes, then turn the oven to broil and broil until deep golden, about 3 minutes.

· Immediately spoon the gnocchi onto warm dishes and drizzle with some of the butter from the pan. Serve immediately.

TO DRINK:
A glass of Morellino di Scansano from Moris Farms. Fruity and young, it's perfect to enjoy with all the butter and cheese.

Kale holds a special place in my heart, and I like to think of Tenuta di Capezzana in Carmignano, Italy, as the epicenter for the modern-day kale obsession. Many years ago, I ate there on separate occasions with my friends Judy Rodgers and Nancy Silverton, and we were served this soup. It was the first time either of them had had kale, and they brought it back to the States in a hurry. Unlike in America, where kale is eaten every month of the year across the country, in Tuscany, kale is only eaten after the first frost, when the leaves are dark green, curled, and full of nutrients. This soup—and it is definitely more of a soup than a thick porridge—is sweet, comforting, and nurturing, ideal for a cold winter night.

Polenta and Kale Soup

FARINATA COL CAVOLO NERO

SERVES 6 TO 8

½ cup plus 2 tablespoons (150 ml | 142 g) robust extra-virgin olive oil

2 leeks, cleaned, quartered lengthwise, and coarsely chopped

1 bunch *cavolo nero* (Tuscan kale), stemmed, leaves thinly sliced

6 cups (1420 ml | 1360 g) Old Hen Broth (page 54)

1 small whole *peperoncini*, or ½ teaspoon red pepper flakes

q.b. coarse sea salt and crushed Tellicherry black peppercorns

½ cup (113 g) coarse polenta

Olio nuovo, for serving

· In a large pot or Dutch oven, combine the olive oil and leeks and cook over medium heat until the leeks are soft, about 10 minutes. Add the kale and cook until the kale has wilted, about 2 minutes, then pour in the broth, add the hot pepper, and bring to a simmer. Cook until the leeks and kale are very soft, about 20 minutes. Season with salt and black pepper.

· Whisking continuously, add the polenta in a steady stream. Switch to a wooden spoon and cook, stirring often, until the polenta is soft and creamy but not overly thick, 30 to 35 minutes. Season with salt and pepper and divide between warm bowls. Top with plenty of *olio nuovo* and serve immediately.

TO DRINK:

A spicy, dark, graphite-flavored bottle of Chianti Classico "Gherardino" from Vignamaggio.

5

As a Main Course

COME PIETANZA

Pietanza—root of the word *"pietà"*—

is to be pious or to show charity and have feelings of compassion toward others. These dishes bestow love and gratitude on yourself and/or others; they fill and nourish your body and soul. Some take a day to make, such as *La Cena del Gran Bollito Misto*, while others, like *Salsiccie con Lenticchie e Cavolo Nero* (page 235), take less than 30 minutes. Some of these dishes are meals in and of themselves, no need for sides (or starters, if you want to be very simple!). Others are meant for pairing with Sautéed Greens (page 60), Mashed Potatoes (page 57), and other dishes *Per Acconpagnare* (page 295). I've listed some of my favorite pairings, but feel free to mix and match depending on your and your guests' tastes!

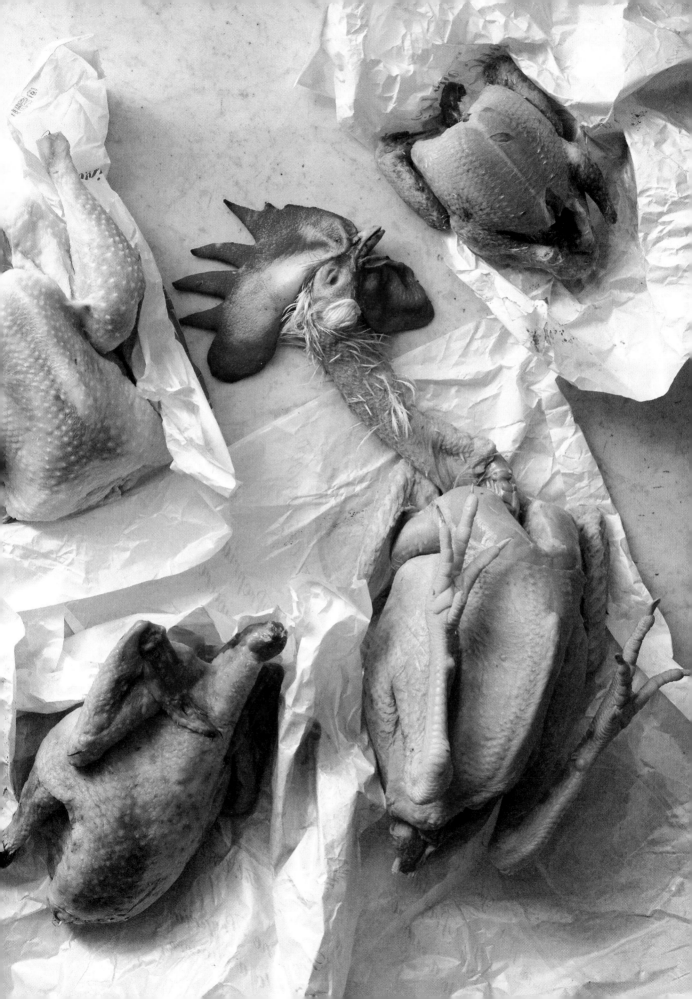

Once a year—typically on a dark, long Sunday in January—I organize a big, raucous dinner party at home in Florence. The revelry revolves around *bollito misto* and is as close to a regal event as I host all year. It is also one of the most heartwarming experiences I have yet to have around the table.

Bollito misto (or, in its less exciting translation, "mixed boiled meats") includes no less than seven types of *tagli* (meat cuts), seven *frattaglie* (side cuts or offal), seven sauces, and a slew of vegetables. It is an incredible tradition in Italy that spans from Piedmont to Emilia-Romagna and is very much loved in the Veneto. If you are ever in Torino, Verona, Bologna, or many of the other cities of the Pianura Padana, there are many restaurants that proudly serve only *bollito misto*.

While this recipe will take most of the afternoon to make, it requires minimal attention, so you can do many other things around the house or make the sauces in the meantime. I tend to split my prep into two days—shopping and making the sauces the day before and cooking the meats the day of.

The Big Dinner of the Mixed Boiled Meats

LA CENA DEL GRAN BOLLITO MISTO

My first stop is always my butcher, Fillipo, at Macelleria Vignoli in the Piazza di San Pierino. He is one of my most vital sources of inspiration when it comes to buying meats, poultry, and salumi. I spend most of my weekly money there (as well as at Rosy's vegetable stand on the square). Entering the butcher shop each week is like coming home—many of the customers know one another and swap recipes, jokes, and advice while waiting their turn—and I never leave without my market totes stuffed to the brim.

The key to a truly excellent *bollito misto* lies both in the quality of the cuts of meat and the broth itself. However, unlike making a standard meat broth—where you want the flavor of the meat to infuse the liquid—the opposite happens. You want an aromatic broth that seals and flavors the meats while cooking them until tender. For the best effect, use less salt in the beginning, and when you are almost done boiling, taste the broth and season.

If you have a big pot that will fit most of the meats, feel free to do it all in one. However, I much prefer to boil the tongue separately (it emits too much scum and the broth has a flavor I don't like, so I discard the liquid once the meat is boiled). I also boil the *cotecchino* (without vegetables) separately for the same reason. Some people boil the old hen separately as well, but I don't, since it gives the broth a flavor like no other.

The morning of the party, I sit down with my coffee and plan out when to add the first meats according to the time I want to serve dinner. As soon as guests begin to arrive, I set out a big bowl of *pinzimonio*—Italian-style crudités served alongside a bowl of *olio nuovo* (see page 11). After a few glasses of wine and plenty of nibbles, the *bollito misto* is nearly ready, and I set out cups of the broth for everyone to enjoy (I add broken fettuccine or tortellini if I have them on hand for extra heft).

Finally, the guests take their seats around the table. There is no happier moment at the party than when everyone has a plate full of sliced meats and sauces, and side dishes are being passed around, plenty of wine is flowing, and everyone is laughing and chatting.

NOTE: *This recipe offers suggestions for the* tagli *(main cuts) and* frattaglie *(side cuts). Feel free to pick and choose between them (even one or two from each of the groups can make a simpler version) or create your own!*

SERVES 6 TO 8

1 large yellow onion, spiked with cloves

2 carrots

1 large celery stalk, halved

2 garlic cloves

1 bunch fresh flat-leaf parsley

1 tablespoon (10 g) whole Tellicherry black peppercorns

q.b. fine sea salt

6½ pounds (2950 g) mixed *tagli* (such as beef shank, beef ribs, brisket, tied chuck roast, bottom round, veal brisket, and/or short ribs)

3 pounds (1360 g) mixed *frattaglie* (such as fresh or cooked sausage, veal tongue, oxtail, beef hoof, a boned and tied veal's head and/or an old hen.)

· Fill a large pot (or pots, depending on the amount of meat you need to cook—just double the amount of vegetables) with water and add the onion, carrot, celery, garlic, parsley, and peppercorns. Season generously with salt. Set over high heat and bring to a rolling boil. Cook for 10 minutes.

· Start adding the meats in order of what takes the longest to cook:

　3 hours: large pieces of meats and muscles with bones

　2 hours: ribs, oxtails, and veal's head

　1½ hours: veal tongue and old hen

　1 hours: fresh sausage

　30 minutes: precooked sausages

· Keep the flame as high as possible when adding a new cut of meat, but as soon as the broth comes back to a rolling boil, reduce the heat to maintain a gentle, steady simmer. Use a slotted spoon or spider to skim off any scum on the surface as needed, adding additional water as needed to keep the meat fully covered.

· Once the meats are cooked, the only one that requires any additional effort is the veal tongue, if you're using one. Remove it from the broth and set aside to cool slightly. As soon as the tongue is cool enough to handle, use a knife to make an incision into the skin and, using your fingers (some people wear rubber gloves), peel off and discard all the skin. Scrape off any bumps and trim off the gristle and fat on the underside.

>>>

· Using a large kitchen fork and very sharp chef's knife, cut each piece of meat on a cutting board and either plate directly for your guests or layer in a large, deep platter and spoon a bit of the broth over the top to keep the slices warm and moist. (Since everyone will want seconds and sometimes even thirds, return the extra meats to the broth, keeping them at a very low simmer so they stay ready for another round of serving.)

· Serve with a few or all of the below sauces and vegetable side dishes:

Sauces
· *Salsa Verde* (page 50)
· Dijon mustard
· *Cren* (horseradish whisked in a bowl with a drizzle of robust olive oil and a pinch of salt)
· *Aioli* or freshly made mayonnaise with extra-virgin olive oil (see page 186)

Vegetable Side Dishes
· Mashed potatoes (page 57)
· *Cipolline in Agrodolce* (page 302)
· Steamed broccoli, romanesco, or cauliflower
· Sautéed greens

TO DRINK:
Start the dinner with a Soave from Pieropan, and then move on to a drinkable red, such as a Chianti Classico from Vignamaggio.

Meat and Mashed Potato Pies, Two Ways

MIEI DUE GATÓ DI PATATE

Starting in the 1700s, most aristocratic Italian households had a chef called a *monzú*—a variation of the word *monsieur*. In fact, a number of French culinary terms influenced the names of many Neapolitan and Sicilian dishes. In this case, the French word for "cake," *gâteau*, became *gató*. It doesn't necessarily mean a sweet cake; in these two recipes, *gató* refers to a savory dish similar to shepherd's pie.

Much of Argentina's cuisine comes from a blend of traditional foods brought over by the large influx of immigrants from Europe. *Gató* was served two different ways at my home. One had a flaky *pâte brisée* crust, a lattice top, and a generous dusting of sugar. The other (more traditional) version blended Neapolitan and Sicilian flavors in a filling more akin to an Argentine *empanada*.

Neapolitan Meat and Mashed Potato Pie

GATÓ DI PATATE RUSTICO

SERVES 4 TO 6

3 tablespoons (42 g) unsalted butter

¼ cup plus 2 tablespoons (42 g) bread crumbs

4 cups (900 g) Mashed Potatoes (page 57)

2 large eggs

¼ pound (113 g) cooked Parma ham or prosciutto, diced

¼ pound (113 g) *mozzarella di buffala*, diced

¼ pound (113 g) *scamorza* (smoked mozzarella), diced

½ cup (60 g) grated Parmigiano-Reggiano cheese, plus more to finish

q.b. coarse sea salt and crushed Tellicherry black peppercorns

TO DRINK:
A red wine with layers of fruit such as plums and dark fruit made with the Aglianico grape, from Azienda Agricola San Salvatore.

• Preheat the oven to 350°F (180°C). Butter a 9-inch square baking dish with 1 tablespoon of the butter and dust the sides and bottom evenly with ¼ cup (31 g) of the bread crumbs.

• In a large bowl, combine the mashed potatoes and the eggs and mix well to combine. Add the ham, mozzarella, *scamorza*, and Parmigiano-Reggiano. Mix gently, using your hands, until just combined. Season with salt and pepper as needed.

• Spoon the mixture into the prepared baking dish and gently spread it evenly to the sides. Using a fork, make ridges on the top, and sprinkle with 2 tablespoons Parmigiano-Reggiano and the remaining 2 tablespoons bread crumbs. Cube the remaining 2 tablespoons butter and scatter evenly over the top.

• Bake for 15 minutes, until it feels a bit firmer to the touch. Turn the oven to broil and broil until the crust is golden and toasted, 3 to 5 minutes (checking often to be sure it doesn't burn). Remove the dish from the oven and let cool for 5 minutes, then cut into 3-inch squares and serve immediately on warm plates.

My Gató di Patate

GATÓ DI PATATE DI CASA MIA

SERVES 6 TO 8

4 tablespoons (56 g) unsalted butter

6 tablespoons (40 g) finely grated Parmigiano-Reggiano, plus more for serving

½ cup (125 ml | 115 g) mild extra-virgin olive oil

2 medium white onions, coarsely chopped

2¼ pounds (1 kg) lean ground beef, broken up with your fingers

½ cup (80 g) pitted and sliced green Castelvetrano, Bella Cerignola, or Ascolane olives

¼ cup (40 g) dried currants

¼ cup (30 g) Italian pine nuts

1 tablespoon sweet Hungarian paprika (optional)

q.b. coarse sea salt and crushed Tellicherry black peppercorns

2 hard-boiled eggs, thinly sliced horizontally

4 cups (907 g) Mashed Potatoes (page 57)

· Preheat the oven to 375°F (180°C). Butter a 9 x 13-inch baking dish with 1 tablespoon (14 g) of the butter and dust the sides and bottom evenly with 3 tablespoons (20 g) of the Parmigiano-Reggiano.

· In a large skillet, combine the olive oil and onions and sweat over medium-low heat until the onions are translucent and tender, 5 to 7 minutes. Add the meat in small batches, breaking it up with your fingers. Stir to combine the meat and onions, then add the olives, currants, and pine nuts. Cook, stirring often, until the meat just becomes evenly brown, about 10 minutes, then immediately remove the skillet from the heat. (Be careful not to overcook the meat or it will dry out when it is baked in the *gató*.) Stir in the paprika (if using) and taste for seasoning. Season with salt and pepper as needed.

· Spread the meat mixture evenly in the prepared baking dish. Arrange the sliced eggs on top of the meat, then gently spread the mashed potatoes evenly over the top. Use a fork to score the top with ridges and dust with the remaining 3 tablespoons (20 g) Parmigiano-Reggiano. Cube the remaining 3 tablespoons (42 g) butter and scatter it evenly over the top.

· Bake until the top is golden and bubbling around the edges, about 25 minutes. Remove from the oven and set aside to cool for 5 minutes before serving with additional Parmigiano-Reggiano.

TO DRINK:
A hearty Sicilian red from Cantina Bennati or a Leone from Tasca d'Almerita.

When you say "a UFO" in Florence, Florentines will understand that you're not talking about spaceships! Instead, *Ad Usum Florentinæ Operæ* ("To Be Used for the Florentine Opera"), or "A UFO," is an expression used when people give something as a gift that took a lot of work. This recipe for *il peposo* comes from one of my most authentic Florentine friends, Lorenzo Augier. He is a walking encyclopedia of Florentine history, and a great cook to boot! This recipe is a true UFO.

Legend says the architect Brunelleschi, who designed the Duomo's tile roof, invented this dish to provide sustenance for the tilemakers at the *fornacina* in Impruneta, right outside of Florence. When the workday was over, they put a terra-cotta dish with *coccio* (a very poor cut of beef), red wine, and a handful of exotic, very precious black pepper in the cooling oven. By the time they came back to work the next day, the stew was perfectly cooked and still warm from the day before.

The key is using a very sinewy, fatty cut of beef, a good Chianti, and tons of good Tellicherry peppercorns. Since black peppercorns are much easier and less pricey to get nowadays, this recipe uses plenty of them (I like to call this black pepper with beef stew, not the other way around!) Add as much as you'd like—since it cooks for so long the peppercorns become incredibly dark, soft, and flavorful.

Tellicherry Black Pepper Beef Stew

IL PEPOSO ALLA FORNACINA DELL'IMPRUNETA

SERVES 6 TO 8

2 pounds (900 g) *muscolo* or beef top shank, or other cuts like top round, bottom round, or chunk roast with lots of cartilage and a sinewy consistency

2 tablespoons (30 ml | 27 g) cooking extra-virgin olive oil

¼ cup (90 g) *Soffritto* (page 40)

3 tablespoons (27 g) whole Tellicherry black peppercorns

2 tablespoons (18 g) crushed Tellicherry black peppercorns

3 juniper berries

2 whole cloves

6 cups (1500 ml | 1500 g) Chianti Classico

3 sage sprigs and 3 rosemary sprigs, tied into a small bundle with butcher's string

q.b. fine sea salt

· Cut the meat into 1- to 2-inch cubes. Save the tendons and sinewy parts to flavor the oil.

· In a large terra-cotta dish with a lid (or in a Dutch oven, if you don't have one) combine the olive oil and the tendons and sinewy parts of the meat. Cook over medium-high heat until they are crisp and fried, about 5 minutes. Remove the bits with a spoon, then start to add the meat, in batches, turning the pieces occasionally until they are golden, about 10 minutes. Transfer the browned pieces to a plate before adding the next batch. Once the meat is all nice and brown, return all the pieces to the pot and mix in the *soffritto*. Once the *soffritto* is warmed through, add the whole and crushed peppercorns, juniper berries, and cloves. Pour in the red wine and add the herb bundle.

· Bring to a boil, then reduce the heat to low, cover the pot, and simmer, stirring often, until the wine is reduced and the meat is tender, about 3 hours. The *peposo* should be very dark, glossy, and thick. I often serve this dish with soft creamy Polenta (page 203) or with toasted crusty bread. Toss leftovers with pappardelle or fettuccine, or mix a tablespoon into my Tomato Sauce (page 42) and toss with spaghetti.

TO DRINK:
A wine made by the king of the Cotto d'Impruneta, Giovanni Manetti, who also owns a wonderful winery called Fontodi, in Panzano in Chianti. I love his "Vigne del Sorbo" Chianti Classico. It has enough depth and structure to stand up to the very peppery stew.

Meat Loaf and Meatballs

IL POLPETTONE E LE POLPETTE

- *Un polpettone, due polpettoni* (one meat loaf, two meat loaves)

- *Una polpetta, due polpette* (one meatball, two meatballs)

- *Una polpettina, due polpettine* (one little meatball, two little meatballs)

With the same meat mixture, you make one *polpettone* about the size of a (deflated) football or 16 *polpettine* the size of Ping-Pong balls.

Serve the *polpettone* with Mashed Potatoes (page 57) and Sautéed or Roasted Vegetables (page 60) and get creative with the fillings—whenever you have a *polpettone* at someone's home in Italy, it is always different and always a fun surprise! I've offered plenty of ideas in the following recipe, but whatever you have in the fridge and your imagination can work! For the *polpette* and *polpettine*, consider serving them two ways, allowing your guests to choose their own adventure!

Whether you're making *un polpettone* or *sedici polpettine*, two things will have great impact on their texture and flavor: the quality of the meat you buy (seek out grass-fed, organic meats) and making sure you don't add too many bread crumbs to bind the meat, which can result in very compact and doughy *polpettone/polpettine* rather than soft and succulent ones.

A Big Meal Meat Loaf

IL POLPETTONE

**SERVES 6 TO 8;
MAKES ONE 5 X 12-INCH
*POLPETTONE***

POLPETTONE

1 cup (90 g) stale bread, crusts removed and break broken or diced into ½-inch cubes

½ cup (120 g) whole milk

1 pound (450 g) grass-fed, very lean ground beef

¼ pound (120 g) ground veal (or ground turkey)

2 (180 g) fresh Italian sausages, casings removed, meat broken into small pieces

1 tablespoon *Soffritto* (page 40)

2 medium eggs

2 tablespoons (10 g) grated Parmigiano-Reggiano cheese

q.b. finely chopped fresh flat-leaf parsley, rosemary, and sage

q.b. fine sea salt and crushed Tellicherry black peppercorns

1 cup (125 g) bread crumbs, plus more to coat

>>>

• Put the bread pieces in a small bowl and cover with the milk. Let soak for 10 to 15 minutes, then, using your fingers, crush the bread until it forms a soft, even mush. Squeeze out all the milk and set the bread aside.

• In a large bowl, gently combine the beef, veal, and sausage with your hands (the final dish will have better texture if you mix gently with your hands rather than pushing into it as if you were making pasta dough or bread). Add the softened bread, *soffritto*, eggs, Parmigiano-Reggiano, and as much chopped parsley, rosemary, and sage as you prefer. Season with salt and pepper and mix until just combined. Start adding the bread crumbs a little at a time until the mixture feels somewhat drier and when you pick up some of the meat mixture, it holds together. You may not need to use all the bread crumbs.

• Place a sheet of parchment paper on a cutting board and transfer the meat mixture to the paper, spreading it evenly across the paper to make a flat rectangle about 8 x 12-inches, and ½ inch thick. Layer with your chosen fillings, and using the parchment to help, gently roll the meat into a long cylinder with the filling on the inside. With the long side facing you, first lift the parchment and use it to roll meat to the center, pressing down to keep it in place. Then lift the parchment on the opposite long side, bringing the meat just past the center to overlap itself slightly. Pinch the "seam" of the meat together to keep the filling in place. Refrigerate the *polpettone* for at least 1 hour.

>>>

FILLINGS AND FINISH

Optional fillings, such as diced
    Provolone cheese and Parma ham,
    spinach and chopped hard-boiled
    eggs, cooked peas and diced
    boiled carrots, or diced zucchini
    and mortadella cubes

2 tablespoons (30 ml | 27 g) cooking
    extra-virgin olive oil

5 garlic cloves, whole and unpeeled

2 rosemary sprigs

2 sage sprigs

2 fresh bay leaves

- Preheat the oven to 375°F (190°C).

- Remove the parchment paper and gently—without pressing too hard—roll the *polpettone* in the remaining bread crumbs to cover evenly.

- Drizzle a baking dish with olive oil and lay the garlic and rosemary sprigs, sage, and bay on the sides of the dish. Place the *polpettone* in the middle, seam-side down, and make sure the herbs are snuggling alongside it. Bake until the *polpettone* is golden brown and just firm to the touch, 40 to 45 minutes.

- Remove the *polpettone* from the oven and set aside to rest for 10 minutes before transferring to a serving platter and serving warm.

TO DRINK:

A hearty Barbera d'Alba from Renato Ratti. It has a wonderful aroma of dark fruit, yet a lively acidity will add a fun spark to your meal.

Would You Like Veal Meatballs with Fresh Peas or with a Tomato and Olive Sauce?

POLPETTINE DI VITELLA CON I PISELLI FRESCHI O IN UMIDO?

SERVES 4; MAKES 16 POLPETTINE

POLPETTINE

2 large eggs

1 cup (125 g) bread crumbs

1 recipe basic *Polpettone* (see page 227), refrigerated

1 cup (250 ml | 230 g) cooking extra-virgin olive oil

PEAS

2 tablespoons (30 ml | 27 g) cooking extra-virgin olive oil

1 scallion, thinly sliced

3 cups (450 g) freshly shelled green peas or frozen green peas, defrosted

¾ cup (170 ml | 170 g) dry white wine

¼ cup (7 g) fresh flat-parsley leaves

q.b. fine sea salt and crushed Tellicherry black peppercorns

OR...

TOMATO AND OLIVE SAUCE

2 tablespoons (30 ml | 27 g) cooking olive oil

1 large red onion, sliced

2 cups (500 ml | 450 g) *Tomato Sauce* (page 42)

1 tablespoon (7 g) Hungarian paprika

2 tablespoons (30 ml | 30 g) dry red wine, such as Chianti

½ cup (100 g) pitted Taggiasca olives

· **To make the polpettine:** In a shallow bowl, whisk together the eggs. Line one plate with the bread crumbs and another with paper towels.

· Remove the *polpettine* mixture from the fridge and form the mixture into 16 (40 g) balls, each about 1½ inches round. Dip the *polpettine* first in the egg mixture, then roll in the bread crumbs to coat evenly.

· In a medium skillet, heat 3 tablespoons of the oil over medium-high heat. Working in batches, adding oil as needed, cook the *polpettine* until golden, 5 to 7 minutes. Transfer to the paper towel–lined plate.

· **To make the peas (if using):** In a medium skillet, heat the oil over medium heat. Add the scallion and cook until softened, 1 to 2 minutes, then add the peas. When the peas are hot and sizzling, about 4 minutes, add the wine and *polpettine*. Cover the pan and reduce the heat to low. Cook, turning the meatballs occasionally, until they are warmed through, about 5 minutes. Sprinkle with parsley, salt, and pepper and serve immediately.

· **To make the tomato and olive sauce (if using):** In a medium skillet, heat the oil over medium heat. Add the red onion and cook, stirring, until soft, about 7 minutes. Add the tomato sauce and bring to a gentle simmer, then stir in the paprika and wine. Cook for 2 minutes, then tuck the *polpettine* into the sauce. Cover the pan and reduce the heat to low. Cook, turning the meatballs occasionally, until the meatballs are warmed through, about 5 minutes. Sprinkle the olives all over the pan and serve immediately.

TO DRINK:
A Castello di Nipozzano Vigne Vecchie from the Marchesi de' Frescobaldi will pair beautifully with both versions.

Del maiale non si butta via niente!

You never throw away anything from a pig!

Every time I eat this delicious, simple dish in Florence, the very mention of the name of the recipe creates a commotion among my Florentine friends: What is it really called?

Rosticciana? Rostinciana? Costoleccio? (*Costa* meaning "rib.")

The upheaval one word can create reflects the very essence of what I love so much about authentic food—and especially what this authenticity means to Florentines. In my own mind, there is "the right way," or "this other way," or "that way," but to them there is only "the one way" (which typically means the recipe was passed down through generations).

And the simpler the dish, the louder and stronger the opinions become.

I firmly believe that this passion is what makes Italy so great. These layers of perception and authenticity, as well as the differences among Italians themselves, come out in both big and small ways, *rosticciana/rostinciana/costoleccio* being one of them.

As for the final recipe title here? My butcher sells *rosticciana* and—since I trust him implicitly—I call this recipe that. Feel free to serve it at home whichever way it serves you.

Sometimes I make *rosticciana* from scratch (and have included the method below—insider tip: make certain to open the windows first, there's bound to be plenty of smoke!).

Other times, if I have made *Arista di Maiale al Forno* (page 239) with the rack of bones, I make *rosticciana* the next day or so after, splitting the ribs open and sautéing them in a cast-iron skillet until hot. Serve directly from the skillet at the table, alongside some simple boiled potatoes. It's so wonderful to pick the bones directly from the pan, eating them with your fingers.

I prefer the *rosticciana* to be on the soft and succulent side. If it becomes dry, toss it with a cup or two of *Pepperonata* (page 49) to "reconstitute," or serve with *Cipolline in Agrodolce* (page 302) mustard, or *Pesto Verdi* (page 158). There is nothing nicer than eating it with your fingers, along with potatoes, sautéed vegetables, and many other greens. Eating off a bone is a typical and most authentic Florentine experience.

>>>

Roasted Pork Ribs

ROSTICCIANA

SERVES 4

Leaves from 3 rosemary sprigs,
finely chopped

Leaves from 2 sage sprigs,
finely chopped

1 garlic clove, finely chopped

4 teaspoons coarse sea salt

4 teaspoons crushed Tellicherry
black peppercorns

3 pounds (1360 g) pork ribs, cut into
4-inch long pieces

¼ cup (60 ml | 57 g) cooking
extra-virgin olive oil

¼ cup (60 ml | 60 g) red wine
vinegar

2 teaspoons fennel pollen (optional)

• In a small bowl, mix together the rosemary, sage, garlic, salt, and pepper. to create a *sale aromatico*. Rub the ribs all over with the *sale aromatico* (herb salt) and place in an airtight container. Refrigerate for at least 4 hours and up to overnight.

• Preheat the oven to 350°F (175°C).

• Rub the ribs with olive oil. Heat a cast-iron skillet over high heat (make sure you've opened your windows and turned your hood exhaust to high). Once the pan is sizzling hot, add the ribs one at a time and cook without moving them, until they are golden brown, 5 to 7 minutes, then flip and brown on the other side. Transfer to a large plate and continue to cook all the ribs until they are crisp and evenly browned. Pour in the vinegar, using a wooden spoon to scrape up any bits stuck to the bottom of the pan. Return all the ribs to the pan, season with fennel pollen (if using), salt, and pepper, and transfer to the oven. Bake until the meat starts to pull towards the center of the rib, exposing bone on both ends, 20 to 30 minutes. Serve hot.

TO DRINK:
A dry, earthy Chianti Classico "Rancia" from Felsina. You and your guests should be able to drink a few bottles of it, since these wines are so drinkable and perfect for this dish—and the glasses should have lots of fingerprints on them by the end!

Going to the *macellaio* (butcher) and the *fruttivendola* (fruit and vegetable seller) is always a wonderful learning experience. I see them both on a weekly (and sometimes daily) basis, and they are always ready to offer advice or suggestions, or share a slice of something they love. Many times my conversations with other patrons in the shop make it more of a social visit than a shopping trip. We all exchange recipes, ideas, and suggest corrections or combinations. These interactions have changed and improved the way I cook.

My butcher is especially helpful when I ask him to cut a rack of pork for this recipe. Follow this same technique with a rack of veal or a rack of beef. Buying a whole rack of pork will allow you to make three dishes from this book. First, serve the *arista*, then with the rack of ribs (the bones and meat in between, similar to what they use for BBQ pork ribs in the United States) serve *Rosticciana* (page 236), and finally, with the leftover cuttings, make *Ceciata di Suino e Bietole* (see page 246). I serve *arista* with slow-cooked beans (see page 29) and Mashed Potatoes (page 57) and layer extra slices from the *arista* the following day between slices of plain focaccia.

Oven-Roasted Pork

ARISTA DI MAIALE AL FORNO

SERVES 8

ROAST

1 (4-pound | 907 g) bone-in pork loin or rib roast

4 garlic cloves, finely chopped

2 teaspoons wild fennel pollen or finely crushed fennel seeds

2 teaspoons cracked Tellicherry black peppercorns

1 teaspoon fresh rosemary

1 teaspoon chopped fresh sage leaves

q.b. fine sea salt

q.b. cooking extra-virgin olive oil

>>>

• **To prepare the roast:** Ask your butcher to make a crack between each vertebrae (my butcher flips the roast over so it is bone-side up and uses his huge butcher cleaver). If I am at home, I use a very sharp chef's knife, and with the help of a rubber mullet or a hammer, I tap between each of the chops until I hear a crack. Once you split the ribs, flip the roast over again, and trim away and set aside some of the fat. Finally, flip the rack to a stand-up position and, using a very sharp knife, begin boning the filet to remove it entirely in one piece. Use the tip of the knife to make a series of incisions and cuts in the meat without piercing all the way though.

• Using a mortar and pestle, mash the garlic, fennel pollen, pepper, rosemary, sage, and salt. Add the olive oil until a thick paste forms.

• Using your hands, rub the mixture on the inside of the bone rack, and all over the *arista*. If you have any left over, rub some on the outside bone rack as well.

>>>

FOR THE PAN

10 rosemary sprigs

10 sage sprigs

20 bay leaves

**1 head pink or regular garlic,
cloves broken apart but not peeled**

q.b. robust extra-virgin olive oil

- Using cooking twine, tie the meat back to the rack, wrapping between each rib to make it easier for you to slice and keep the *arista* tight and whole. Wrap in plastic wrap and refrigerate for at least 8 hours or up to overnight.

- Preheat the oven to 400°F (200°).

- In a large baking dish, combine the rosemary sprigs, sage, bay leaves, and garlic. Cut the reserved pork fat into cubes and scatter over the top. (If you don't have enough fat for the size of the rack, drizzle with additional cooking extra-virgin olive oil.)

- Tranfer the *arista* to the baking dish and roast until a thermometer inserted into the center of the rack reads 130°F (55°C), about 40 minutes. Remove from the oven, cover with aluminum foil, and set aside to rest for 20 minutes.

- Cut the string as you slice, leaving the others tied up if you are not serving the whole *arista*. Drizzle with pan juices and robust extra-virgin olive oil and serve warm. I like to save the bones to make *Rosticciana* (page 236).

TO DRINK:

A Brunello di Montalcino from Casanova di Neri, the wine made my friend Giacomo Neri. His Brunelli is a class of its own, and an *arista* deserves such accompaniment.

With *soffritto* and cooked lentils in the fridge, this is an easy weeknight meal that can be on the table in less than 30 minutes. All you need to do is pick up some fresh Italian sausages from the butcher. Rather than frying the sausages, I cook them in a shallow water bath and deglaze the pan with hearty red wine. If you have leftover sausages, tuck them between pieces of focaccia and you have a hearty lunch ready to go!

Sausages with Lentils and Tuscan Kale

SALSICCIE CON LENTICCHIE E CAVOLO NERO

SERVES 6 TO 8

Coarse sea salt

2 large bunches *cavolo nero* (Tuscan kale), stemmed

4 (90 g each) fresh Italian pork sausages

½ cup (125 g) *Soffritto* (page 40)

1 cup (250 ml | 270 g) *passata di pomodoro* or *Salsa di Pomodoro* (page 42)

1 cup (250 ml | 250 g) plus 2 tablespoons Chianti or dry red wine

2 cups (200 g) cooked lentils, warmed

Fresh flat-leaf parsley, rosemary, and sage leaves, for serving

q.b. crushed Tellicherry black peppercorns

- Bring a large pot of salted water to a boil. Add the kale leaves, cover the pot with a lid, and boil until tender, 4 to 5 minutes. Drain the kale in a colander and set aside to cool slightly. When it is cool enough to handle, squeeze out any excess moisture and coarsely chop the kale.

- Using a fork, poke the sausages on all sides to pierce the skins. Arrange the sausages snugly in a medium saucepan with high sides (rather than a skillet, to keep the fat from splattering all over the stove) and add just enough water to cover the sausages. Place over medium-high heat and cook until the water becomes cloudy and foamy, about 5 minutes. Use a pair of tongs to turn the sausages over and reduce the heat to medium. Cook, turning the sausages frequently, until the liquid has evaporated and the sausages are brown, 12 to 18 minutes (depending on the thickness of the sausages). Pour in 2 tablespoons of red wine and stir to deglaze the pan.

- While the sausages are cooking, in a large saucepan, heat the *soffritto* over medium heat until it begins to bubble. Stir in the cooked kale, tomatoes, and the rest of the red wine and stir to combine. Season with salt.

- Divide the lentils among four plates and top with the kale sauce. Add a sausage to each plate and sprinkle with herbs and pepper. Serve hot.

TO DRINK:
A Nipozzano from Frescobaldi.

Pork belly wasn't always as prevalent as it is now. Nowadays, you can find it on restaurant menus, simply grilled on a charcoal fire, or braised slowly so that when you eat it, you only need a fork. It's especially nice to make this dish and have *avanzi* (leftovers!), which then can be used in panini, or cut into cubes for a new twist on *Spaghetti alla Carbonara* (page 133), or when making Spaghetti Frittata of Spagetti, Pancetta, and Beans (page 281). Seek out wild fennel pollen from Tuscany—it is essential to the perfect success of this recipe.

Roast Pork Belly with Wild Fennel

PANCETTA STESSA CON FINOCCHIO SELVATICO

SERVES 4 TO 6

PORK BELLY

1 tablespoon wild fennel pollen, or 2 tablespoons crushed fennel seeds

3 garlic cloves, finely chopped

2 tablespoons finely chopped fresh rosemary

2 tablespoons finely chopped fresh sage leaves

2 fresh bay leaves, finely chopped

1 tablespoon robust extra-virgin olive oil

q.b. coarse sea salt and freshly ground Tellicherry black peppercorns

2 pounds (900 g) skin-on pork belly

>>>

- **To make the pork belly:** In a large mortar, combine the wild fennel pollen, garlic cloves, rosemary, sage, bay, and olive oil and crush with the pestle until very finely mashed. Season with salt and pepper.

- Make a long, deep cut on the skin of the pork, and then across diagonally in the opposite direction to create a cross. Rub the fennel mixture all over the pork belly, place in an airtight container, and refrigerate for at least 4 hours or up to overnight.

- When you're ready to roast, remove the pork belly from the refrigerator and set aside for 30 minutes.

- Preheat the oven to 375°F (190°C).

- In a large roasting pan, combine the celery, carrots, red onions, garlic, rosemary, bay, sage, and whole peppercorns. Drizzle with the olive oil.

- Heat a large cast-iron grill pan over high heat. Once the pan is smoking hot, add the pork belly, skin-side down, and grill, without moving, until it is golden and crispy, about 2 minutes. Flip the pork belly over and sear quickly until golden, about 2 minutes more. Transfer the pork belly to the vegetable-filled roasting pan, skin-side down, and pour the wine and broth over the meat. Cover the pan with aluminum foil and roast for 30 minutes.

VEGETABLES

3 celery stalks, chopped into
  1-inch pieces

4 carrots, sliced on an angle into
  1-inch pieces

2 red onions, diced into 1-inch pieces

5 garlic cloves, unpeeled

6 rosemary sprigs

6 fresh bay leaves

6 fresh sage leaves

q.b. whole Tellicherry black
  peppercorns

½ cup (125 ml | 115 g) cooking
  extra-virgin olive oil

1 to 2 cups (250–500 ml | 250–500 g)
  dry white wine

½ cup (125 ml | 125 g) *Brodo di
  Costata di Manzo* (page 55)

2 tablespoons (30 ml | 56 g)
  red wine vinegar

· Remove the foil and flip the pork belly so it is skin-side up. Increase the temperature of the oven to 400°F (200°C). If the liquid has almost evaporated, add a bit more wine or stock and baste the skin side of the pork belly. Return the pan to the oven and roast until the skin is sizzling and cracking, about 10 minutes.

· Remove the pan from the oven and transfer the pork belly to a plate. Cover with aluminum foil and set aside to rest in a warm place. Remove the vegetables from the pan and place over low heat. Pour in the vinegar and, using a wooden spoon, scrape up any bits stuck to the bottom of the pan carefully over low heat.

· Cut the pork belly into squares and place them on a serving platter. Surround the pork belly with the vegetables and pour the sauce over the top. Serve immediately.

TO DRINK:
One of my favorite red wines from Tuscany, the Villa di Trefiano from the Contini-Bonacossi family. It has wonderful minerality and violet notes, as well as a beautiful acidity that helps clean your palate so you can enjoy the flavors of the pork and the crunch of the skin.

Chiara Massiero has been serving *Ceciata di Suino e Bietole* since her grandfather opened Trattoria Cammillo in Florence in 1947. The dish embodies the simple perfection of a one-course meal, and I often find myself at one of her tables to eat solely this dish. The success lies in the perfect proportion of meat to chickpeas to beet greens, a generous amount of garlic, and a final—heavy—pour of robust extra-virgin olive oil

Chickpeas, Beet Greens, and Pork

CECIATA DI SUINO E BIETOLE

SERVES 4

1 cup (250 ml | 230 g) cooking extra-virgin olive oil

6 garlic cloves, thickly sliced

1 pound (453 g) pork shoulder, cut into ½-inch cubes

2 cups (473 ml) of cooked chickpeas with their broth (page 45)

1 medium bunch beet stems and greens, chopped coarsely

q.b. fine sea salt and cracked Tellicherry black peppercorns

Robust extra-virgin olive oil

· In a large skillet, combine the olive oil and garlic and sauté over medium heat for 2 minutes. Add the pork, increase the heat to high, and cook until the cubes are browned on all sides, 5 to 7 minutes. Reduce the heat to medium and add the chickpeas and their broth. Bring the broth to a simmer and stir in the beet stems and greens. Simmer until the liquid evaporates and the stems are tender. Season with salt and pepper and drizzle generously with olive oil. Serve immediately.

TO DRINK:

A bottle from the Maremma Toscana, such as Fattorie Le Pupille or Avvoltore from Moris Farms. The fruitiness of the Sangiovese grape in southern Tuscany goes well with the dark and bitter flavors of the dish.

La Pecora guarda sempre se ha dietro l'Agnello.

A sheep will always look to see if her lamb is behind her.

TRAFFIC ON THE ROADS OF BASILICATA

Agnello Dolce Forte is one of my favorite classic dishes to make when it's cold and dark outside. *Dolce*, or "sweet," refers to the citrus, while *forte,* or "strong," suggests the generous amount and array of spices, brought to Italy and other parts of Europe from Asia and North Africa by spice route traders, used in the dish. In fact, when I made this stew at an event in New Delhi, the food editor of the *Times of India* told me that a similar dish is popular in the Kerala, the Southern Indian state on the Malabar coast. Kerala has been growing and selling its spices—cinnamon, nutmeg, black peppers, cloves, and more—for thousands of years, so the Italian-Indian connection in this dish is easy to trace.

When I make *Agnello Dolce Forte* I use a fatty cut of lamb or veal, preferably from the shoulder, or short ribs. Carlo Cioni of Da Delfina in Tuscany makes his with cubed veal tongue and serves it as an appetizer. (To do this, simmer the tongue in water for 1½ hours, then when cool enough to handle, peel and cube it.) Whatever you use, make the stew a day or two in advance; the flavors get better with age. Serve with wedges of Grilled Polenta (page 203) or a scoop of slow-cooked beans (see page 29), lentils, or Rice (page 59).

Sweet-and-Strong Lamb Stew

AGNELLO DOLCE FORTE

SERVES 10 TO 12

2 tablespoons (30 ml | 28 g) robust extra-virgin olive oil

2 pounds (900 g) lamb shoulder, cut into 1- to 2-inch pieces and patted dry with paper towels

1 tablespoon (20 g) tomato paste

3 cups (765 g) *Soffritto* (page 40), reheated

2 cups (500 ml | 500 g) dry red wine

1½ tablespoons (8 g) unsweetened cocoa powder

1 teaspoon Demerara sugar

½ teaspoon whole cloves (about 10)

½ teaspoon juniper berries (about 8)

1 (2-inch) cinnamon stick

1 star anise pod

5 fresh or dried bay leaves

2 *peperoncini,* or ¼ teaspoon red pepper flakes

1 teaspoon whole Tellicherry black peppercorns (about 10–12)

A few gratings of nutmeg

2 strips of orange zest (peeled with a vegetable peeler; each about 2 inches long)

½ teaspoon coarse sea salt

¾ cup (100 g) flame or golden raisins

¼ cup (70 g) chopped candied orange peel

½ cup (70 g) Italian pine nuts, toasted

>>>

· In a skillet, heat the olive oil over medium heat. Add the lamb and cook, turning the pieces occasionally, until they are browned on all sides. Add the tomato paste and cook, stirring, for 1 minute. Stir in the *soffritto* and cook over medium heat to warm through. Pour in the wine and bring to a boil, then reduce the heat to maintain a simmer and pour in 1 cup (250 ml | 250 g) water, the cocoa powder, sugar, cloves, juniper, cinnamon, anise, bay, peppers, peppercorns, nutmeg, orange zest and salt. Cook the stew, uncovered, over the lowest heat possible, until most of the liquid has evaporated and the meat is tender and can be shredded with a fork, about 3 hours.

· Stir in the raisins and orange peel and cook for 10 to 12 minutes more, until the raisins and orange are plumped and warmed through. Remove the bay leaves, cinnamon stick, juniper berries, and star anise and spoon the stew into warm bowls. Sprinkle with pine nuts before serving.

TO DRINK:
A gutsy, powerful Amarone, such as Allegrini or Dal Forno.

Antonietta Marrone married Sergio di Zio almost fifty years ago and moved to his home, a farm in Abruzzo, where he had a gas station. Antonietta is such an amazing cook that they decided to open a small restaurant called La Bilancia in 1972.

To me, their restaurant is one of the most authentic restaurants in Italy. Cranky Sergio commands the dining room as a dictator (but his heart is full of love and generosity), and Antoinetta runs the kitchen with so much heart and soul (and deliciousness!). Their daughter, Ute, is the custodian of all Antonietta's traditions and culinary secrets and, together with Ute's daughter, Benedetta, those traditions will carry on well into the future. It's a magical place. Antonietta's juicy breaded lamb chops, along with other recipes from her in this book including *Cac e Ov* (page 258) and *Misticanza di Abruzzi* (page 76), are all magical and all work so well together as a meal!

Antonietta's Breaded Lamb Chops

COSTOLETTE D'AGNELLO COME MI HA INSEGNATO ANTONIETTA

SERVES 4 TO 6

6 small (340-g) lamb chops with the skin attached

2 large eggs

q.b. fine sea salt and crushed Tellicherry black peppercorns

2 cups (250 g) bread crumbs

1 tablespoon (15 g) unsalted butter

2 tablespoons (30 ml | 27 g) cooking extra-virgin olive oil, plus more as needed

Mashed Potatoes (page 57), for serving

TO DRINK:

A juicy red Montepulciano d'Abruzzo from one of the most important wine houses of Italy, Valentini. It's a unique privilege to go to La Bilancia to eat, since they are very close friends with the Valentini family and serve the wines of Valentini as their house wine! Worth the trip to Abruzzo, if you are an Italian-wine lover.

• Use a sharp paring knife to separate the meat and skin from the top part of the lamb chop and expose the bone as much as possible, keeping it all in one piece. I tend to cut the top first, then make an incision along the length of each side of the bone from the inside, taking into account the thickness of the bone. Once it's all separated, I put the paring knife below the bone while holding the side of the meat down (see following page).

• Once you have this little flap of meat, wrap the flap right at the top of the fillet, and make a knot. Do the same to each of the chops.

• Now, using a meat pounder, pound the meat and the flap part gently so that it is all one even piece, about ½-inch thick.

• Line a plate with paper towels. In a shallow medium bowl, whisk the eggs with salt and pepper. Pour the bread crumbs into a second bowl. In a large skillet, melt the butter and olive oil together over medium-high heat. Dip each of the lamb chops first into the egg, then in the bread crumb mixture, then set the chops in the pan. Fry until golden on the first side, 3 to 5 minutes, then flip and repeat on the second side.

• Serve hot with mashed potatoes.

Every Easter, Antonietta makes *Cac e Ov* for three hundred guests at La Bilancia. For one (very big) batch, she uses 23 kilos lamb, 150 farm-fresh eggs, 1 kilo Parmegiano-Reggiano, and 2 liters *passata*. Her daughter, Ute, kindly scaled the recipe down for *Autentico*, and I can attest firsthand that the dish is worth making for the leftovers the next day for breakfast alone. Serve it as a second course with crusty Italian bread.

Lamb, Cheese, and Eggs

CAC E OV

SERVES 10 TO 12

3 tablespoons (45 ml | 41 g) cooking olive oil

1 carrot, finely chopped

1 celery stalk, finely chopped

1 leek, cleaned well and finely chopped

Leaves from 2 rosemary sprigs

Leaves from 2 thyme sprigs

2 tablespoons chopped fresh flat-leaf parsley

3 pounds (1500 g) lamb shoulder, chopped into 1-inch pieces

8 large eggs

½ cup (50 g) finely grated Parmigiano-Reggiano cheese

1 cup (240 ml | 250 g) *passata di pomodoro*

Crusty Italian bread, for serving

• In a large pot, combine the olive oil, carrot, celery, leek, rosemary, thyme, and parsley. Cook, stirring, until the vegetables are tender, 7 to 10 minutes. Add the lamb and cook over high heat, stirring occasionally, until the lamb is nicely browned on all sides, 20 to 30 minutes. Reduce the heat to low and add 2 cups (500 ml | 500 g) water, using a wooden spoon to scrape up any brown bits from the bottom of the pan.

• In a medium bowl, whisk together the eggs and Parmigiano-Reggiano.

• Add the egg mixture to the lamb and use a spatula to scrape and break up the eggs until they are softly scrambled, 3 to 4 minutes. Pour in the *passata* and stir to combine. Serve with crusty bread.

TO DRINK:
A robust and succulent red Montepulciano d'Abruzzo "Chronicon" from Zaccagnini.

Abruzzese tradition holds that during the first year of marriage, a woman should make 365 bottles of *passata*, one for every day of the coming year. If she uses all 365, then she makes the same amount the following year. If she only has 300 bottles left at the end of that first year, then she makes an additional 65 bottles to bring the total number back up to 365 for the second year. Stefania Peduzzi preserves far more of her rich tomato *passata di pomodoro* every summer because she cooks with it so frequently throughout the rest of the year.

For her *Brodetto Abruzzese*, or fish stew, Stefania uses several bottles of her *passata*, rather than a broth of fish trimmings commonly used in other fish stews such as *bouillabaisse* or *cioppino*. The result is an almost sweet, slightly spicy tomato broth that helps showcase and enhance the brininess of the ten varieties of seafood she's added.

The day Stefania decides to make *Brodetto Abruzzese*, her husband, Giancarlo d'Annibale, drives twenty minutes from their home to Pescara—a seaside city on the Adriatic. At the seafood market, Giancarlo asks the owner for fish and shellfish to make *brodetto* for four people, knowing that he will fill a white Styrofoam box with enough of the day's catch to feed a dozen. The box is always different but, depending on the day, Giancarlo returns home with *vongole* (clams), *granghi* (spider crabs), prawns, calamari, *merluzzo* (cod), *pescatrice* (monkfish), *triglia* (red mullet), and more. Stefania cooks the dish in one large pot, or *tegame di coccio*, adding the seafood slowly and layering the briny flavors on top of one another. It's a multisensory experience for her, and she smells as she cooks, noting how each addition changes the scent and enhances the final dish (her favorite addition: shrimp) until the smell is so intoxicating you can't help but bring the pot directly to the table.

Stefania also let me in on a bonus recipe for her *brodetto*: After you've eaten all the fish, toss the leftover sauce with spaghetti and serve it as a second course. This may be the only time you eat pasta as a third (or fourth) course in Italy, and it's well worth bending the cardinal rule for.

Fish Stew from Abruzzo

BRODETTO ABRUZZESE

SERVES 4 TO 6

½ cup (125 ml | 115 g) mild
extra-virgin olive oil

3 garlic cloves, peeled and left whole

1 sweet dried pepper, broken
into pieces

3 pounds (1.4 kg) cleaned mixed
shellfish and fish (such as shell-on
shrimp, squid, octopus, cod fillets,
tilapia fillets, mussels, and small
whole fish)

>>>

• In a large Dutch oven (or a *tegame di coccio*), combine the olive oil and garlic and heat over medium heat until the garlic begins to sizzle, about 2 minutes. Add the dried pepper and stir to combine. Add the squid and octopus and cover the pot. Cook until the squid start to lose their opacity, 5 to 6 minutes. Cut the fish fillets into 2- to 3-inch pieces and add to the pot. Cook until the fish turns white and firms up, 3 to 5 minutes. Tuck the mussels and shrimp into the mixture, making sure they don't sit on top, reduce the heat to low, and cover the pan. Cook until the mussels

>>>

4 cups (950 ml | 900 g) *passata
di pomodoro*

q.b. fine sea salt

Toasted white bread, for serving

open and the shrimp are pink, 2 to 3 minutes. Add the *passata* and stir to combine, then add the small whole fish (if using) and cover the pot again. Raise the heat to medium-high and bring to a boil. Once the stew is boiling, remove the lid and cook, uncovered, until the tomato sauce is very red and there is no more foam, about 5 minutes. Taste the *brodetto* and season with salt, if necessary.

• To serve, place a piece of toasted bread in each bowl. Top with *brodetto* and serve with an additional piece of toasted bread.

TO DRINK:
A rosé Cerasuolo d'Abruzzo from Valentini.

When you think of Toscana, rolling hills covered in olive groves, vineyards, old farmhouses, and villas comes to mind. But in addition to all this, there is a 247-mile-long (397-km) coastline running along the Tyrrhenian Sea that provides coastal Toscana with an abundance of seafood. This simple, regional stew, made with calamari, tomatoes, and red wine, is rich, earthy, and deeply flavored.

Tender calamari is cooked in one of two ways: quickly, for just under a minute; or long and slow, for 60 to 90 minutes. Here, I cook them in a flash. I find the contrast in texture between the quick-cooked squid and long-cooked greens perfect. Served over slices of toast covered in robust sauce, it's the ideal dish for any season. If you can't get your hands on calamari, substitute cooked pieces of cod, clams, or mussels in place of the squid.

Squid with Tomatoes, Bitter Greens, and Red Wine

CALAMARI IN'ZIMINO

SERVES 6

2 cups (450 g) *Soffritto* (page 40)

1 pound (450 g) tomatoes, peeled and diced

1 tablespoon red pepper flakes

q.b. fine sea salt

2 cups (500 ml | 450g) Chianti or other dry red wine

2 bunches (1.3 kg) chard, stems and leaves coarsely chopped

1 large bag (650 g) mixed braising greens, such as kale, beet greens, and collards, coarsely chopped

3 tablespoons chopped garlic chives or scallions

1 pound (450 g) calamari, cleaned and sliced into ½-inch pieces

12 slices rustic Italian bread, toasted

Robust extra-virgin olive oil, for serving

• In a large saucepan, heat the *soffritto* over medium heat until it begins to bubble. Stir in the tomatoes and red pepper flakes, season with salt, and cook until the mixture is warmed through. Pour in the wine and stir to combine, then add the chard and chives or scallions to the pan and cover with a tight-fitting lid. Cook over medium heat until the greens wilt, 3 to 5 minutes, then reduce the heat to low and remove the lid. Cook, uncovered, stirring occasionally, until the leaves and stems are tender, about 20 minutes. Taste the sauce for seasoning. Stir in the calamari, cover the pan with the lid, and immediately turn off the heat. Set aside until the calamari is fully cooked, turns opaque, and begins to curl around the cut edges, about 1 minute.

• To serve, place a heaping spoonful of the stew in each dish, top with a slice of toasted bread, and cover the bread with an additional spoonful of the stew. Drizzle with olive oil and serve immediately.

TO DRINK:
A hearty Tuscan red, such as Rosso di Montalcino from Casanova di Neri or Vino Nobile di Montepulciano from Avignonesi.

Triglie (red mullet) abound in the Mediterranean, but beware! There are two varieties: *triglie* from the sand banks (as they are bottom-feeders, their flavor is a bit muddy), and *triglie* from the *scogli* (deep-water rocky bottom or cliffs), which taste as clean as the deep blue sea.

About the size of red trout, rock *triglie* are briny, easy to debone, and leave you with so much bright flavor in your mouth that you feel as if you just went for a swim in the Mediterranean.

My friend Gianfranco Becchina, who lives on the outskirts of Castelvetrano, a small city in southwestern Sicily, is the producer of an incredible, intense *olio verde*. He is also the man who introduced me to the best *triglie* I've ever had at La Bettola in Mazara del Vallo. The recipe below is my at-home take on the chef, Pietro Sardo's, dish. I hope you enjoy it as much as I did!

Rock Red Mullet with Crushed Cherry Tomatoes and Caperberries

TRIGLIE DI SCOGLIO ALLA GRIGLIA CON POMODORI PACHINO SCHIACCIATI E CUCUNCI

SERVES 4

q.b. robust extra-virgin olive oil, preferably Sicilian

4 cups (1100 g) coarse sea salt

Four 2-pound (900 g) large red mullet fillets (branzino or red snapper may be substituted), cleaned and patted dry

2 cups (300 g) very small cherry tomatoes, halved

½ cup Sicilian caperberries packed in olive oil or salt, rinsed and dried if salt-packed, coarsely chopped

2 sprigs Sicilian oregano blossom

q.b. fine sea salt

TO DRINK:
A beautiful "Rajàh" from Gorghi Tondi. This wine is made from Zibibbo, but is dry and scented with orange blossoms and citrus.

• Preheat the oven to 500°F (260°C). (You want it blasting hot.)

• Line a baking dish large enough to fit the fish with parchment paper and drizzle with olive oil. Make a little bed for the fish with the coarse sea salt.

• Rub the inside and outside of the fish fillets with olive oil and place on top of the salt bed. Cover the pan with aluminum foil and bake until the fish is firm to the touch, about 15 minutes.

• In a medium bowl, stir together the tomatoes, caper berries, and oregano. Season with fine sea salt and drizzle in a generous few tablespoons of olive oil, sprinkle with the oregano blossoms and fine sea salt, and cover with the robust olive oil. Set aside, stirring occasionally, while the fish roasts.

• Remove the *triglie* from the oven, discard the aluminum foil, and, with the help of a spatula, carefully flip the fish. Drizzle each fillet with olive oil and cook longer, 1 to 5 minutes, depending on the size of the fish.

• Serve the *triglie* topped with additional olive oil and the tomato-oregano sauce.

The island of Pantelleria is one of the most fascinating islands in the Mediterranean. Although technically part of the Sicilian region, it is closer to North Africa than to Sicily. The island is made of black lava, and the houses are made with the black lava rocks with very ornate whitewashed domes to keep the inside of the house naturally cool during the blistering summer months. You truly feel as if you are in another country.

Many, many years ago, a friend who had a vacation home in Pantelleria made this for me, and I've been making it ever since. The complexity of flavor between the tuna, tomatoes, olives, and oregano is thrilling each and every time. After many tries, I think the secret to keeping the final dish soft and succulent is to cook it very slowly and very long in an earthenware dish (see Resources, page 352). A 10-inch dish fits four thick slices of tuna perfectly, and it's beautiful to serve directly at the table.

Pantelleria-Style Slow-Braised Tuna

TONNO ALLA PANTESCA

SERVES 4

3 tablespoons (45 ml | 40 g) cooking extra-virgin olive oil

1 large red onion, finely chopped

2 small whole chile peppers, or 1 teaspoon red pepper flakes

2 cups (500 ml | 540 g) *passata di pomodoro*

2 cups (500 ml | 500 g) robust dry red wine, such as a Nero d'Avola, plus more as needed

4 (½-pound | 225-g) tuna fillets, each about 1 inch thick, rinsed and dried

½ cup (60 g) Nocellara or Castelvetrano olives, pitted and sliced

¼ cup (35 g) salted capers, rinsed and dried

2 sprigs dry Sicilian oregano blossoms

q.b. fine sea salt

• Pour the olive oil into the earthenware dish (or a 10-inch ovenproof skillet) and place over medium heat. Add the onion and chile peppers and sauté until the onion is transparent but not golden, about 7 minutes. Pour in the *passata* and bring to a simmer. Pour in the wine and simmer until the sauce thickens and reduces by about half, 10 to 15 minutes.

• Carefully add the tuna fillets to the pan, covering them gently with the sauce. Add the olives and capers and, again with the spoon, submerge them in the sauce. Sprinkle with the oregano and remove the pan from the heat. Cover the dish with aluminum foil and bake for 20 minutes. Remove the foil and, if the sauce has reduced too much, carefully whisk in a bit more wine. Bake, uncovered, until the sides of the pan have a nice, almost burnt crust and the tuna is cooked through, about 10 minutes. Remove the pan from the oven and set aside to cool slightly before serving.

TO DRINK:
A bold, super-intense, and gutsy SP68 Rosso 2015 from Arianna Occhipinti (a legendary female winemaker in Sicily!).

One of my favorite Italian singers is Paolo Conte. His amazing little song "Pesce Veloce del Baltico" sings of polenta with salt cod:

Pesce Veloce del Baltico	**Fast Fish of the Baltic**
dice il menù, che contorno ha?	**says the menu, what's the side dish?**
"Torta di mais" e poi servono	**"Corn Cake" and they serve**
polenta e baccalà	**Polenta with Cod**
cucina povera e umile	**Poor and humble kitchen**
fatta d'ingenuità	**made of naïveté**
caduta nel gorgo perfido	**fallen into the whirlpool**
della celebrità	**of treacherous celebrity**

Baccalà is for the graduate fish eater. If you love anchovies, bottarga, or anything fishy, you will certainly enjoy its bold, complex flavors. *Baccalà*, as Paolo Conte says, has had a bit of a renaissance, and a dish that was typically reserved for the poor now has celebrity status and a place at restaurant tables. This version with prunes and tomato sauce—which I've had many times in Tuscany—is a variation of a theme that can be found all over Italy: You prepare the salt cod with something to neutralize it, mask it, or make it sweet and salty. For another version, use dried figs in place of the prunes (*baccalà con i ficchi*), or do like the lovely Chiara of Cammillo in Florence and simply boil it, serve with perfectly cooked chickpeas and top with enormous amount of *olio nuovo*.

I serve this with polenta as an homage to Paolo Conte, but I also love it alongside Mashed Potatoes (page 57).

Salt Cod with Prunes
BACCALÀ CON LE PRUGNE

SERVES 6 TO 8

1¾ pounds (795 g) salt cod, soaked overnight (be sure to change the water frequently during soaking)

1 cup (30 g) fresh herbs, such as rosemary sprigs, parsley, sage, and fresh bay

1 cup (250 ml | 250 g) dry white wine

2 tablespoons (32g) *estratto di pomodoro* (tomato paste)

>>>

• Check the soft, soaked cod for bones as if you are trying to find a splinter in your finger or the palm of your hand. Use a pair of tweezers to remove any bones, then, using a very sharp knife, remove the skin and discard.

• Place enough water in the bottom of a pot to come 1 inch up the sides of the pan. Add the herbs. Place the cod pieces in a steamer basket and set it in the pot. Bring to a simmer, then reduce the heat to low, cover the pot, and steam until the cod is shiny and soft to the touch, about 10 minutes. To test for doneness, cut into one of the pieces and feel if it is warm inside.

q.b. cooking extra-virgin olive oil

¼ cup (60 g) *Soffritto* (page 40)

1 cup (250 ml | 270 g) *passata di pomodoro*

10 (80 g) dry prunes, pitted and halved

• While the cod is steaming, set a small saucepan over medium heat and whisk together the wine and *estratto* until the *estratto* has completely dissolved and the wine is warm, about 3 minutes.

• In a medium skillet, combine the olive oil and *soffritto* and heat over medium heat until the *soffritto* is warmed through. Pour in the *passata* and, once it starts to bubble, add the warm wine-*estratto* mixture and stir well to combine. Cook until the sauce has slightly thickened and reduced, about 7 minutes. Stir in the prunes and simmer on very low heat until the *baccalà* is ready.

• Once the cod is ready, use a spatula to very gently transfer the cod to the prune sauce. Snuggle the pieces in and use a spoon to baste them with some of the juices. Cover the pan and set aside for 20 minutes. Serve warm.

TO DRINK:
A succulent Sagrantino di Montefalco from Umbria from Arnaldo Caprai. The complex and dark fruity notes of this wine complement the salty and sweet vigor of the cod.

This is a very simple version of a classic and usually quite complicated dish: the *Timballo Del Gattopardo*. Savory-sweet *timballo* embodies all the complex flavors that are so uniquely Sicilian: pine nuts, currants, Castelvetrano or Nocellara olives, and *cacio ragusano* (a strong, salty Sicilian cheese similar to very aged pecorino). Incredibly, this tort manages to combine fish and cheese, effectively debasing the myth that the two don't go together. I love to make this *timballo* for dinner on a Friday night when I am home in Florence, for most of my friends observe the tradition of "Fish on Fridays," and this dish is a one-dish meal and a true celebration. I especially love to serve this dish in the winter months after a course of the Blood Orange, Lemon, and Red Onion Salad (page 88).

Swordfish Torte

TIMBALLO DI PESCE SPADA

MAKES ONE 9-INCH *TIMBALLO*

PASTA FROLLA SALATA
SALTY PASTRY DOUGH

3 cups (450 g) "00" flour (see Resources, page 352), plus more for rolling

q.b. fine sea salt

q.b. freshly grated nutmeg

16 tablespoons (226 g) very cold unsalted butter, cut into ¼-inch cubes

4 medium eggs

3 medium egg yolks

FILLING

2 tablespoons (20 g) durum wheat flour (Semolina)

1 pound (450 g) swordfish fillet, skin removed, fillet washed and dried

q.b. cooking extra-virgin olive oil

3 tablespoons (70 g) *Soffritto* (page 40)

2 cups (550 g) *passata di pomodoro*

1 tablespoon (8 g) toasted Italian pine nuts

>>>

- **To make the dough**: Chill a large bowl in the refrigerator for 20 minutes.

- First add the salt and nutmeg to the flour in the chilled bowl, then working quickly, add the butter and using clean fingers, pinch the butter into the flour until the mixture resembles polenta or a coarse-ground cornmeal. Add the eggs and egg yolks and mix until thoroughly incorporated. Gather the dough into a ball. Dust a clean surface with flour and, using the bottom of your hand, knead the dough for a few minutes until it is smooth and shiny, about 5 minutes.

- **Separate the dough into two parts**: one about two-thirds of the dough, the other about one-third. Flatten them into ½-inch-thick rounds, wrap in plastic wrap, and refrigerate for at least 1 hour and up to 2 days.

- **To make the filling**: Scatter the flour in a shallow dish and dredge the swordfish fillet thoroughly in the flour.

- In a medium skillet, combine 1 tablespoon of the olive oil and the *soffritto* and heat over medium heat until the *soffritto* is warmed through. Pour in the *passata* and once it starts to bubble, add the pine nuts, currants, capers, and olives and season with salt as needed. Set aside until you are ready to assemble the *timballo*.

1 tablespoon (8 g) dried red currants

1 tablespoon (9 g) salted capers, rinsed and dried

¼ cup (30 g) pitted Nocellara or Castelvetrano olives

½ cup (100 g) *cacio ragusano* or a very aged Sicilian pecorino cheese, cut into ½-inch cubes

1 tablespoon (15 g) unsalted butter

1 large egg

TO DRINK:
A glass of Nerello Cappuccio, an amazing wine from Bennanti in the Mount Etna area.

- In a medium skillet, heat 3 tablespoons of the olive oil over medium heat. Once the oil is hot, add the swordfish and fry until the fish is golden on both sides, about 5 minutes per side. Transfer the fish to a cutting board and cut it into 1-inch cubes. (As always, I prefer surprises when I eat, so I do not make the cubes equal—you might get some big pieces or small pieces in every slice.) Set aside until you are ready to assemble the *timballo*.

- Preheat the oven to 375°F (180°C). Generously butter a 9-inch springform pan.

- Sprinkle a clean surface with flour. Remove the larger piece of dough from the fridge and, working quickly, roll the dough out with a rolling pin to a 14-inch-wide circle about ¼-inch thick. Line the pan with the dough. Using a fork, poke holes all around the bottom and edges of the dough.

- Add the swordfish in an even layer. Stir the pecorino into the cooled sauce and spoon it into the pan, filling in the spaces between the swordfish; you should see spots of fish, cheese, green, and a bit of everything all over the pan.

- Roll out the second disc of dough into an 11-inch-wide circle and place it over the top of the *timballo*. Use a paring knife to trim the edges. Use your index fingers to press against the seams and seal the edges together. If you have extra dough, make small flowery decorations or roll them like spaghetti and layer them across the top of the pie in a decorative pattern.

- Whisk the egg until frothy in a small bowl and, using a pastry brush, brush the *timballo* with the egg wash. Bake until the crust is golden and firm, 35 to 40 minutes.

- Remove the *timballo* from the oven and set aside to cool for a few minutes before unmolding and serving.

This vegetarian dish is the perfect winter dish. Inspired by the flavors from the Valtellina, a high valley that follows the Swiss border in Northern Lombardia, the combination of cabbage, farro, and fontina is just right for a cold winter day. You can also place the rolls on a well-buttered baking dish dusted with plenty of Parmigiano-Reggiano and cover with a light *besciamella* sauce. See Lasagna (page 167), and bake in the oven as you would *Pasticcio* (see page 167).

Savoy Cabbage and Fontina Rolls

INVOLTINI CAVOLO VERZA E FONTINA

SERVES 4

CABBAGE

¼ cup (60 ml | 55 g) mild extra-virgin olive oil

10 large savoy cabbage leaves

1 cup (200 g) cooked farro (see page 193)

1 large egg, lightly whisked

¼ cup (40 g) ¼-inch-dice Italian fontina cheese

¼ cup (5 g) chopped fresh flat-leaf parsley

1 tablespoon (2 g) fresh sage

1 tablespoon (2 g) fresh rosemary

SAUCE

1 cup (160 g) ¼-inch-dice Italian fontina cheese

1 cup (250 ml | 225 g) heavy cream

2 tablespoons (10 g) grated Parmigiano-Reggiano cheese

• *To make the cabbage:* Arrange one oven rack in the bottom third of the oven and a second rack in the middle. Preheat the oven to 350°F (180°C). Oil a 9 x 13-inch baking dish generously.

• Bring a large pot of salted water to a boil. Fill a large bowl with ice and water. Add the cabbage leaves to the boiling water and blanch until they are wilted and soft, 2 to 3 minutes. Drain the cabbage and transfer to the prepared ice bath. Dry one of the cabbage leaves and thinly slice. Place in a medium bowl along with the farro, egg, fontina, parsley, sage, and rosemary. Season with salt and pepper.

• Place a drained and dried cabbage leaf on a clean work surface and use a sharp knife to remove the hard triangular rib from the base of the leaf. Pile 2 tablespoons of the filling near the rib edge of the leaf and roll up toward the outer edge, tucking in the sides, as if you're making an egg roll. Arrange the cabbage rolls, seam-side down, in the prepared baking dish. Fill and roll the remaining cabbage leaves.

- Place a large baking dish on the lower rack in the oven. Fill it three-quarters full with hot water. (This will ensure a warm, steamy environment so the filled cabbages won't dry out while baking.) Put the dish with the cabbage rolls on the middle rack and bake until they are dry and slightly firm to the touch, about 30 minutes.

- **To make the sauce:** In a small saucepan, combine the fontina and cream and cook over medium heat, stirring frequently and taking care that the mixture does not boil, until the cheese has melted and the cream is hot. Strain through a fine-mesh sieve and drizzle over the baked cabbages before serving.

TO DRINK:

A Pinot Nero made in the Dolomites by my friends Fiorentino Sandri and Mario Pojer. The wine has the color of an eggplant, and wonderful notes of spices and tobacco. Or any other Pinot Noir or Lagrein grape–based wine from the Dolomites, such as the one by Frank Haas.

Just before the first frost of the year, there's the briefest of moments when the green tomato plants are just about to end and the first white wine grapes (such as Malvasia Bianca, Trebbiano, and San Colombano) start to ripen. This perfect connection between the end of one season and the beginning of another is the ideal time to make *Pomodori Verdi Con L'uva*.

My friend and guru, Carlo Cioni of Da Delfina, introduced me to this short-season recipe and explains it as such: "Nobody but a wise *contadino* [peasant] can get it right. You never waste anything, and nothing goes to waste. This to me is the purest example of the *economia rurale,* or for a lack of a better word: a cuisine that saves and preserves, that cherishes anything that grows and makes full use of it."

The combination of crispy acidic tomatoes and sweet white grapes (using ones with seeds adds a touch of nuttiness to the dish) is ideal alongside Oven Roasted Pork (page 239) or Mashed Potatoes (page 57). For even more flavor, spread a few tablespoons of *Soffritto* (page 40) or tomato paste on the bottom of the baking pan.

Fried and Baked Green Tomatoes with Grapes

POMODORI VERDI CON L'UVA

SERVES 4 TO 6

q.b. cooking extra-virgin olive oil, plus more to brush the pan

1 cup (160 g) all-purpose flour

q.b. coarse sea salt and crushed Tellicherry black peppercorns

1 tablespoon *Soffritto* (page 40)

4 very firm green tomatoes, cut crosswise into 1½-inch-thick slices, tops and bottoms finely diced and reserved

3 cups (600 g) white grapes with seeds (such as Malvasia Bianca, Chardonnay, or Sauvignon Blanc): 1 cup halved, 2 cups left whole

2 cups (500 ml | 500 g) fruity white wine (such as Trebbiano, Malvasia Bianca, or Vermentino)

1 teaspoon *estratto di pomodoro* (tomato paste)

- Preheat the oven to 350°F (180°C). Brush a baking sheet with olive oil. Line a platter with paper towels.

- Put the flour in a medium shallow bowl and season with salt and pepper. Dredge the tomato slices in the flour mixture.

- Pour olive oil into a large straight-sided skillet to a depth of ¼ inch. Heat the oil over medium-high heat. Once the oil is hot, add the tomato slices and fry until golden on one side. Add additional olive oil, if needed, and flip to fry on the other side until golden. Transfer the tomatoes to the paper towel–lined platter and set aside to drain.

- Heat a small saucepan over medium heat. Add 1 tablespoon of the olive oil and the *soffritto*. Once the *soffritto* is heated through, add the halved grapes and the reserved tomato ends. Pour in ½ cup (125 ml | 125 g) of the wine and cook until the alcohol has evaporated, about 3 minutes. Reduce the heat to low, cover the pan, and simmer until the grapes are very

soft. Stir in the *estratto di pomodoro*, then remove the pan from the heat and press the mixture through a *passatutto* (food mill). Taste for seasoning (it should be fairly acidic).

· Drizzle some olive oil in a large baking dish large enough to fit all the tomatoes. Lay them in one layer, leaving plenty of space to place the white wine grapes in between.

· Scatter the whole grapes all over the tomatoes, then drizzle with the thick grape-tomato sauce. Pour the remaining wine over

the top and bake until the grapes are shriveled and the tomatoes are golden brown, using a spoon to occasionally baste the tomatoes with the liquids, about 30 minutes. Serve hot.

TO DRINK:
A bottle of Barco Reale di Carmignano from Villa Artimino. The wine is mostly Sangiovese, which gives it a nice acidity, but it has a small percentage of Cabernet Sauvignon to offer a nice backbone and structure to stand up to the acidity of this dish.

When the first small tender zucchini with their blossom still attached arrive at the market in early spring, I rush home to make this dish.

The simple combination of two eggs and seasonal vegetables is a very typical dish in Florence. At Ristorante Sostanza, they cook the eggs in a *tegamino* with half a fried artichoke directly over hot coals. My friend Chiara at Ristorante Cammillo does the same—again with just two eggs—and serves them with a very thin layer of porcini mushrooms or thinly sliced artichoke hearts, and—if they're in season—fresh white truffles.

My friend Connie loves this dish, but she doesn't like runny eggs, so I cook hers a little longer. Her beautiful daughters, Paulina and Fabbiene, like it runny as I do, and we have our own, sopping the eggs up with crusty Italian bread. Yet another friend of mine in Italy, Elizabeth Minchilli, who lives in Rome, caught me on video doing this dish at her beautiful home, and you can see it today in her blog, elizabethminchilliinrome.com.

Handkerchief of Zucchini and Its Blossoms

FAZZOLETTO DI ZUCCHINE E FIORI

SERVES 2 TO 4 AS AN ANTIPASTO

2 medium or 4 small zucchini

4 zucchini blossoms

2 large eggs

q.b. fine sea salt and crushed Tellicherry black peppercorns

1 cup (250 ml | 230 g) cooking extra-virgin olive oil

q.b. fresh basil leaves

q.b. fresh flat-leaf parsley leaves

½ cup (70 g) grated Parmigiano-Reggiano cheese

- Line a plate with paper towels and set aside. Cut the zucchini in half crosswise, then in thirds lengthwise, creating triangular-shaped sticks each about 5 inches long. Using a sharp paring knife, make an incision in each of the blossoms and remove the pistil and stem, then thinly slice.

- Put the eggs in a small bowl. With the point of a sharp paring knife, cut the yolks in a few places, mixing them lightly but keeping the yolks and the whites somewhat separated. Season with salt and pepper.

- Heat a 7-inch nonstick pan over medium-high heat. Add ½ cup (125 ml | 115 g) of the olive oil. Once hot, place the zucchini sticks in the pan and fry until al dente, turning so one side is very golden, one is lightly golden, and one not at all, 8 to 10 minutes. Carefully transfer the zucchini to the paper towel–lined plate and discard the olive oil (it is bitter and will overwhelm the delicate flavor of the eggs and zucchini).

>>>

- Add the remaining olive oil to the pan. Once it is hot, pour in the broken eggs, starting from the middle and slowly pouring until you get the eggs evenly all the way to the edges. Turn the flame off right away and start adding the zucchini sticks, pointing them toward the center of the egg *fazzoletto* as radii and making sure they all have different sides facing up. Sprinkle in the zucchini blossoms, basil, and parsley leaves, and then generously cover with the Parmigiano-Reggiano—especially on the spots where you can see more of the runny egg (the cheese will melt into it and become deliciously runny).

- Carefully slide the *fazzoletto* onto a large round serving dish, cut it into slices, and serve immediately.

TO DRINK:
A crisp glass of Prosecco from Mionetto.

I purposely make extra spaghetti in order to make this frittata. It is a perfect lunch when I'm working from home and need a quick meal. It's also delicious served cold, cut into wedges, at the beach or as part of a summertime buffet. Toast the spaghetti until very golden and nutty and serve alongside *Misticanza di Firenze* (page 76) for a complete meal.

Frittata of Spaghetti, Pancetta, and Beans

FRITTATA DI SPAGHETTI, PANCETTA E FAGIOLI

SERVES 2

½ cup (170 g) diced pancetta

3 large eggs

½ cup (50 g) finely grated Pecorino Romano cheese

2 tablespoons (30 ml | 27 g) cooking extra-virgin olive oil

1 cup (141 g) cooked spaghetti

½ cup (105 g) slow-cooked beans (see page 29)

q.b. crushed Tellicherry black peppercorns

TO DRINK:
A fruity red wine from Abruzzo, such as a Cerasuolo from Emidio Pepe.

• Line a plate with paper towels. In a large skillet, cook the pancetta over medium heat, stirring often, until browned and crisp, about 5 minutes. Use a slotted spoon to transfer the pancetta to the paper towel–lined plate. Discard or reserve the excess fat.

• In a medium bowl, gently whisk the eggs and cheese with a fork—try to keep the yolks and egg whites separate so you have a beautiful array of colors in the frittata when it is cooked.

• Turn the broiler on high and heat an ovenproof nonstick pan over medium-high flame. Add the olive oil and spaghetti to the pan and cook, stirring occasionally, until you start to see a little color and crispness develop on the spaghetti, 7 to 8 minutes. Spread the spaghetti as widely and evenly as you can on the bottom of the pan and lower the heat. Add the beans and the pancetta, distributing them evenly over the pasta and season with black pepper.

• Pour in the eggs slowly and evenly and return the pan to medium-high heat. Cook until the edges are golden and crispy, 5 to 7 minutes. Place the skillet under the broiler and cook until the top is just set, 1 to 2 minutes. Remove the pan from the oven, set a large plate on top of the skillet and, with the help of oven mitts, carefully turn the skillet over and unmold the frittata.

• Cut into wedges and serve immediately, or let cool completely and serve at room temperature.

Disclaimer: I don't like turkey. While we're at it, I don't like chicken, either.

So what is this American bird doing in an authentic Italian cookbook? This is evidence of the last "Great Food Invasion" that Italy has undergone: the American Food Invasion! In Tuscany and around Italy, the turkey has become another form of white meat, and I see many people in Florence buying *fessa di tacchino* (thinly sliced turkey breast), which they use in place of veal when making saltimbocca or breading them to make a perfect Milanese.

I was first served this dish in a farmhouse outside of Pomarance, in Tuscany. The house had no electricity and you could only arrive there by foot or by horse. The eightysomething-year-old *nonna* made us lunch and served the turkey straight from her smoky, wood-fired oven.

I made the recipe many times for many visiting American friends at home in Florence, but the most memorable time was when my dear friend, the late Judy Rodgers, chef and owner of Zuni Café in San Francisco, came to stay. Judy was shocked by the dish and couldn't stop eating it. She asked for the recipe, and I told her that I have only had it in homes since it's a "one-shot" dish—not something you can put on the menu and deliver throughout the evening. But Judy being Judy—the most inquisitive, talented, and truly amazing chef I've ever met—drew forth her "I can make that work" mentality and figured out a way to do it. Sure enough, the dish made it to Zuni's menu and gained much approval among her faithful clients.

This dish is not pretty. In fact, quite the contrary. It's white, and the curds are ugly; I don't imagine any food stylist or photographer can make it look worthy of a cookbook, let alone serve it in any fancy way. At home, I serve the turkey sliced on a white platter, and surround it on both sides with the roasted potatoes, or with potatoes on one side and warm beans on the other. Using a slotted spoon, I gather as many of the fluffy, succulent curds from the pot as I can and pour them, along with a little milk, all over the turkey. A final drizzle of mild extra-virgin olive oil and it's ready to serve—for Thanksgiving or otherwise!

Turkey Breast Cooked in Milk with Herbs

TACCHINO AL LATTE

SERVES 4 TO 6

2 tablespoons (30 ml | 27 g) cooking extra-virgin olive oil

1 (2-pound | 900-g) turkey breast, deboned, tied up with kitchen twine, and strung with 2 whole rosemary sprigs

• In a Dutch oven large enough to hold the turkey breast, heat the olive oil over high heat. Add the turkey and reduce the heat to medium. Sear until the turkey is lightly golden on all sides, about 5 minutes per side.

• Pour in the milk and cream, making sure the turkey breast is covered by at least one or two fingers' worth

16 cups (3785 ml | 3629 g) organic
whole milk, plus more as needed

1 cup (250 ml | 225 g) heavy cream

4 fresh sage leaves

2 fresh or dried Tuscan bay leaves

2 rosemary sprigs

1 tablespoon fine sea salt

1 generous tablespoon coarsely
crushed Tellicherry black
peppercorns

TO DRINK:
I love this dish with a very rustic
Morello di Scansano from the
Maremma in Toscana, such as
the one from Tenuta di Belguardo
from my friends the Mazzei family.
The earthy and fruity notes of the
Sangiovese grape from this part
of Tuscany complement the creamy
notes of the milk curds beautifully.

of liquid, as it will reduce as the turkey cooks. Add the sage, bay leaves, and rosemary. Season with 1 tablespoon of salt and the pepper, cover the pan, and bring to a boil. Once the milk starts to boil, remove the lid and reduce the heat to maintain a very gentle simmer. Cook, flipping the breast occasionally and using a wooden spoon to gently scrape the sides and bottoms of the pot. (Unless you are continuously stirring, the milk may develop a crust underneath, which is okay—just make sure you don't scrape it directly before serving.) Cook the turkey until it is slightly warm to the touch and a meat thermometer inserted into the center of the breast reads 155°F (68°C), 30 to 40 minutes.

· Preheat the oven to 185°F (85°C).

· Remove the turkey from the milk and place it in a medium baking dish. Cover with aluminum foil and place in the oven to keep warm. Place the Dutch oven with the milk-cream mixture over medium-high heat and cook, stirring occasionally to create more curds, for 10 minutes.

· Remove the turkey from the oven, remove and discard the strings, and slice the turkey on an angle into ¼-inch-thick slices. Arrange on a platter and spoon the curds all over the turkey. Drizzle with some of the milk, then a small drizzle of olive oil. Transfer the remaining curds and milk to a bowl or small pitcher and serve immediately.

Faraona means "pharaoh's hen" and when you see them, they really do look like a pharaoh. I am extremely fond of this bird. The meat is elegantly dark, very lean, and cooks very fast. The first time I tried this tasty bird was at Ristorante Da Delfina, where Carlo had very simply roasted it in the oven and topped it with gravy made from deglazing the roasting pan with *vin santo*. This is the basic way I roast a bird, which is very similar to what I do with *Arista di Maiale* (page 239).

Guinea Fowl Braised with Pearl Onions and Red Peppers

FARAONA BRASATA CON CIPOLLINE E PEPERONI

SERVES 4

1 (2-pound | 900-g) guinea fowl, quartered

q.b. coarse sea salt and crushed Tellicherry black peppercorns

4 tablespoons (60 ml | 54 g) cooking extra-virgin olive oil

6 garlic cloves, unpeeled

6 fresh bay leaves

2 rosemary sprigs

2 sage sprigs

1 cup (250 ml | 225 g) *Peperonata* (page 000)

2 cups (500 ml | 450 g) *Cipolline in Agrodolce* (page 302)

1 tablespoon (15 ml | 15 g) dry red wine

TO DRINK:

A delicious Barbera from Odero in Piemonte, which has a fruity acidity that will help accompany the sweetness of the onions, the smokiness of the *peperonata*, and the succulent dark meaty flavors of the *faraona*.

• Preheat the oven to 500°F (260°C). Season the guinea fowl with salt and pepper. In a large cast-iron skillet, heat 2 tablespoons of the olive oil over high heat until very hot. Add the guinea fowl quarters, skin-side down and cook, without moving them, until the skin is browned and crisp, about 5 minutes. Flip the pieces over and cook for 5 minutes more. Transfer to a plate and discard the rendered fat from the pan. Use a paper towel to wipe out the pan and return it to the stovetop.

• Add the remaining 2 tablespoons olive oil, the garlic, bay, rosemary, and sage to the pan. Set the browned guinea fowl on top, skin-side up, and place the pan in the oven. Roast until the guinea fowl is cooked through and a thermometer reads 155°F (68°C), 20 to 25 minutes. Transfer the guinea fowl to a plate and cover with aluminum foil. Remove the garlic cloves and carefully peel them, removing the soft, creamy roasted insides.

• Place the cast-iron skillet over high heat and pour in the wine to deglaze the pan. Cook until the wine is emulsified, about 5 minutes. Add the Agrodolce and the roasted vegetables and heat over medium heat until warmed through, about 5 minutes, then pour over the guinea fowl. Serve immediately.

My grandma had a little secret when cooking *frataglie* (innards). She would cover all organ meats (especially sweetbreads, kidneys, tripe, and tongue) with very cold ice water, add a fistful of coarse sea salt and plenty of vinegar, and marinate them for at least 4 hours in order to "purge" them. She said the brine-vinegar bath took away most of the ureic flavor that can turn people off to eating organ meats. With her brine, she also cut down the cook time, since the salt and the vinegar partially cure the meat. I also follow her advice to serve the livers barely cooked—still pink inside—over soft, creamy white polenta, a plating very typical of the Veneto-Friuli area. They are also delicious served on a bed of a *Risotto in Bianco* (page 179).

The first written recipe for liver dates to 1790 in the *L'Apicio Moderno* by Francesco Leonardi and calls for milk-fed veal liver and sweet onions from Chioggia (though I have been told numerous times that it was traditionally made with the pork liver).

Venetian-Style Chicken Livers with Onions

FIGÀ ÀEA VENESSIANA (IN AUTHENTIC VENETIAN DIALECT)
FEGATINI ALLA VENEZIANA, MA . . . DI POLLO

SERVES 4

1 pound (450 g) chicken livers and hearts, rinsed and fat removed

5 tablespoons (75 ml | 75 g) white wine vinegar

2 tablespoons (20 g) coarse sea salt, plus more as needed

2 tablespoons (30 ml | 27 g) mild extra-virgin olive oil

8 tablespoons (113 g) unsalted butter

4 medium sweet white onions, thinly sliced

q.b. crushed Tellicherry black peppercorns

q.b. fresh flat-leaf parsley leaves, coarsely torn

Cooked polenta (page 203) or *Risotto in Bianco* (page 179), for serving

· In a large bowl, combine the livers and hearts with 1 cup (250 ml | 250 g) cold water, 4 tablespoons (60 ml | 60 g) of the vinegar, the salt, and ice. Refrigerate for 4 to 5 hours. Drain and dry the livers and hearts with a towel.

· In a large skillet, combine the olive oil and the butter and heat over medium-high heat until the butter melts. Add the onions, cover, and cook until they start to soften, about 5 minutes. Reduce the heat to medium-low and cook until the onions are very soft and tender, about 5 minutes more. Add the livers and hearts and stir to combine. Pour in the remaining 1 tablespoon vinegar and season with salt and pepper. Cover and cook, stirring occasionally, until the livers are browned and firm to the touch, about 7 minutes. (If the livers start to become dry, add a splash of white wine or water to the pan.)

· Sprinkle with parsley and serve immediately with polenta or risotto.

TO DRINK:
A nice red from the Veneto, such as Palazzo della Torre from my friends Marilisa and Silvia Allegrini.

We need to talk about rabbit. . . . Many of my friends in Florence prefer it and eat it more often than chicken. However, the very mention of it to *stranieri* (literally "strangers," but meaning foreigners) elicits an *awww* and a sad look—I think Walt Disney had something to do with it. However, when it comes to lean white meat, there is nothing like it. Grill it like my friend Chiara does at Trattoria Cammillo—over very hot coals and served with lots of rosemary and copious amounts of robust extra-virgin olive oil—or make it into a stew—the most famous of which being *alla cacciatora*, or "hunter's style," made with plenty of Chianti, tomatoes, and olives.

Here, I braise it in Aleatico. Think of Aleatico as a sweet red Moscato wine. It's lightly ruby red (almost like very light Pinot Noir), aromatic, and different from any red wine you've ever had. It tastes as if it has been infused with cinnamon, allspice, nutmeg, and pepper, but that's just the grape! The grape works well with the sweetness of figs and rosemary-infused rabbit.

Rabbit Stewed in Aleatico with Figs from the Island of Elba

CONIGLIO STUFATO ALL'ALEATICO DELL'ISOLA D'ELBA CON FICHI

SERVES 6 TO 8

MARINADE

2 (2½-pound | 1134 g) rabbits, cut into 8 pieces each

4 rosemary sprigs

2 fresh bay leaves

3 garlic cloves, thinly sliced

Zest of 1 lemon

¼ cup (60 ml | 54 g) mild extra-virgin olive oil

q.b. fine sea salt and cracked Tellicherry peppercorns

>>>

- *To make the marinade:* In a large airtight container combine the rabbit, rosemary, bay, garlic, lemon zest, and olive oil. Season with salt and pepper. Use your hands to coat the rabbit pieces with the mixture then cover and refrigerate overnight. If you can remember, try to mix it every now and then while it marinates.

- About 2 hours before you are ready to cook and serve the rabbit, remove it from the fridge and, using your hands, remove all the marinade. Transfer the rabbit pieces to a clean plate.

- Heat 3 tablespoons of the olive oil in a large, high-sided skillet over high heat. Add the rabbit, a few pieces at a time, taking care not to crowd the pan. Sear until all sides are evenly golden in color, about 10 minutes. Transfer the seared pieces to an oven-proof dish and cover with foil. Repeat until all the rabbit pieces have been browned.

>>>

SAUCE

½ cup (125 ml | 115 g) cooking extra-virgin olive oil

2 tablespoons (60 g) *Soffritto* (page 40)

3 cups (750 ml | 750 g) Aleatico di Toscana (Elba, Pitigilano, or Sorano)

15 fresh bay leaves

q.b. fine sea salt and cracked Tellicherry peppercorns

10 (310 g) fresh black figs, quartered

• *To make the sauce*: Since rabbit is so lean, you will not have to deglaze the pan. I like to use a piece of paper towel to gently remove the cooking oil from the pan, taking care not to scrape the beautiful crunchy bits stuck to the bottom.

• Return the same pan to a medium flame, add the remaining oil and the *soffritto* and heat until warmed through. Return the rabbit to the pan in an even layer and pour the wine in to cover the rabbit. (If there is not enough wine, add some water to cover it.) Add the bay leaves, season with salt and pepper, and bring to a boil. Lower the heat to very low, cover the pan and gently simmer until the rabbit is cooked through, about 30 minutes. Check the rabbit occasionally, turning the pieces to make sure they cook evenly or adding more water if the rabbit isn't covered. Once the rabbit is cooked, layer the figs on top of the rabbit and cover the pan. Let steam for 3 minutes, then serve warm.

TO DRINK:
A wonderful bottle of Nambrot, a Tuscan wine from my friend Ginevra Venerosi-Pesciolini of Tenuta di Ghizzano.

6

To Accompany

PER ACCONPAGNARE

While an excellent one-dish meal

(*Gató di Patate Rustico*, page 221, *Timballo di Pesce Spada*, page 272, or *Brodetto Abruzzese*, page 261, for example) is nothing to scoff at, a well-executed side dish can elevate the main course and, at times, be the best thing on the table!

From potatoes to beans to every kind of vegetable and salads, hundreds of little side dishes seem to fly out of restaurant and home kitchens when serving a *pietanza*, particularly when either fish or meat are the main course of the event. There are too many to include (my friend David Lebovitz says there should be a book of only *contorni*!) but these recipes are my favorites, and from Stewed Potatoes to a thoughtfully prepared *Caponata* (page 313), I imagine you'll find a thing or five to love as well.

Umido, which means "stewed" in Italian, refers to cooking food by adding some liquid, then once it has been absorbed, adding more. The technique is similar to making risotto, except that potatoes are used in place of rice and the pot is covered. When the potatoes have absorbed the *brodetto*, another ladleful is poured in. Serve with grilled steak, fish, or with *Il Peposo* (page 255), as Patrizio does at Capezzana in Carmignano, Tuscany. Patrizio also offers an easy fix should you make too much—just press through a food mill and serve the next day or use as a filling for tortellini.

Stewed Potatoes

PATATE IN UMIDO

SERVES 4

½ cup (125 ml | 110 g) mild extra-virgin olive oil

2 small red onions, quartered and thinly sliced

½ cup (125 ml | 110 g) *pelati di pomodoro*, pressed through a food mill, or *passata di pomodoro*

1 cup (250 ml | 250 g) *Brodetto* (page 261) or Old Hen Broth (page 54), warmed

7 medium (1000 g) russet potatoes, peeled and cut into 1-inch cubes

q.b. coarse sea salt and crushed Tellicherry black peppercorns

Handful of fresh flat-leaf parsley or basil leaves, torn

· In a large Dutch oven, combine the olive oil and onion and sauté over medium heat, stirring, until the onions are soft, about 5 minutes. Stir in the tomatoes and heat until they begin to bubble, about 5 minutes, then add 1 cup of the *brodetto*. Gently stir in the potatoes and return to a simmer. Cook, refraining from stirring (so the potatoes stay whole), adding another ladleful of *brodetto* whenever the liquid has been absorbed, until the potatoes can be pierced with a knife without falling apart, 20 to 30 minutes total. Season the potatoes with salt and pepper, sprinkle with parsley or basil, and serve warm.

Crunchy, steamed broccoli, high-quality anchovies, and the freshest *olio nuovo* are the perfect start to a meal in late November and early December. This dish is so satisfying, green, and fresh, yet the umami flavor of the anchovies and the dark bark flavors of black walnut wake up your appetite and prepare you for the meal to come.

Broccoli with Black Walnuts and Anchovy Relish

BROCCOLI CON SALSA ACCIUGATA

SERVES 4

1 large head broccoli

1 garlic clove, crushed

Leaves from 1 large bunch fresh flat-leaf parsley, stems reserved for another use

5 anchovy fillets

½ cup (50 g) black walnuts, chopped and toasted, plus more to finish

½ cup (125 ml | 115 g) mild extra-virgin olive oil plus more as needed

½ teaspoon white wine vinegar

q.b. sea salt and crushed Tellicherry black peppercorns

½ cup (125 ml | 115 g) robust extra-virgin olive oil, preferably *olio nuovo*

- Cut the broccoli in half lengthwise using a small paring knife, sliding it in between the florets and cutting toward the bottom of the head until the broccoli is cut into florets of equal size. If you see a tough part of the skin, peel it without getting completely into the whiter core of the stem. Keep a keen eye on trying to make them all as even and as equal as possible, so when you steam them, they will be ready somewhat at the same time. Keep the florets in a bowl of cold water until you are ready to steam them.

- In a mortar, crush the garlic and parsley leaves and one anchovy together with the pestle. Add the walnuts and a drizzle of olive oil to emulsify. Once the paste is ready, transfer it to a glass bowl, mix in the vinegar, and season with pepper. Taste and adjust the seasoning as needed. The relish should be fairly intense. Whisk in additional olive oil until you achieve a saucy consistency and set aside.

- Put the insert into a pasta pot. Add just enough water to come just above the holes and bring the water to a boil. Add the broccoli, cover, and steam until just before al dente, 2 to 3 minutes. Remove the pan from the heat, drain the water, and transfer the broccoli to a serving platter. Let it cool down a bit.

- Spoon the sauce over the broccoli and dot the remaining anchovies and a few walnuts over the broccoli. Drizzle with more olive oil just before serving.

Cipollini are small red and white onions that are flat and oval in shape and have a sweet flavor. They're easiest to peel when blanched for two or three minutes, then shocked in a bowl of ice water. Although granulated sugar can be used, Demarara imparts a gorgeous amber color to the onions. This is the time to use that special bottle of quince or cherry vinegar in place of red wine vinegar. The *cipolline* can be made several hours ahead, but reheat them just before serving so the butter doesn't congeal. Keep a jar of these on hand and you'll find plenty of uses for them: Serve alongside a platter of salumi or as a side dish with roasted meat or fish.

Sweet-and-Sour Onions

CIPOLLINE IN AGRODOLCE

SERVES 4 TO 6

1 pound (450 g) *cipolline* onions

8 tablespoons (115 g) unsalted butter

½ cup (113 g) Demerara sugar

½ to 1 cup (125–500 ml | 125–500 g)
   red wine vinegar or fruit vinegar

· Bring a large pot of water to a boil over high heat. Fill a large bowl with water and ice.

· Add the onions to the boiling water and cook for 3 minutes. Using a slotted spoon, transfer the onions to the ice bath. As soon as the onions are cool enough to handle, use a paring knife to peel them.

· In a large, straight-sided skillet, melt the butter over medium heat. Arrange the onions in the skillet and stir to coat with the butter. Sprinkle in the sugar and vinegar and stir to combine. Cover the pan and reduce the heat to low. Cook, stirring occasionally, until the onions can be pierced with a knife, but still hold their shape, 12 to 15 minutes. The *cipolline* can be made several hours ahead. Reheat just before serving so the butter melts and caramelizes again.

The rugged island of Pantelleria is known for its abundant capers. Whether you dine in a local restaurant or in someone's home, chances are good that you will be served this simple potato salad as an accompaniment to grilled swordfish or tuna. While one cup of capers may seem like a lot, they are essential to the dish (but do taste carefully before adding salt; it may not be necessary!). Make this at least 8 hours before serving or the day before.

Steamed Potatoes with Red Onions and Capers

INSALATA PANTESCA

SERVES 4;
MAKES ABOUT 5 CUPS

1 pound (450 g) new potatoes, each about the size of a large egg, peeled and ends cut off

1 medium red onion, halved and thinly sliced on a mandoline

½ cup (175 g) salted capers, rinsed and thoroughly dried

½ cup (90 g) robust extra-virgin olive oil

¼ cup (45 g) white wine vinegar

1 tablespoon dried Sicilian oregano

q.b. coarse sea salt and crushed Tellicherry black peppercorns

· To prepare the potatoes, hold a paring knife in your dominant hand and place a potato in your other hand, between the tip of the thumb and index finger. Rotate the knife in a smooth motion to slice a thin layer, from the top to the bottom, creating a slight curve. Turn the potato slightly and repeat around until six facets have been cut.

· Place the pasta insert inside a large pot. Add just enough water to be visible through the holes. Add the potatoes, cover the pot, and steam until the potatoes can be pierced with a knife. Lift up the insert and allow the potatoes to drain well. Transfer the potatoes to a bowl. Gently mix in the onions and capers. Toss with the olive oil and vinegar; sprinkle with the oregano. Taste and season with salt and pepper.

In Sicily, there are these amazing, huge *broccolo*, which is somewhat of a cross between cauliflower and broccoli, about the size of a baseball. Since I can't find the huge *broccolo* at home in Florence, I make a mixture of broccoli and cauliflower and steam them together, and then serve them all tossed up with the same ingredients of a traditional Sicilian pasta dish. I like to serve as a side alongside sliced swordfish steaks or sardines.

Mixed Broccoli and Cauliflower

VRUOCCULI ARRIMINATI

SERVES 4 TO 6

½ cup (125 ml | 125 g) warm water

3 threads Italian saffron

2 tablespoons (30 ml | 27 g) cooking extra-virgin olive oil

1 small onion, finely chopped

1 medium head cauliflower, separated into florets

1 medium head broccoli, separated into florets

2 anchovy fillets, torn with your hands, or 1 teaspoon *colatura di alici* (anchovy essence)

½ cup (50 g) bread crumbs, toasted

½ cup (75 g) Italian pine nuts, toasted

½ cup (75 g) dried currants

½ teaspoon wild fennel pollen or fennel seeds, crushed in a mortar and pestle

q.b. robust Sicilian extra-virgin olive oil

• In a small glass bowl, combine the warm water and saffron. Set aside.

• In a small skillet, combine the olive oil and onion and cook over medium heat until the onion is soft and tender, about 5 minutes. Pour in the saffron water and cook until the liquid has mostly evaporated, 4 to 5 minutes. Remove the pan from the heat and set aside to cool to room temperature.

• Place the colander insert in a large pasta pot and add just enough water to be visible through the holes in the bottom. Add the cauliflower and broccoli florets and set over high heat. Cover the pot and steam until the florets can be sliced into with a paring knife while still finding some resistance, about 3 minutes. Drain the cauliflower and broccoli and transfer to a large bowl. Pour the onion-saffron mix overtop and, using your hands, mix to coat them evenly.

• Transfer to a serving platter and top with the anchovy fillets (or *colatura*). Sprinkle with warm toasted bread crumbs, pine nuts, currants, and a generous dusting of fennel pollen. Drizzle with olive oil and serve warm or at room temperature.

Scarola, also known in the area around Napoli as *indivia scarola*, is elongated like endive with very light white leaves that boast a little green at the bottom, and a huge white thick rib that comes together like a big rosette. The beautiful crown of the *Latifolium* varieties is a wonder to serve during the autumn and winter. Raw, it has a very crisp texture, juicy pulp, and—what I love the most—a good, bitter flavor. I love it shredded and tossed with good olive oil and a splash of lemon juice. Cooked, it loses the bitter taste I so dearly love, but will pick up quite a bit of kick and flavor from additional ingredients. Serve as a side dish to any meat, or with salumi platters and mozzarella as an antipasto.

Sautéed Green Endive with Lemon, Olives, and Capers

SCAROLA RIPASSATA

SERVES 4 TO 6

½ cup (125 ml | 115 g) cooking extra-virgin olive oil

1 garlic clove, finely chopped

1 anchovy fillet

Pinch of red pepper flakes

½ lemon, sliced into thin wedges

1 head green endive, carefully washed and leaves separated

½ cup (65 g) large salted capers, soaked, rinsed, and towel dried

½ cup (70 g) Gaeta black olives, pitted and halved

q.b. coarse sea salt

• In a large skillet with a tight-fitting lid, heat the olive oil over medium heat. Add the garlic, anchovy, red pepper flakes, and lemon. (Be careful because the lemons will cause the oil to splatter, so you might want to cover the pot until you hear the fireworks subside.)

• Using a fork, crush the anchovy until it melts into the oil. Add the endive, a handful of leaves at a time, covering the skillet with a lid occasionally to help wilt the leaves. Cook, tossing often, about 5 minutes for crunchy or 8 minutes for more cooked. Cook as much endive as you need (*quanto basta!*), then add the capers and olives and turn off the flame. Cover with the lid again and set aside until ready to serve. Season with salt as needed and serve warm or at room temperature.

When *broccolo romanesco* arrives at Grazia's vegetable stand on Borgo San Jacopo, I know autumn is here. She is my seasonal vegetable barometer, and I am always mesmerized by the fractal symmetry the romanesco brings to her stand. It's a dazzling vegetable to look at—pyramids of green sitting atop a basket of dark green leaves. Its flavor is just as fascinating: Think of it as a cabbage with broccoli flavor, but cauliflower texture.

The start of *broccolo romanesco* season coincides with the first press of *olio nuovo*, and I can't help but think their green energy is made to be eaten together to fuel our bodies for the winter to come.

Snap-Snap Pan-Roasted Romanesco Broccoli

BROCCOLO ROMANESCO AL VAPORE ZAP-ZAP

SERVES 4

1 large head (455 g) *broccolo romanesco*

¼ cup (60 ml | 56 g) mild extra-virgin olive oil

Robust *olio nuovo*, for serving

q.b. coarse sea salt and crushed Tellicherry black peppercorns

• Soak the romanesco in a large bowl under cold running water for 5 minutes. Using your fingers, very gently open the leaves enfolding the romanesco and see if you can remove any remaining inside grit. Using a paring knife, cut the end of all the branches and the bottom heart, and very carefully, make a pyramidal incision in the core, somewhat parallel to the edges of it. Be careful to not go in too far or deep so that it won't break.

• Put the steamer insert in a large pot and fill with just enough water to come about ¼ inch above the bottom of the steamer basket. Add the romanesco, cover the pot, and place over high heat to bring the water to a boil. Reduce the heat slightly and cook until the romanesco is just tender when poked with a paring knife, 5 to 8 minutes. Use tongs to very carefully transfer the romanesco to a platter and set aside to cool.

• When you are ready to serve, cut the romanesco from the top down into wedges (including the leaves) about ⅔-inch-thick at the very bottom of the edge.

• Heat a large nonstick pan over medium heat and add the olive oil. Once the oil is hot, add the wedges, and fry until lightly golden and crisp, 3 to 4 minutes on each side. Season with salt and pepper and transfer to a large oval serving dish. Drizzle generously with *olio nuovo* and serve immediately.

With its bright *agrodolce* flavor, good *caponata* depends on cutting eggplant, celery, carrots, tomatoes, and onions into the same size pieces and cooking them one by one, so they retain their individual textures. When done properly, the eggplant is cooked—but not mushy—the celery and carrot have a bit of crunch, and the onion remains soft. A dash of cocoa powder adds just the right touch of bitterness for my palate.

Caponata

CAPONATA

MAKES ABOUT 3 CUPS

2 (400-g) Japanese eggplants cut into ½-inch cubes

1 teaspoon coarse sea salt, plus more to season

2 to 3 cups vegetable oil, for frying

1 tablespoon (20 g) *estratto di pomodoro* (tomato paste)

2 celery stalks, cut into ½-inch pieces

2 carrots, quartered and cut into ½-inch pieces

1 yellow onion, cut into ½-inch pieces

2 large tomatoes, peeled, seeded, and cut into ½-inch pieces

¼ cup (30 g) salted capers, rinsed and dried

¼ cup (30 g) dried currants

1 tablespoon (4 g) unsweetened cocoa powder

½ cup (125 ml | 85 g) red wine vinegar

¼ cup (30 g) Italian pine nuts, toasted

q.b. fine sea salt and crushed Tellicherry black peppercorns

10 to 12 fresh basil leaves, torn

- Line a baking sheet with paper towels and arrange the eggplant cubes in a single layer on top. Sprinkle with the salt and set aside for 1 hour to draw out the water. When the eggplant cubes start to sweat, cover them with more paper towels. Dry the eggplant thoroughly before frying.

- Fill a large, straight-sided skillet with vegetable oil to a depth of ½ inch. Heat the oil over medium heat. Add the tomato paste, stirring to melt, then add the eggplant cubes and cook, stirring frequently, until the pieces are golden on all sides, 8 to 10 minutes. If necessary, add more oil to the skillet. Use a slotted spoon or a spider to transfer the eggplant to clean paper towels and set aside. Discard the cooking oil from the skillet.

- Add 2 tablespoons of fresh cooking oil and the celery to the skillet and sauté until the celery is tender but not soft, 3 to 4 minutes. Using a slotted spoon or a spider, transfer the celery to paper towels and discard the cooking oil from the skillet. Repeat—adding 2 tablespoons of oil to the skillet each time and discarding it after each use—with the carrots and onions. Once the vegetables are cooked and drained, combine them in a bowl with the tomatoes, capers, and currants. Add the cocoa powder, vinegar, and pine nuts and toss to combine. Season with salt and pepper and let the mixture sit at room temperature for 6 to 8 hours. Sprinkle with the torn basil leaves just before serving.

- The *caponata* will keep in the refrigerator for up to 1 week.

PECORINO CHEESE RUBBED WITH *PEPERONCINO* AND OLIVE OIL WHILE IT AGES.

To Finish With

PER FINERE

A good glass of wine

is my preferred way to end a meal, but there are occasions that require slightly more than a corkscrew and flowing conversation. Italian desserts are best when simple: cheese drizzled with honey, dried fruit and nuts, a few Biscotti, a scoop of Pistachio gelato, or a slice of Pear Torte or Olive Oil cake. To stay authentically Italian all the way through the end of your meal, wait to serve coffee and after-dinner drinks (like amaro or grappa). Instead, serve dessert alongside a selection of sweet wines. I've listed a few favorites here:

- An old vintage Marsala from De Bartoli (one of my all-time favorite producers in Sicily)
- Vin santo from Capezzana or Avignonesi (a rare find and a true luxury to enjoy) from Tuscany
- Picolit by Livio Felluga from Friuli
- Passito di Pantelleria Bukkuram from De Bartoli or the Ben Rye' from Donnafugata
- Aleatico from Acquabona from the Island of Elba in Tuscany
- Moscato d'Asti from Paolo Saracco in Piemonte

Amaro:

A SWEET NOTE ON SOMETHING BITTER

One of Florence's most controversial journalists, the late Oriana Fallaci, used to save her best argument for last, or in *dulcis in fundo*, "the sweet things for last." While I don't agree with all her points of view, I love the idea that she always saved the strongest point for last (and sometimes it was more bitter than sweet). At the end of a big meal, I think of this and try to serve something with a bit of a bitter or umami edge.

Italian amaro is the ideal way to do this. *Amaro*, or bitter, flavors jumpstart your digestive system and are key in helping you feel a sense of relief after a particularly rich meal. One of my favorite places to try something new is at Café degli Artisti in Pianella, Italy, which opened in 1988. The owner, Elio, stocks an astounding 12,800 bottles that scale the walls of the large room, 120 of them being amari. Amari, the charismatically aromatic, bittersweet set of liqueurs, come in all shapes and sizes: They range from light to very dark in color, thin to incredibly viscous in body, and at all price points. Look for classic Italian amari like Averna, Lucano, Meletti, and Amaro Nonino, or seek out something you've never seen before—choosing just by the label alone is fun in its own right!

Macedonia is a labor of love and patience. There are very few places in Italy still serving *Macedonia*, but up until not too long ago, a beautiful *macedonia* was served mostly in *pizzerie* or at home. I still remember my mother patiently cutting each fruit directly over a big salad bowl. The type of fruit always varied, and at the end, she would sprinkle on some sugar and add a splash of Marsala. I personally think that having a big, beautiful bowl of fruit is so much more loving to your guests than serving something overly sweet and filling. I have to admit that one of the reasons why I love my friend Antonio's Ristorante Da Nazzareno in Rome is that they always have a big bowl of fruit salad in the antipasti and *dolci* bar, and it's almost exactly the same as the one my mother used to make!

Fruit Salad

MACEDONIA

SERVES 4

¼ cup (60 ml | 60 g) light-colored
    dessert wine (such as Marsala or
    vin santo)

Juice of 2 oranges

Juice of 1 lemon

2 tablespoons Demerara sugar

1 tart green apple (such as Granny
    Smith), peeled, cored, and cut into
    ¼-inch cubes

1 red apple, peeled, cored, and cut
    into ¼-inch cubes

1 cup (200 g) red grapes, halved

1 firm but ripe banana, peeled and
    sliced into ½-inch pieces

• In a medium bowl, combine the dessert wine, orange juice, lemon juice, and sugar. Whisk until the sugar has dissolved. Add the green and red apple, grapes, and banana and toss just to combine. Serve at room temperature.

The complex flavors of grilled stone fruit, chestnut honey, and bitter cocoa in this recipe make it easy to serve alongside a glass of red wine or a few Biscotti (page 337). Sprinkle in any other type of spice you might like: cinnamon, crushed black pepper, or nutmeg work well. A sprinkling of chopped pistachios from Bronte or toasted Sicilian almonds are also perfect.

Summer Fruit Caponata

CAPONATA DI FRUTTA

SERVES 8

2 ripe peaches

4 ripe apricots

2 ripe nectarines

2 tart green apples, halved, cored, and cut into 8 equal pieces

2 bananas, cut into ½-inch slices

1 cup (130 g) diced watermelon or cantaloupe

2 cups (250 g) diced fresh pineapple

1 tablespoon cooking extra-virgin olive oil

½ cup (125 ml | 180 g) Italian chestnut honey

1 to 2 tablespoons (15–30 ml | 14–28 g) quince vinegar

½ cup (60 g) unsweetened cocoa powder

1 cup (150 g) pomegranate seeds

1 cup (120 g) Italian pine nuts, toasted

q.b. crushed Tellicherry black peppercorns

q.b. torn basil or mint (optional)

• Bring a large pot of water to boil. Use a sharp paring knife to cut a small X in the bottom of each apricot, peach, and nectarine. Add the stone fruits to the boiling water and boil for 30 seconds. Use a slotted spoon to remove the fruit from the water and set aside to cool slightly. Remove and discard the skin from each fruit, then halve them, remove the pits, and slice each half into three or four equal pieces.

• In a large bowl, combine the apricot, peach, and nectarine slices, the apple, bananas, watermelon, pineapple, and olive oil. Toss to coat.

• Preheat a ridged grill pan over high heat. Once the pan is very hot, add the fruit in batches until grill marks form, 2 to 4 minutes on each side. Transfer the grilled fruit to a large serving bowl and add the honey. Gently toss the fruit with your hands to coat it evenly with the honey (I also sing a nice happy song or listen to a nice song while I am doing this and sing along!), then stir in the vinegar and cocoa powder. Add the pomegranate seeds and pine nuts and season with pepper. Cover with plastic wrap directly on the *caponata* and refrigerate for at least 4 hours and up to 1 day before serving.

• To serve, remove the dish 1 hour before serving and let it come to room temperature. Sprinkle the basil or mint on the fruit, if desired, as well as an additional splash of the vinegar, should the *caponata* need a little bright note at the end.

Whenever you have leftover red wine in the summer, make this dish. A bit like Tuscan sangria, it's good to use an acidic wine to ensure the tannic pucker to cut through the sweetness of in-season peaches, but whatever you have on hand will work. Usually I make and serve the peaches day-of, but a while back I threw together the dish just before taking a weeklong trip down to the south of Italy, and a week later it had the most unbelievable color and flavor.

Peaches in Chianti with Black Pepper and Basil

PESCHE IN CHIANTI CON PEPE AND BASILICO

SERVES 4

4 ripe peaches

1 tablespoon raw turbinado sugar

Freshly ground Tellicherry black peppercorns

8 fresh basil leaves, torn in half

2 cups (500 ml | 453 g) Chianti or other dry red wine

· Bring a large pot of water to a boil. Use a sharp paring knife to cut a small X in the bottom of each peach. Add the peaches to the boiling water and cook until the skin splits, about 30 seconds. Use a slotted spoon to remove the peaches from the water and set aside to cool slightly. Remove and discard the skin from each fruit, then halve each of the peaches, remove the pits, and slice each half into four equal pieces.

· Place the peach slices in a medium bowl and sprinkle with the turbinado sugar and pepper. Toss to coat. Add the basil leaves and cover with wine. Refrigerate for at least 24 hours and up to 1 week. Serve slightly chilled.

Eating *boffoli* reminds me of eating the filling of an apple strudel. Carla Bani, the Tuscan wine producer at the incredible fifteenth-century renaissance villa Villa Vingamaggio—where *Much Ado About Nothing* was filmed and where it's said the "Mona Lisa" was painted by Leonardo da Vinci—shared this recipe with me. Baking apples are cored, filled with Demerara sugar, pine nuts, and raisins, and topped with vin santo, an amber-colored dessert wine from Toscano, before being roasted until tender, tender, tender. The skins on the apples burst or *boff* (blow up) and are served with a few spoonfuls of vin santo–infused mascarpone.

Tuscan Baked Apples

BOFFOLI

SERVES 4

2 tablespoons (56 g) unsalted butter, plus more for the baking dish

4 tart green apples (such as Granny Smith)

4 teaspoons (32 g) Demerara sugar

2 teaspoons (8 g) Italian pine nuts

2 teaspoons (12 g) flame or golden raisins

1 cup plus 2 tablespoons (280 ml | 280 g) *vin santo*

½ cup (113 g) mascarpone

• Preheat the oven to 375°F (190°C). Butter a 7 x 10-inch baking dish (it should be large enough to hold the apples without touching). Use a paring knife or apple corer to cut about two-thirds of the way into each apple. (The opening should be 1 inch wide.)

• Spoon ½ teaspoon of the sugar into each hole, followed by ½ teaspoon of the pine nuts, then ½ teaspoon of the raisins. Cut the butter into four pieces and set one piece on the top of the filling in each apple. Pour some *vin santo* into the cavities and on the bottom of the baking dish, reserving 2 tablespoons of the wine for the mascarpone. Sprinkle the remaining sugar over the apples. Bake until the apple skins have burst and the sugars have been caramelized, and the apples can be pierced easily with a knife, about 45 minutes.

• While the apples bake, in a medium bowl, whisk together the mascarpone and the remaining 2 tablespoons *vin santo*.

• Serve the apples warm or at room temperature, topped with a heaping spoonful of mascarpone and a drizzle of the caramelized wine from the baking dish.

If there was one fruit I could take to a desert island (off the coast of Sicily, of course!), it would be the fig. You can use it in so many ways—savory and sweet. Carlo Cioni at Ristorante Da Delfina always serves one or two of these figs during the wine grape harvest season along with a slice of *schiacciata con l'uva*, a flat bread stuffed with Sangiovese grapes and dusted with sugar and fennel seeds. I love to serve them with a little sprinkle of crushed black pepper and a scoop of Silvana's *Crema Gelato* (page 333).

Poached Spiced Figs in Wine

FICHI GIULEBBATI

SERVES 8 TO 10

½ cup (125 g) Demarara sugar

40 figs | 2¼ pounds (1020 g) fresh figs

15 fresh Italian bay leaves

1 lemon, thinly sliced into rounds

¾ cup (180 ml | 180 g) dry red wine (such as Chianti or Sangiovese)

· Spread the Demarara sugar in a thin, even layer over the bottom of a 10-inch straight-sided skillet. Add the figs to the pan, stems up, in a circular pattern, making sure the figs are touching. Tuck the bay and lemon slices in between the concentric circles of figs, alternating lemon-bay-lemon-bay until you reach the center circle. Gently pour in the red wine (it should come about halfway up the sides of the figs) and top with enough water to come two-thirds of the way up so only the stems are showing.

· Set the skillet over high heat. Once the liquid starts to bubble, reduce the heat to medium-low and cook until the liquid has reduced by about half, about 15 minutes. Carefully turn the figs with a pair of tongs to caramelize all the sides, about 6 minutes per side. Once the figs are caramelized, tender, and very sticky, remove from the heat and set aside to cool. Store the cooled figs, preserved in their syrup, for up to 2 weeks in the refrigerator.

At Trattoria Cammillo in Firenze, Chiara Massiero runs the show. Not only is she the third-generation owner, but for nineteen years she's been on the floor directing traffic—customer and staff alike—and in the kitchen, she makes all the specials every morning before the restaurant opens. Despite what some might see as a grueling schedule, during service she's all smiles. "I'm very lucky," she says. "I love to cook and then I get to see how people enjoy it."

Her food, just like her management style, is simple, straightforward, and unfussy. Her crustless pear torte is composed of mostly pears (make sure they're firm and just underripe) with the barest amount of sweet batter holding them together. The resulting flavor is fruit, pure fruit. Its natural sweetness needs no embellishment—leave the sauce, gelato, and cream aside. In the summer, Chiara makes the torte with firm fresh peaches from the market or, when the pears aren't the right texture, she substitutes firm, tart apples.

Chiara's Pear Torte

LA TORTA DI PERE DELLA CHIARA

**MAKES ONE 10-INCH TORTE;
SERVES 10 TO 12**

1 tablespoon (15 g) unsalted butter, softened

1 cup plus 2 tablespoons (260 g) Demerara sugar

½ cup (63 g) all-purpose flour

½ teaspoon aluminum-free baking powder

¼ teaspoon fine sea salt

2 large eggs, lightly beaten

½ cup (125 ml | 122 g) heavy cream

2 tablespoons (30 ml | 30 g) dark rum

1½ teaspoons (7 g) pure vanilla extract

5 or 6 medium (1500 g) Bartlett, Bosc, or other firm pears, peeled, cored, and thinly sliced

· Preheat the oven to 350°F (175°C). Using a paper towel or a pastry brush, thoroughly butter a 10-inch springform pan. Sprinkle the pan with 2 tablespoons of the sugar to evenly coat the bottom and sides of the pan.

· In a large bowl, whisk together 1 cup of the sugar with the flour, baking powder, salt, eggs, cream, rum, and vanilla, just to combine. Using your hands, gently fold the pear slices into the batter to coat them evenly. Pour the mixture into the prepared pan, making sure the pears are evenly spread. Sprinkle the top with the remaining 1 tablespoon sugar. Place the pan on a baking sheet and bake until the top is golden and firm to the touch, about 2 hours. Remove from the oven and place the pan on a wire rack to cool for 5 minutes, then run a dinner knife around the sides of the pan to make sure the torte comes away easily. Remove the sides of the pan and serve the torte warm or at room temperature. If you can stand it, allow the torte to cool completely, wrap it in plastic wrap, and store for 1 to 2 days before serving. This allows the flavors to meld and creates an even more flavorful dessert.

The beautiful, vivacious Silvana Vivoli is the third-generation owner of the famous Vivoli Gelateria in Florence. Vivoli was the first gelateria in Florence, and Silvana still churns her famed crema in the ice cream machine her grandfather bought to celebrate her birth, fifty-odd years ago. Vivoli's gelato is made daily and with only the best ingredients. The *crema*, a rich custard made of eggs, milk, sugar, and a pinch of salt, is made with farm-fresh eggs and organic milk (in the summer, Silvana goes through 100 liters of milk a day!), and doesn't have any flavors like vanilla or lemon added. Silvana says, "You have to be able to taste the eggs." Her remarkable pistachio gelato is made with a paste of Bonte pistachios from Sicily, which are more gray than green and the finest you can find.

To me, Silvana's gelato is the ultimate dessert. Her crema, served with Biscotti (page 337), some poached fruit, or syrup, is always a perfect way to end the meal. Her pistachio is fantastic on its own, but I have a special way of serving it with a generous drizzle of robust olive oil, a few plucks of fresh basil, some toasted whole pistachios, *fleur de sel*, and grated bitter dark chocolate. The genius of it is in its proportions, and it has been the most-copied dessert among my friends.

Silvana Vivoli's Gelato

IL GELATO DI SILVANA VIVOLI

Crema Gelato

IL GELATO DI CREMA

MAKES 1 QUART

1¼ cups (250 g) granulated sugar

6 large egg yolks

q.b. fine sea salt

4 cups (950 ml | 907 g) whole milk, warmed

• Fill a large bowl with ice and water.

• In a medium saucepan, whisk together the sugar, egg yolks, and a pinch of salt. Add 2 cups of the warm milk, whisking constantly. Place the saucepan over medium-low heat and slowly add the remaining 2 cups hot milk. Cook, stirring with a wooden spoon, until the mixture is thickened and coats the back of the spoon, 7 to 10 minutes. Remove the pan from the heat and transfer the custard base to a medium bowl. Set into the prepared ice bath and stir until cooled. Remove from the ice bath, place a piece of plastic wrap directly on top of the custard base, and refrigerate for at least 6 hours and up to overnight.

• Follow the instructions on your ice cream or gelato maker and churn until the gelato is thick. Transfer to a stainless-steel container and freeze until firm.

Pistacchio Gelato with Olive Oil and Fleur de Sel

GELATO DI PISTACCHIO, OLIO E SALE

MAKES 1 QUART

4 cups (1 L ml | 907 g) whole milk

Pinch of fine sea salt, plus more
    to serve

6 large egg yolks

1¼ cups (250 g) sugar

2 cups (269 g) toasted and ground
    Sicilian pistachios, plus more whole
    toasted pistachios for serving

q.b. robust extra-virgin olive oil

q.b. basil leaves

q.b. fleur de sel

1 small bar bittersweet chocolate,
    grated on a Microplane

• Fill a large bowl with ice and water. Then, in a small saucepan, warm the milk over medium heat until it is almost at a boil. Whisk in the sea salt and remove from the heat.

• Place the egg yolks and sugar in a separate large high-sided saucepan and whisk vigorously until the mixture is pale yellow and fluffy, about 2 minutes. Whisking continuously, pour the warm milk into the egg mixture and place over medium-low heat. Switch to a wooden spoon and stir the custard continuously until it thickens enough to coat the back of the spoon, 7 to 10 minutes.

• Strain the custard through a fine-mesh sieve into the bowl. Add the pistachios, stirring continuously, until the color of the gelato turns from white to gray. (Pistachio gelato is not green, but gray!) Set into the prepared ice bath and stir until cooled. Remove from the ice bath, place a piece of plastic wrap directly on top of the custard base, and refrigerate for at least 6 hours and up to overnight.

• Follow the instructions on your ice cream or gelato maker and churn until the gelato is thick. Transfer to a stainless-steel container and freeze until firm.

When it's time to serve the gelato, I set the following on the counter:

1. The gelato with a gelato scoop and a glass of warm water
2. A bottle of robust extra-virgin olive oil
3. A bowl of basil leaves
4. A bowl of warm toasted pistachios
5. Fleur de sel
6. A bar of bitter chocolate and a Microplane

Make sure to serve a small scoop in each bowl, with a generous drizzle of grassy, green olive oil, and just a bit of the basil, pistachios, salt, and bitter chocolate.

Biscotti (bis, or twice, and *cotti*, cooked) are the cookie of Tuscany. *Biscotti di Prato* from my friends the Pandolfini siblings, Francesco and Elizabetta, who own the Biscottificio Antonio Mattei in the city of Prato, make the benchmark of *biscotto* (also known as *cantucci* or *mattonelle*, "little bricks," due to their hard consistency). This recipe is the closest I can make to theirs (although be sure to check them out online). The quality of the almonds (add a few bitter almonds if you can find them) and the freshest, most orange-yolked eggs you can find, will give you the best *cantucci* outside of Prato.

Almost Biscotti from Prato

QUASI BISCOTTI DI PRATO

MAKES 48 COOKIES

6 cups (850 g) cake flour, plus more for dusting

2 ⅔ cups (600 g) sugar

3 large egg yolks

5 whole large eggs

1½ teaspoons baking soda

1½ teaspoons baking powder

1 teaspoon kosher salt

Zest of 1 orange (about 1 tablespoon)

1 cup (225 g) unsalted butter, melted

1 cup (230 g) whole almonds, toasted

• Preheat oven to 350°F (175°C). Line two large baking sheets with parchment paper or nonstick mats.

• Mound the flour on a clean work surface. Make a well in the center and add the sugar, 1 egg yolk, the whole eggs, baking soda, baking powder, salt, and zest. Add the melted butter and, using a fork, gradually beat the egg-butter-sugar mixture into the flour until it is all incorporated. Use your hands to mix just until smooth. Knead the almonds into the dough. Do not overwork.

• Divide the dough into quarters. Use your hands to form each piece on a floured surface into a 2- to 2½-inch-wide by 12- to 14-inch-long flat log. Place the logs at least 2 inches apart on the prepared baking sheet pans. In a small bowl, beat the 2 remaining egg yolks until smooth and use a pastry brush to brush the yolk over the tops of the dough.

• Bake until the top is firm and the edges are golden, 35 minutes. Remove the baking sheets from the oven and reduce the oven temperature to 325°F (160°C). Use a serrated knife to carefully slice the logs on an angle into ¾-inch-thick slices and lay them on the baking sheets, cut-side down. Bake until golden and dry, about 20 minutes more, turning the cookies over halfway through. Transfer the biscotti to wire racks and cool completely.

• Once the biscotti are cool, store in an airtight container in a cool, dry place for up to 1 month.

When I think of a *budino di riso*, I think of my dear friend Conte Paolo Salvadori di Weisenhoff, the *primogenito* of Contessa Rosetta Clara Cavalli d'Olivola and heir of the Principato di Lucedio in Piemonte. I have so much admiration and respect for Paolo, who is the most authentic Piemontese (if not true Italian) I know. He has such deep roots, passion, and love for his land as well as his family history and tradition. Every time I am with him, I am in awe of his sense of place and belonging, even when the entire system seems to be working against him. I truly believe that he is one of the iconic men of Italy. Many years ago in their beautiful home on the Costa Smeralda in Sardegna, they served this beautiful dessert in wide Champagne coupes, topped with a mixture of exotic fruit. The proportions were half rice pudding, half fruit on top, and it was just what I didn't know I needed on a hot summer day.

If you want to make *gelato di riso*, follow the *crema* recipe that Silvana gave us (page 333), and mix in a few tablespoons of *budino di riso* before churning. Serve the sweet, starchy gelato in beautiful cups topped with amaro, coffee liqueur, or a simple dusting of cocoa powder. While you're at it, drink a glass of *Passito di Pantelleria* along with it.

Rice Pudding

BUDINO DI RISO

SERVES 6

½ cup (100 g) Arborio rice

3 cups (750 ml | 680 g) whole milk

½ cup (125 ml | 125 g) heavy cream

½ cup (100 g) Demerara sugar

¾ cup (75 g) sliced almonds, toasted, plus more to finish

4 tablespoons (113 g) unsalted butter, at room temperature

2 tablespoons (30 ml | 30 g) grappa

· In a large pot, combine the rice and milk. Cook over low heat, stirring occasionally, until the rice has absorbed almost all the milk (it should be custardy and puddinglike), 30 to 40 minutes. Remove the pot from the heat and set aside to cool for 10 minutes (this allows the temperature to stabilize and not burn you when transferring!). Add the sugar, almonds, butter, and grappa and stir well to combine. Press the mixture through a food mill, discarding any solids, then pour into a quart-size mold, cover with plastic wrap and refrigerate for at least 2 hours and up to overnight.

· Remove the mold from the fridge and turn the pudding out onto a plate, giving the mold a gentle shake to release the pudding from the pan. Sprinkle with sliced almonds and serve.

During the holiday season, large displays of too-beautiful-to-unwrap panettone can be found artfully piled in food shops across Italy. Some packages actually look like giant jewelry boxes with Old World lettering and colorful ribbons. Panettone is a twentieth-century invention, created by bakers in Milano. The cylindrical sweet bread, studded with candied and dried fruit, is a traditional holiday gift meant to be served after the Christmas meal along with a glass of dessert or sparkling wine and alongside mixed nuts, dried fruit, *torrone*, and other holiday confections. Leftover panettone is sliced, toasted, and enjoyed with a cup of coffee or tea for breakfast or as an afternoon snack.

If you receive too many *panettoni* for the holidays, this bread pudding is an ideal place to put them to use. Or, if there's not enough, substitute cubes of challah or brioche bread tossed in a mixture of chopped candied oranges, raisins, and dried cranberries before adding the other ingredients. Since the bread is quite sweet, whipped cream, gelato, or even a dusting of *zucchero al velo* (confectioners' sugar) can be too much. Instead, a spoonful of *amarena* (sour) cherries makes a nice finish.

Panettone Bread Pudding

BUDINO DI PANETTONE

SERVES 10 TO 12

1 (1½-pound | 760-g) panettone, cut into 2-inch cubes

2 cups (450 g) Demerara sugar

4 cups (1 L ml | 900 g) whole milk

8 large eggs

1 teaspoon pure vanilla extract

• Preheat the oven to 375°F (190°C).

• On a large baking sheet, arrange the panettone cubes in a single layer. Toast in the oven until light brown, using tongs to gently toss the pieces, 20 to 25 minutes. Remove the baking sheet from the oven and set aside to cool. Do not turn off the oven.

• Pour 1 cup sugar into a 9 x 13-inch baking pan. Wearing oven mitts, place the pan over medium heat. Swirl the pan continuously, until the sugar melts and turns caramel in color, about 5 minutes. Take care; the sugar will be extremely hot! Once the sugar is caramelized evenly on the bottom of the pan, turn off the heat and set the pan aside on a wire rack. As the caramel cools, it will make cracking sounds.

• In a large saucepan, whisk together the milk, eggs, the remaining 1 cup sugar, and the vanilla until it is smooth and frothy, like eggnog, and heat over medium heat until you can see a little steam rising, about 10 minutes. Remove the pan from the heat.

>>>

- Place a baking dish large enough to hold the baking pan on the lower rack of the oven. Carefully fill the baking dish with 1 inch of hot water to create steam.

- Gently arrange the panettone cubes inside the baking pan on top of the caramel, taking care not to break it. Slowly ladle the milk-egg mixture over the panettone pieces to soak them. Use the back of a spoon to submerge the cubes in the milk-egg mixture. Place the mold in the baking dish with the hot water and bake until the bread pudding is firm to the touch when gently pressed, about 45 minutes. Remove the pan from the oven and set aside to cool on a wire rack. Once cool, place in the refrigerator and chill for at least 1 day and up to 3 days before unmolding.

- When you are ready to unmold the *budino*, remove the pan from the refrigerator and set aside at room temperature for 30 minutes. Set the pan in a deep skillet and fill the skillet with water. Bring to a boil—the caramel will make cracking sounds as it warms up. Run a dinner knife around the edge of the *budino di panettone* and, after 30 to 45 seconds, remove the pan from the water. Place a large serving dish with slanted edges on top of the mold and, wearing oven mitts, flip the mold over and with one big *colpo* (forceful shake), release the cake from the pan. Reheat the mold in the water-filled skillet to melt any remaining caramel and pour the caramel over the *budino*. Set the unmolded *budino di panettone* aside to cool.

- Serve at room temperature or cover the *budino* lightly with plastic wrap and refrigerate for 6 hours or overnight before serving so it doesn't dry out.

When you are introduced to Contessa Beatrice Contini Bonacossi of Tenuta di Capezzana, she asks that you called her Bea. Down-to-earth Bea travels the world representing her family's olive oil and wines. At home, she frequently bakes bread using years-old yeast starter as well as this light olive oil cake. It can be served alone or accompanied by pears poached in red wine or brandy-soaked cherries or prunes. Bea insists that the success of the cake depends on using a top-quality olive oil and I don't disagree!

Extra-Virgin Olive Oil Cake

TORTA DI CAPEZZANA

SERVES 12

2 cups (320 g) all-purpose flour

½ teaspoon (2 g) baking powder

¾ teaspoon (6 g) baking soda

Pinch of fine sea salt

3 large eggs

1¼ cups (425g) honey

1¼ cups (375 ml | 275 g) robust unfiltered extra-virgin olive oil (preferably *olio nuovo*)

1¼ cups (300 ml | 300 g) whole milk

Zest of 3 oranges

Confectioners' sugar (optional)

1 orange, thinly sliced into rounds

• Preheat the oven to 325°F (165°C).

• Line a 9 x 13-inch baking pan with parchment paper and butter and flour the paper and sides of the pan.

• In a medium bowl, whisk together the flour, baking powder, baking soda, and salt. Set aside. In a large bowl, whisk together the eggs and honey until combined and frothy. Add the olive oil, milk, and orange zest and whisk well to combine. Switch to a spatula and fold the dry mixture into the wet, stirring just until combined.

• Pour the batter into the prepared pan and bake until a toothpick inserted into the center comes out clean, 35 to 40 minutes. Transfer the pan to a wire rack and let cool completely. Run a butter knife around the sides of the pan and invert the cake onto a serving platter. Cut into 3 x 3-inch squares with a knife, dust with confectioners' sugar, and serve with orange slices, if desired.

Meringata (meringue cake) is a kaleidoscope of textures and flavors—crunchy/soft/bitter/sweet/salty—every bite is different. The meringue is airy and just a little bit salty. The lightly sweetened cream is laced with bitter chocolate before being frozen between the layers of crisp meringue. At Sostanza in Firenze they serve their three-layer *meringata* with a heap of tiny wild strawberries—feel free to do so here or stick with a final drizzle of warm chocolate-espresso sauce over the icy cake. The cold-hot contrast solidifies it as a dessert fit for celebration.

Meringue and Chocolate Chip Torte with Bitter Chocolate Sauce

LA MERINGATA CON SALSA DI CIOCCOLATO AMARO

SERVES 8 TO 10

6 large egg whites, at room temperature

1½ teaspoons fine sea salt

½ teaspoon cream of tartar

1½ cups (300 g) granulated sugar

½ teaspoon pure vanilla extract

2¼ cups (560 ml | 506 g) heavy cream

¼ cup (32 g) confectioners' sugar

1 pound (450 g) dark chocolate (70% cacao), finely chopped

¼ cup (60 ml | 60 g) hot brewed espresso or other strong coffee

· Position the oven racks in the lower and middle thirds of the oven. Preheat the oven to 225°F (110°C). Trace two 10-inch circles on parchment paper and place them on two baking sheets.

· In the bowl of a stand mixer fitted with the whisk attachment, beat the egg whites, salt, and cream of tartar on medium speed until foamy. Increase the speed to high and slowly add the granulated sugar, 3 tablespoons at a time, beating for 5 seconds between additions. Beat until soft peaks form, then add the vanilla and beat until combined.

· Transfer half the meringue to a pastry bag fitted with a ½-inch plain round tip. Pipe a ring of meringue just inside each drawn circle. Spoon the remaining meringue into the circles and use an offset spatula to spread it ½ inch thick. Bake the meringues until firm and dry, about 1½ hours. Turn off the oven, prop the door open slightly, and let the meringues cool in the oven for at least 6 hours, until dry and crisp. (The meringues can be made the day before and stored at room temperature.)

>>>

- In the bowl of a stand mixer fitted with the whisk attachment, beat 2 cups (500 ml | 450 g) of the cream with the confectioners' sugar until stiff peaks form. Gently fold ¼ cup (113 g) of the chopped chocolate into the cream.

- To assemble the cake, place one meringue circle on a serving platter. Spread all the whipped cream evenly over the meringue circle to the edges. Top with the second meringue circle, pressing lightly so it doesn't break. Freeze until the cream is firm, about 2 hours.

- In a glass or metal bowl set over saucepan of barely simmering water (do not allow bottom of bowl to touch water), stir the remaining chocolate until melted and smooth. Remove the pan from the heat and whisk the remaining ¼ cup (60 ml | 56 g) cream (at room temperature) and the espresso into the chocolate.

- Carefully remove the cake from the freezer. In order to avoid breaking the meringue, rinse the blade of a very sharp knife with hot water then dry it carefully before beginning to cut the cake into 2-inch wedges. Continue to rinse and dry the knife before cutting each slice. Let stand for 10 minutes (the frozen cream will temper slightly and be more enjoyable to eat), then spoon some of the chocolate sauce on each wedge and serve.

RESOURCES

I firmly believe you should be close (if not best!) friends with your food purveyors.

They are the ones who you trust the most in anything you bring into your kitchen. I strongly believe we have to support these independent brick-and-mortar shops specialty food shops, farmers markets, and stores, both physical and online—and keep them from extinction if we want to continue to eat AUTHENTIC food. They are the ones who can guarantee and bestow upon your table incredible, diverse flavors that you might never have tasted otherwise. They do, and love doing this, for a living and the simple act of looking straight into their eyes and making that connection is what builds a stronger, better world. Trust them and support them by buying a bottle of great extra-virgin olive oil and giving it as a gift. This both supports and shares your love and excitement of GOOD FOOD. We can do it one person—and one bottle—at a time.

Today, there are too many layers of separation between nature and what we put in our mouths to nourish us and our loved ones. Trying to get as close as possible to your food's natural form and making sure you purchase, eat, and share the best products—no matter where in the world they are from—all of which are made with heart, tradition, integrity, and most of all, authenticity, is the best way to close the gap of that separation and forge the way ahead.

Food is PEACE and food brings LOVE and TOGETHERNESS.

Lately, Italian foods in the United States have taken a beating. There are a lot of fake *MADE IN ITALY* food products (just as much as there are fake designs, furniture, fashion, machines, etc. *Made in Italy* is the best branding in the world). It sells. But the best way to protect it and make sure it maintains that *Made in Italy* quality is by making sure you buy the AUTHENTIC Italian products. That's the best and easiest way to support the real deal, and ask the fakes to go their own merry way.

For the last thirty years, and for as long as I can breathe, I have and will continue to do my best to support the true artisans of Italy, protect them, and promote them. PLEASE embrace and support this vision and path with me.

And, I promise you, your food will taste GREAT!

If you are a wholesaler, specialty food shop, or a chef, your authentic food supplier should be your best friend.

Cook with authentic Italian food ingredients and come to Italy as often as possible to share a meal with them. That is the best way to be part of the web we have all become a part of.

Unfortunately, due to many trade and restrictions between countries, you will be unable to find some, and be scolded for asking for others. I've gotten into a whole lot of trouble with Customs many times, but if you don't push and sometimes break some rules then we would all still be eating butter lettuce! The best way to make products and food happen, is by SHARING. Keep that pressure up! I am forever grateful to the United States of America for their hunger and curiosity, and continue to learn about great foods from all over the world. Can you imagine the culinary world without the United States?

Yes, I am biased—and rightfully so—after thirty years of representing some of the best of Italy, along with other amazing Italian artisan food importers, here is my "Secret List":

- **MANICARETTI**
  manicaretti.com
  My "family." You will find a part of the website that lists stores and restaurants and many online retailers across the country.

- **GUSTIAMO**
  gustiamo.com
  The very charismatic and truly Italian Beatrice on her website.

- **RITROVO**
  ritrovo.com
  Ron Post and Ilyse Rather bring an enormous assortment of products, mostly labeled under their brand. Available to order on line directly from them.

- **VIOLA IMPORTS**
  violaimports.com
  Alessandro Bellini in Chicago has a wide range of products from authentic producers.

If you are a FOODIE, ask your favorite store to carry the ingredients you need.

Just as when the cookbook *Jerusalem* by Yottam Ottolenghi came out—I never knew half of the ingredients—now many specialty food stores stock them all the time. Curiosity is a wonderful thing!

- **CORTI BROTHERS**
  cortibrothers.com
  Even when I was a starving student at UC Davis, I saved money and made a trip once a month to Sacramento to buy a bottle of authentic extra-virgin olive oil, which had to last for a month. Darryl Corti, whom I consider my "Cal-Ital" Food Oracle is an iconic figure in my life. I am so grateful for Darryl's friendship and his overly abundant generous and overly beyond-belief knowledge and sharing; I can't imagine someone more AUTENTICO than him. I wish he would write a book, but it would be more like an Encyclopedia Brittanica! Buy anything he tells you; it's authentic. He knows!

- **DEAN AND DELUCA**
  deandeluca.com
  Giorgio de Luca was our first client thirty years ago in New York City, and even though Joel